Dictionary of International Security

Paul Robinson

T0087511

polity

First published in 2008 by Polity Press

Polity Press
65 Bridge Street
Cambridge CB2 1UR, UK.

Polity Press
350 Main Street
Malden, MA 02148, USA

ISBN-13: 978-07456-4027-3
ISBN-13: 978-07456-4028-0 (pb)

A catalogue record for this book is available from the British Library.

Typeset in 11 on 13 pt Scala
by SNP Best-set Typesetter Ltd., Hong Kong
Printed and bound in Great Britain by MPG Books Ltd, Bodmin, Cornwall

For further information on Polity, visit our website: www.polity.co.uk

Contents

Defining International Security: A Guide on How to Use this Book

What is Security?

This book aims to provide readers with an easily understood introduction to the major concepts, issues, actors, and institutions in the world of international security. Such an introduction is necessary because growing interest in international security coincides today with a period of rapid change in perceptions about what security means or should mean. The book is not a dictionary in the strict sense, as it goes beyond giving definitions. Each entry gives readers the basic information that they require to understand the significance of the subject in question. In some cases this information will be purely factual. In other cases, when scholars disagree about the subject's meaning or significance, the entry will include a summary of the main opinions which different experts hold about it. This should offer readers the tools to help them make some initial sense of the topic and investigate it further.

All of the entries, of course, relate to security. But what is that? Security implies an absence of threat. This can be viewed as an absolute – either one is secure or one is not, threats exist or they do not – or, as is more usual, as a relative condition – one can have varying degrees of security, more or less protection from threat. One can also view security in objective and subjective terms, in other words as an evaluation of how many threats people and institutions actually face and how much protection against them they actually have, versus how secure they feel.

Based on this definition of security, 'international' security implies a situation in which things which happen in one part of the world do not threaten people who live in another part. This means, for instance, safety from the threat of war between states, of terrorists crossing international boundaries, of conflicts in certain areas restricting international trade or curbing the flow of necessary resources such as oil, or of oppressive government, environmental disaster, or some other problem causing massive flows of refugees across borders. Many other potential threats could be added to this list.

On the surface, this seems absolutely clear. Nevertheless, experts bitterly disagree over the scope of international security. Indeed, academics who declare themselves followers of the school of 'critical security studies' argue that the concept of security is 'essentially contested'.[1] The implication is that there is something about the essence of security which ensures that it will never be possible to reach agreement about its meaning. Not everybody accepts this proposition. David Baldwin, for instance, argues that the idea that security is essentially contested is itself contestable.[2] Certainly, nearly all definitions of security come down to some variation of the words 'absence of threat'. This can be seen in a list of definitions by numerous authors provided in Barry Buzan's 1991 book *People, States and Fear*. The list includes such expressions as 'relative freedom from war', 'ability to withstand aggression from abroad', 'relative freedom from harmful threats', and 'absence of threats to acquired values'.[3]

Security can apply to almost anything or anybody, and to almost anything or anybody which threatens them. Disputes about the concept arguably relate not to its basic meaning – absence of threat – but to which aspects of security belong rightly within the realm of international security studies. Ill-health and unemployment threaten individuals. States provide them with some protection from these threats by means of health care and unemployment benefits. We call this 'social security', but few consider social security to be an appropriate subject for study under the title of 'international security'. What this example shows is that the disputes are not over the basic concept of security but over the referent object of international security – who and what is being threatened – and over the threats – by whom and what they are being threatened. Should the referent object

---

[1] For discussions of critical security studies, see Keith Krause and Michael C. Williams (eds), *Critical Security Studies: Concepts and Cases* (London and New York: Routledge, 2003), Ken Booth (ed.), *Critical Security Studies and World Politics* (Boulder: Lynne Rienner, 2005), and Richard Wyn Jones (ed.), *Critical Theory and World Politics* (Boulder: Lynne Rienner, 2001)

[2] David A. Baldwin, 'The Concept of Security', in Paul F. Diehl (ed.), *War*, vol. 1 (London: Sage, 2005), pp. 1–24

[3] Barry Buzan, *People, States and Fear* (London: Harvester Wheatsheaf, 1991), pp. 16–17

be the international system as a whole, the nation state, or the individual human being? Which of the things we need to protect should take first priority – national sovereignty, territory, culture and religion, economic resources, quality of life, or something else? Should security policy focus on traditional military matters, or should it be broadened to encompass other threats to well-being, such as economic underdevelopment, environmental degradation, human rights abuses, and so on? Analysts disagree fundamentally about the answers to these questions, and thus about where the focus of international security studies and international security policies should lie.

For many years the dominant mode of thought was the one described as 'Realism'. For Realists, the answers to the above questions were clear: the focus should be on the nation state and on military threats. There were good reasons for this choice. Nation states were the most powerful actors on the international stage, with enormous potential to cause harm to each other and to each others' citizens. The most important problem for international security was thus seen as preventing war between states. Other issues paled into insignificance in comparison. In the aftermath of two world wars, and in the face of the threat of nuclear annihilation during the Cold War, this view of international security was understandable.

Over the past twenty or so years the number of voices calling for a reinterpretation of international security has grown. Critics of Realism argue that we need to both broaden and deepen our understanding of the subject – broaden it to include issues such as environmental security, societal security, and economic security, and deepen it to move the point of reference away from the nation state and down to the level of the individual. This has given rise to concepts such as 'human security'. The human security approach argues that individuals and not states should be the primary concern of international security policies, because states exist solely to serve individuals, not as ends in themselves. Furthermore, if the condition of individuals can be improved, by alleviating poverty, ensuring human rights, and so on, the root causes of international conflict will be addressed, making the world in general more secure. National security is thus ultimately dependent on the human security of people throughout the world.

This new approach calls in turn for new means and institutions to be created to foster security. It has been argued that a narrow focus on national security will tend to produce policies which put nation states at loggerheads with one another. States should instead establish new multilateral institutions, or strengthen such institutions as already exist, so as to cooperate in the solving of mutual problems. The days may be past when a state could defend itself entirely by its own means; problems such as climate change, which potentially threaten the lives of millions, can only be cured by global action. Leaders should also be more ready to prevent conflict before it erupts or to limit its spread once it begins. An increased emphasis on multilateral conflict prevention, conflict resolution, peacemaking, and peacebuilding is necessary.

The arguments in favour of broadening and deepening the scope of the concept of international security are controversial. There is much logic to them. In terms of deepening the concept, one can make a fair case that globalization has reduced the powers of nation states. Non-state actors, such as international corporations, terrorists, and transnational criminal organizations, exert increasing influence. Restricting discussions of international security to nation states ignores these important developments in the reality of international life. At the same time, the argument that security should be concerned with individuals, and that states' interests should not trump those of their citizens, is emotionally and morally appealing. States, it is sometimes said, are often the main threats to individuals' security, not the main protector of it. In large parts of the globe, people fear their own state much more than they fear attack by a foreign one. Insisting that security should concern itself only with enabling states to defend themselves may contribute to the insecurity of individuals, and not enhance it.

In addition, given the current international security environment, it makes some sense to argue that the traditional military-orientated concept of security is obsolescent. In most countries, the chances of a person being killed as a result of war are remote. Since the end of the Cold War, the magnitude of armed conflict, both internal and external, has declined dramatically (by over 60 per cent according to the most reliable statistics).[4] There are fewer wars and fewer people being killed in them than at any other time in the past sixty years. If security refers to something other than the absence of threats to life, but includes also threats to one's general well-being, war is not the major problem. Nor is terrorism, a subject which since 2001 has

---

[4] Monty G. Marshall and Ted Robert Gurr, *Peace and Conflict 2005* (College Park: Center for International Development and Conflict Management, 2005), p. 11. See also *Human Security Report 2005: War and Peace in the 21st Century* (New York and Oxford: Oxford University Press, 2005)

occupied a dominant position in public discourse about international security. Terrorism in fact kills very few people.[5] Poverty, disease, environmental degradation, and oppressive government threaten the well-being of far more people in a far more obvious manner. In addition, those violent conflicts which do occur are, according to some commentators, in part products of these other problems – environmental degradation, for instance, can lead to resource scarcity which in turn causes violence. Policymakers seeking to enhance both national and international security would arguably do far better to focus on addressing these issues than on seeking solutions to problems such as terrorism.

The broadening of the concept of security also serves a political purpose. By labelling an issue a security issue, one makes a statement about its importance and its urgency (a practice referred to as 'securitization'). Those who support an expansion of the concept hope that the result will be a redistribution of resources. If, for instance, policy makers can be persuaded to regard environmental threats as matters of national and international security, they may devote more resources to eliminating them. Security, according to Ole Waever, is a 'speech act. . . . By saying "security" a state representative moves the particular case into a specific area; claiming a special right to use the means necessary to block this development.'[6]

The first difficulty with expanding the definition of security is that the concept becomes so all-encompassing as to be meaningless. It ceases to be a tool which can provide directions for practical action. The threats of war and terrorism may be less than they once were, but they still exist. There needs to be some separate field of study and policy to address them. Conflating them with the general well-being of individual humans is unhelpful. In addition, the idea that globalization has reduced the significance of the nation state is disputable. Even if it is partially true, states remain extremely important players on the international scene, and reducing conflict between them remains a matter of primary importance. While one can see the attraction of focusing on the individual and not the state, many would

---

[5] For statistics on the incidence of international terrorism, see Anna Sebasteanski (ed.), *Patterns of Global Terrorism, 1985–2005* (Great Barrington, MA.: Berkshire, 2005)

[6] For a more detailed discussion of this issue, see Ole Waever, 'Securitization and Desecuritization', in Ronnie D. Lipschutz (ed.), *On Security* (New York: Columbia University Press, 1995), pp. 46–86

say that strong states are essential to human society, that the one thing worse than an oppressive state is having no state structure at all. Efforts to bypass states in pursuit of some notion of human security may therefore prove counterproductive. In addition, the human security agenda provides renewed justification for the use of force to end human rights abuses, through military humanitarian intervention. While one may see this as a positive development, it is also possible to see it as a negative one, leading to more inter-state war.

Securitization is similarly problematic. In the first place, there is no solid evidence that labelling issues as security problems has the desired effect of persuading politicians to devote more resources to them. Second, the security label can have negative political consequences. Barry Buzan, Ole Waever and Jaap de Wilde warn that the term 'national security' 'works to silence opposition and has given power holders many opportunities to exploit "threats" for domestic purposes, by claiming a right to handle issues with less democratic control and restraint'.[7] Third, securitization can produce counterproductive solutions. In the example of migration, for instance, one can make a reasonable claim for calling it both a national and an international security issue. Mass movement of refugees across borders can have a seriously destabilizing effect. Large-scale immigration can provoke racial tensions, threaten national culture and identity, and provide a conduit for transnational criminal organizations and terrorists to infiltrate host societies. But calling migrants a 'threat' encourages people to treat them as such, hindering their integration into their new societies and thereby aggravating all the problems mentioned above. The attitudes engendered by the use of the word 'security' are not always desirable.

Contents

It is not my purpose in this introduction or in the dictionary to resolve these debates about the concept of security, merely to highlight them. They are of more than purely academic interest, and can have a genuine influence on the politics of international security. For the most part, states remain wedded to the national security model and the traditional military-orientated view of international security. Security policies continue to concentrate on issues such as: preventing,

[7] Barry Buzan, Ole Waever, and Jaap de Wilde, *Security: A New Framework for Analysis* (Boulder: Lynne Rienner, 1998)

deterring, and fighting wars; counter-terrorism; and combating the proliferation of weapons of mass destruction. Because of this, these issues dominate this dictionary. This is not an ideological endorsement of this perspective, merely a recognition of its reality.

Despite the continued dominance of traditional thinking, some of the newer ideas of security have begun to have an impact on state practice. A few middle-ranking states, most notably Canada, endorsed and promoted a human security agenda during the 1990s, resulting in the passage of the Ottawa Convention banning landmines and the adoption by the United Nations of the theory of the 'responsibility to protect'. In Asia, many other states have adopted the concept of 'Comprehensive Security'. While not ignoring the requirement for military defence, this insists that analyses of national security must include all relevant issues, including economic security, energy security, environmental security, human security, and societal security (see the dictionary for definitions). For this reason, this dictionary looks beyond older views of international security and also includes entries on such topics.

For ease of use, entries in the dictionary appear alphabetically rather than thematically. Roughly speaking, however, they fall under nine headings:

1   entries relating to types of security, such as collective security, cooperative security, information security, and national security;
2   entries relating to concepts often referred to in discussions of international security, such as anarchy, balance of power, national power, and unipolarity;
3   entries relating to threats to security, such as biological and chemical weapons, insurgency, proliferation, and terrorism;
4   entries related to responses to these threats, such as arms control, containment, and regime change;
5   entries related to the main terrorist and non-state organizations which are believed to pose a threat to national and international security, such as Al Qaeda, Hamas, and the Liberation Tigers of Tamil Eelam;
6   entries related to peace and peacebuilding, such as conflict prevention, peacekeeping, and war termination;
7   entries related to key international treaties and arms control initiatives, such as the chemical weapons convention, missile technology control regime, Ottawa Convention, and proliferation security initiative;

8   entries related to prominent domestic security and intelligence organizations, such as the Central Intelligence Agency, Government Communications Headquarters, and Joint Intelligence Committee;

9   and entries related to international organizations, such as the African Union, North Atlantic Treaty Organization, and United Nations.

Inevitably, it is impossible to be entirely comprehensive. In making my selection of which subjects to include and which to leave out, I have tried as much as possible to focus on those matters which are of greatest contemporary relevance. So, for instance, historic treaties which no longer apply, such as arms control treaties of the 1920s and 1930s, do not appear unless some knowledge of them is necessary for those wishing to understand another issue. Thus, I have included the Anti-Ballistic Missile Treaty, even though it is no longer in force, because students undertaking research into ballistic missile defences will often find reference to it in their readings and so may find it useful to have a brief summary of its provisions here.

In writing each entry, I have tried as much as possible to be aware of my own biases and prejudices and to put them to one side, and in cases where the issue is contentious, to present all sides of the argument fairly and with equal weight. I will not always have succeeded. It is never possible to be entirely objective. In his book *The Psychology of Intelligence Analysis*, Richards J. Heuer comments that, 'Objectivity is gained by making assumptions explicit so that they may be examined and challenged, not by vain efforts to eliminate them from analysis.'[8] In this spirit, I will conclude with a bout of self-reflection which will, I hope, help readers counter any such biases as have crept into the selection and content of the dictionary entries.

My background is a military one; I have served as an officer in both the British and Canadian armies, and even since taking up academic life have spent much of my time in the company of military personnel. This inevitably means that the core of my knowledge of international security is military in orientation. It also means that, like so many soldiers, I tend to have a practical rather than a theoretical frame of mind, a tendency reinforced by the fact that my academic training is as a historian not a security studies theorist. Robert Cox

[8] Richards J. Heuer Jr, *The Psychology of Intelligence Analysis* (Center for the Study of Intelligence: Central Intelligence Agency, 1999), pp. 40–41

has spoken of a clear division within the sphere of security studies between 'problem solvers' and critical theorists.[9] I would put myself firmly in the camp of the former, thus distancing myself from the camp of critical security studies.

Having said all that, I have some considerable sympathy with those who find traditional conceptions of international security inadequate and even dangerous. All too many security experts tend towards worst-case scenario thinking. As Canadian security analyst Gwynne Dwyer has noted, this is their 'professional deformation'.[10] Experts tend to exaggerate the dangers posed by threats such as terrorism, weapons of mass destruction, 'rogue' states, and 'failed' states, and make excessive use of highly dubious jargon such as the latter two terms, which serve to paint the picture of a world growing ever more dangerous and to justify military responses. Unfortunately, the nations who follow the advice tendered by worst-case-scenario analysts, and who carry out such military responses, generally end up being less rather than more secure as a result.

That conclusion does not mean that I necessarily support efforts to broaden and deepen the concept of security. While I understand these efforts, I more naturally find myself lining up with those opposed to securitization of issues such as the environment. I am unconvinced that extending the use of the language of security is a productive activity; on the contrary, my natural scepticism makes me suspicious that it may have some negative consequences.

Overall, I would tend to the view that an approach to international security which analysed threats and risks more realistically, and distanced itself from military solutions, would be far more effective than that adopted by many states at this point in time. The idealist in me would like to think that I could somehow persuade leaders of the logic of this position. However, the hard-headed realist in me has to admit that those in power do not share my opinions. It may be regrettable, but, as mentioned above, traditional concerns continue to dominate national and international security discourse. We must write about the world as it is, not as we would like it be, and I have written this dictionary with that thought in mind.

---

[9] Robert W. Cox, 'Social Forces, States, and World Orders: Beyond International Relations Theory', in Robert W. Cox and Timothy J. Sinclair (eds), *Approaches to World Order* (Cambridge: Cambridge University Press, 1995), pp. 85–123
[10] Gwynne Dyer, *With Every Mistake* (Toronto: Vintage Canada, 2006), p. 90

A–Z of International Security

ABSOLUTE WAR

Absolute war is a term coined by the Prussian general and military theorist Carl von Clausewitz. It shares some characteristics with **total war**, but is not identical to it. Absolute war describes a form of **war** in which all political and moral restraints have been abandoned after a process of reciprocal **escalation**. Clausewitz pointed out that war will naturally move towards extremes as each side exerts the maximum effort to impose its will on the other. In practice, various restraining factors always moderate this tendency towards the absolute form of war. Clausewitz contrasted the theoretical state of absolute war with what he termed 'real war', which is the kind of war which armies actually fight. In the process, he not only stated his opinion that absolute war is impossible but also commented that it is a political absurdity to engage in practices which are out of all proportion to the supposed political purpose of war.

Further reading
Carl von Clausewitz, *On War*, edited and translated by Michael Howard and
    Peter Paret (Princeton: Princeton University Press, 1976)

AFRICAN UNION

The African Union (AU) is an international organization of 53 African countries, whose supreme governing body is an assembly of the heads of state and of government of the member states. The AU came into being in May 2001 as a successor to the previous Organization of African Unity (OAU), which was deemed to be inadequate to cope with the challenges of the post-**Cold War** international environment. The replacement of the OAU with the AU was designed to strengthen central authority and enhance the ability of African states to act in concert to solve mutual problems. The stated objectives of the AU are: to defend the sovereignty and territorial integrity of its members; to accelerate the political and socio-economic integration of the continent of Africa; to promote **peace**, **security**, and stability on the continent; to protect human rights; to promote democratic institutions; and to work with international partners to eradicate preventable diseases and promote good health. In the realm of security, the AU has already deployed **peacekeeping** forces to Burundi and to the Darfur region of Sudan. The AU aims to establish by 2010 a permanent standby military force which will be able to undertake peacekeeping and other missions when required.

Further reading
African Union website, www.africa-union.org/root/au/index/index.htm
Pusch Commey, 'African Union: So Far So Good', *New African*, July 2004,
   pp. 12–15
Corinne A.A. Packer and Donald Rukare, 'The New African Union and its
   Constitutive Act', *The American Journal of International Law*, vol. 96, no.
   2, April 2002, pp. 365–379

AIDS, see PANDEMIC

AIR POWER

Air power is a measurement of the ability to deliver troops, equipment and weapons from the air. The first application of air power in
war was the use of balloons to observe battlefields in the nineteenth
century, but it was in the First World War that air power acquired
major importance. Initially, aircraft were used primarily for reconnaissance, but by the end of the First World War they were being
used also for air-to-air combat, artillery observation, and the strategic
bombing of enemy cities.

To make effective use of air power, it is first necessary to obtain 'air
superiority', in other words sufficient control over the air to be able to
carry out one's own air operations with little interference from the
enemy, while at the same time denying the enemy the same opportunity. Once air superiority has been achieved, air power may be used
in a number of roles: strategic bombing, including attacks on enemy
cities, vital infrastructure, and command and control centres; **intelligence** gathering and target acquisition; close air support (in other
words air attacks on enemy ground forces which are in close contact
with one's own); electronic warfare, such as the use of aircraft to jam
enemy communications; logistics, including the transport of troops,
equipment, and supplies; and support of naval operations, including
attacks on enemy shipping and anti-submarine operations.

Air power theorists disagree as to the priorities among these roles.
Broadly speaking, they divide into two schools of thought: those who
believe that air power should concentrate its efforts on destroying
enemy land forces, and thus see air power's main role as being an
adjunct to **land power**; and those who believe that air power should
focus on strategic attacks on enemy infrastructure behind the front
lines. An early proponent of the latter strategy was the Italian air
power theorist Giulio Douhet in his 1921 book *The Command of the*

Air. Douhet envisioned a future war which would begin with a decisive battle for air superiority, after which the victor would launch massive aerial assaults on the enemy's cities, forcing the latter to surrender rapidly. In this way, air power would make land power redundant. The experience of the strategic bombing campaign in the Second World War showed, however, that civil populations can be remarkably resilient to aerial bombardment and that air power cannot provide victory on its own. An updated version of air power theory was developed by the American Colonel John A. Warden III, who envisaged a model of five rings moving outwards from the enemy's central leadership to his fielded forces, each ring being of decreasing importance. Warden argued that air power should concentrate its efforts as much as possible on attacking the innermost ring, although if it had sufficient resources it could engage in parallel attack across all five rings. In this way it could paralyse the enemy's decision-making process and cause his collapse without the need for a costly land battle.

Since the Second World War, air power has been the dominant force in conventional war, although some commentators believe that space power is beginning to supersede it. Despite this dominance, the air campaign waged by the **North Atlantic Treaty Organization (NATO)** against Yugoslavia in 1999 is to date the only example of air power achieving strategic success without the need for land combat, and even in this case land forces were required to occupy Kosovo once the Yugoslavs had capitulated. Air power is less able to influence outcomes in conflicts other than conventional war, such as **guerrilla warfare** and **insurgency**, and is of still more limited use against **terrorism**. In such situations, land power continues to play the dominant role.

Further reading
M. J. Armitage and R. A. Mason, *Air Power in the Nuclear Age*, 2nd edition (Basingstoke: Macmillan, 1985)
Timothy Garden, 'Air Power: Theory and Practice', in John Baylis, James Wirtz, Eliot Cohen, and Colin S. Gray (eds), *Strategy in the Contemporary World: An Introduction to Strategic Studies* (Oxford: Oxford University Press, 2002), pp. 137–57
Colonel John A. Warden III, 'The Enemy as System', *Airpower Journal*, vol. 9, no. 1, Spring 1995, pp. 40–55
Robert A. Pape, *Bombing to Win: Air Power and Coercion in War* (Ithaca: Cornell University Press, 1996)

AL AQSA MARTYRS BRIGADE

The Al Aqsa Martyrs Brigade is a Palestinian terrorist organization associated with the **Fatah** movement. Despite denials by Fatah of involvement with the Al Aqsa Martyrs Brigade, the organization has almost certainly received support and backing from senior figures within the Palestinian Authority. The brigade first appeared in late 2000, following the start of the second Palestinian uprising (*intifada*) against the Israeli occupation of the West Bank and Gaza Strip. Initially, it focused its attacks on Israeli soldiers and settlers within the occupied territories, but from 2002 it undertook **suicide terrorism** against targets within Israel. Its increasing militancy may in part have been due to internal Palestinian political dynamics, and the need to prove to Palestinians that Fatah was as committed to the armed struggle as its rival **Hamas**. Unlike Hamas, the Al Aqsa Martyrs Brigade is a secular rather than an Islamic organization. Its aim is not to bring in Islamic law, but to expel the Israelis from the occupied territories and to establish a Palestinian state.

Further reading

Edward V. Linden (ed.), *Foreign Terrorist Organizations: History, Tactics, and Connections* (New York: Nova Science, 2004)

Yonah Alexander, *Palestinian Secular Terrorism* (Ardsley: Transnational Publishers, 2003)

AL QAEDA

Al Qaeda ('The Base') is the name of a terrorist organization most famous for its attacks on the World Trade Center in New York and the Pentagon in Washington DC on 11 September 2001.

Led and founded by Saudi dissident Osama bin Laden, Al Qaeda grew out of a network of Arabs who had participated in the fight against the Soviets in Afghanistan during the 1980s. Although some commentators date the birth of Al Qaeda back as far as 1988, there is little evidence of the organization being involved in significant terrorist activities until the mid-1990s. In 1996, bin Laden set up a number of training camps for Islamic militants in Afghanistan and established links with the then-ruling **Taliban** regime. Al Qaeda came to public notice in August 1998, when it was responsible for bombing US embassies in Nairobi and Dar es Salaam. It also organized an attack on the American destroyer USS Cole in Aden in October 2000, killing 17 US servicemen. After the 11 September 2001 attacks, a US-led coalition destroyed Al Qaeda's bases in Afghanistan, and many of its leaders and supporters were killed or captured. Those who survived, including bin Laden, were dispersed, and since that time have been fugitives. It is generally felt that Al Qaeda's capacity to operate as a centrally-directed terrorist organization has been badly damaged. Nonetheless, its continued ability to survive and to coordinate and inflict damage on its enemies has made it an ideological inspiration for Islamic militants around the globe.

Al Qaeda is noted for its use of **suicide terrorism**, often against multiple targets simultaneously. It stands out among other terrorist organizations because of its global reach. Experts disagree about its aims and motivations. Some see it primarily as religious in orientation, devoted to the creation of an Islamic caliphate in the Middle East, and driven by a visceral hatred of Western culture. Others see its aims as primarily political, albeit wrapped in religious rhetoric, and view its actions as being directed against very specific targets for specific goals, rather than against the West in general. A statement issued in 1998 by bin Laden and others under the name of the 'World Islamic Front' stated that it was the duty of all Muslims to kill Americans, and cited three specific grievances: the occupation of the holy lands in the Arabian peninsula by US forces; the **economic sanctions** and air campaign against the Iraqi people; and the oppression of the Palestinians.

It is difficult to characterize Al Qaeda. In part, it can be seen as a hierarchical terrorist organization whose operations have been planned and financed by a central leadership. In part, it can be seen more as a network of loosely connected terrorist groups which draw inspiration and perhaps occasionally some practical support from it, but which largely operate independently. The importance of Al Qaeda in this regard is increasingly seen as ideological rather than organizational. In recent years a number of groups, such as that previously led by Abu Musab al-Zarqawi in Iraq, have announced that they have merged with or joined Al Qaeda, but it is not clear how meaningful such declarations actually are. In addition, it is not clear what connection, if any, Al Qaeda has had with recent terrorist attacks in Europe, such as those in Spain in March 2004 and in the United Kingdom in July 2005. The current size, shape, and modus operandi of Al Qaeda is uncertain.

Further reading
Jason Burke, *Al Qaeda: The True Story of Radical Islam* (London: I. B. Tauris, 2003)
Rohan Gunaratna, *Inside al Qaeda: Global Network of Terror* (New York: Columbia University Press, 2002)

ANARCHY

Anarchy is a central concept in the school of international relations theory known as **realism**. Anarchy refers in this instance not to chaos, but to the absence of world government standing above nation states. Seen in these terms, anarchy is a simple fact – there is no world government. However, the implications of this fact are not entirely clear. For neo- or structural realists, anarchy of this sort is *the* core feature of the international system. It is what distinguishes international from domestic politics. Without a world government possessing the means and legitimacy to enforce international order, states exist in a condition of uncertainty and cannot rely on others for their safety. They will tend to assume the worst about the intentions and capabilities of others, and will take measures to enhance their **security**, such as increasing their military expenditure. This leads to the **security dilemma** – states' efforts to protect themselves cause alarm among others who see their own security as lessened by those efforts, and who then increase their own defences. The result, according to the proponents of a subset of Realism known as 'offensive realism', is inevitable conflict. Other theorists contest this, arguing that the security dilemma is not inevitable, and that, in the absence of central authority, actors may consider the benefits of cooperation as much as of conflict.

Anarchy, defined in terms of lack of government, does not imply complete international disorder. It is not incompatible with the existence of a limited form of international society, with international laws and institutions. These may exist without any overarching government to enforce order. The existence of such a society, along with its norms and institutions, arguably affects the behaviour of states just as much as the absence of a world government. This casts doubt on whether anarchy should be assigned the central importance given to it by Realist theorists. It is only one of several factors determining state behaviour.

Further reading
Hedley Bull, *The Anarchical Society: A Study of Order in World Politics* (Basingstoke: Macmillan, 1977)

Helen Milner, 'The Assumption of Anarchy in International Relations Theory', *Review of International Studies*, vol. 17, no. 1, January 1991, pp. 67–85

Kenneth N. Waltz, 'Anarchic Orders and Balances of Power', in Robert O. Keohane (ed.), *Neorealism and its Critics* (New York: Columbia, 1986)

ANTARCTIC TREATY

The Antarctic Treaty was signed in Washington DC on 1 December 1959 and entered into force on 23 June 1961. It was the first major **arms control** treaty after the Second World War. The treaty applies to the area south of 60 degrees latitude, declares that 'Antarctica shall be used for peaceful purposes only', and prohibits 'any measures of a military nature, such as the establishment of military bases and fortifications, the carrying out of military manœuvres, as well as the testing of any type of weapons'. Article V of the treaty also specifically prohibits any nuclear explosions in Antarctica and the disposal there of nuclear waste. States who have signed the treaty are permitted to send observers to inspect each others' facilities on Antarctica, and all areas and installations on Antarctica are open to such observers at all times. Prior to the treaty, a number of countries had already staked claims to parts of Antarctica. The treaty stipulates that they and others may not stake new claims to Antarctic territory or enlarge existing claims while the treaty is in force, but also notes that nothing in the treaty should be considered as a renunciation or diminution of any such claims as already exist.

Further reading

Arms Control and Disarmament Agreements (New Brunswick: Transaction, 1984)

Coit D. Blacker and Gloria Duffy (eds), *International Arms Control: Issues and Agreements* (Stanford: Stanford University Press, 1984)

Thomas Graham Jr and Damien J. LaVera, *Cornerstones of Security: Arms Control Treaties in the Nuclear Era* (Seattle: University of Washington Press, 2003)

ANTI-BALLISTIC MISSILE TREATY

The 'Treaty Between the USA and the USSR on the Limitation of Anti-Ballistic Missile Systems', commonly known as the Anti-Ballistic Missile (ABM) Treaty, was signed on 26 May 1972 and entered into force on 3 October 1972. Its purpose was to enhance nuclear **deterrence** by preventing either party from developing an effective defence system against **ballistic missiles** which would weaken the other party's ability to respond to, and thus deter, a nuclear attack. The treaty was also intended to eliminate the need to develop and deploy very expensive ballistic missile defences. For the purposes of the treaty, an anti-ballistic missile system was considered to be any system designed to counter ballistic missiles or their elements in flight trajectory, including interceptor missiles, ABM launchers, and ABM radars. Each of the two parties to the treaty was prohibited from deploying more than two ABM systems or their components. One system could be centred on the national capital, with a maximum effective radius of 150 kilometres; the second, also with a radius of 150 kilometres, could be deployed to protect one area containing intercontinental ballistic missile silo launchers. No more than 100 ABM launchers and 100 ABM missiles were to be deployed in either system. Both parties agreed not to develop, test or deploy mobile, or sea-, air- or space-based ABM systems, and not to deploy radars for early warning of strategic ballistic missile attack except along the periphery of their national territories and oriented outward. The USA and USSR subsequently signed a protocol to the treaty in 1974 which reduced the number of permissible ABM systems from two to one. In practice, the United States, having initially deployed an ABM system at Grand Forks, North Dakota, dismantled it, and until the development of the **National Missile Defence** system did not create another. The Soviets, by contrast, did deploy one ABM system to protect Moscow.

Each party had the right to withdraw from the treaty at six months notice. On 13 December 2001, the US government provided such notice, and on 13 June 2002 Washington formally withdrew from the treaty, which is no longer in effect. The cause of the American withdrawal was the US government's desire to develop and deploy the National Missile Defence system, which could not be done while the USA was bound by the terms of the ABM treaty.

Further reading
Arms Control and Disarmament Agreements (New Brunswick: Transaction, 1984)
Coit D. Blacker and Gloria Duffy (eds), *International Arms Control: Issues and Agreements* (Stanford: Stanford University Press, 1984)

Thomas Graham Jr and Damien J. LaVera, *Cornerstones of Security: Arms Control Treaties in the Nuclear Era* (Seattle: University of Washington Press, 2003)

APPEASEMENT

Appeasement is a **strategy** of **conflict prevention**, with which one party to a conflict aims to reduce tensions and avoid **war** by recognizing the legitimacy of some of the other party's demands and making concessions. Appeasement has acquired highly pejorative connotations due to its association with the policy adopted by the British government of Neville Chamberlain towards Nazi Germany prior to the Second World War, and in particular the Munich agreement between Britain and Germany in 1938. The concessions made to Germany failed to prevent war, and the example has been used to discredit appeasement ever since. Nowadays supporters of war often attach the word to the policies of their opponents with the intent of suggesting cowardice and convincing the public of the need for military action.

Critics of appeasement argue that the strategy will almost inevitably fail, because the making of one-sided concessions will be interpreted as a sign of weakness. Rather than being satisfied, they say, the party which is being appeased will imagine that it can exploit this weakness and so will increase its demands, leading to further aggression. Rather than preventing aggression, appeasement encourages it. Other analysts argue that appeasement can succeed, and in the past regularly has succeeded, in preventing conflict and reducing tension. Often the demands of states are limited, and can be satiated. Appeasement provides reassurance of one's own peaceful intentions, thereby overcoming problems associated with the **security dilemma**. It can also alter the political dynamics within the appeased country, strengthening the position of those who favour **peace**. Much depends on the nature of the regime being appeased, the type of concessions offered, and the incentives for the regime to accept the concessions as sufficient.

Further reading
Ralph B. A. Dimuccio, 'The Study of Appeasement in International Relations', *Peace Research*, vol. 35, no. 2, 1998, pp. 245–59
Peter Neville, 'The Dirty A-Word', *History Today*, vol. 56, no. 4, April 2006, pp. 39–41
Stephen R. Rock, *Appeasement in International Politics* (Lexington: University of Kentucky Press, 2000)

ARMS CONTROL

Arms control is the term for international efforts to limit quantities and types of weapons, the technologies and supplies associated with them, their deployment, or their use. As such it is form of **cooperative security**. Arms control takes numerous forms, including formal treaties, export controls, and **confidence and security building measures**. It may include, but is not synonymous with, **disarmament** – on occasion arms control may even permit increases in numbers of weapons. States engage in arms control not for idealistic reasons, but in order to enhance their own **security**. They are likely to agree to arms control when they believe that they have more to gain from mutual limitations on their weapons than from an **arms race**. During the **Cold War**, analysts believed that arms control served three purposes: to reduce the likelihood of **war**; to reduce the cost of preparing for war; and to reduce the harm done by war should it occur. The last of these aims may conflict with the first, as it may lessen **deterrence** and so make war more likely. This has led some commentators to reject arms control as undesirable, but this is a minority view. States may engage in arms control in order to satisfy domestic public opinion and in order to gain goodwill internationally. The very act of engaging in arms control negotiations with other parties may also help to create networks and personal ties which will help to reduce tensions and aid communication in times of crisis.

States have endeavoured to control the spread and use of weapons for hundreds of years. An often-cited early example is a treaty in ancient Greece between the cities of Chalcis and Eretria outlawing the use of missile weapons. In the modern era, the golden age of arms control was in the period from 1960 to 2000, when the threat of nuclear war made it highly desirable for the USA and USSR to reduce tensions. Three types of arms control treaties were signed during the Cold War: the first, such as the **Antarctic**, **Outer Space**, and **Seabed Treaties**, restricted the places in which certain types of weapons could be deployed; the second, such as the **SALT I** and **SALT II** treaties, limited the quantities of weapons each side was permitted to have; and the third, such as the **Biological and Toxin Weapons Convention**, prohibited the production and use of certain types of weapons.

The expansion of arms control during the Cold War was in part made possible by the development of **intelligence** technologies that made it possible to verify compliance, but even with improved **verification** techniques, some degree of trust was, and still is, required for successful arms control. All arms control agreements involve an element of **risk**.

A number of important arms control negotiations have been undertaken since the end of the Cold War, producing for instance the **Chemical Weapons Convention** and the **Strategic Offensive Reductions Treaty**. In the early years of the twenty first century the focus has shifted from arms control to counter-**proliferation**. This implies a more aggressive approach, which aims to prevent other states from gaining certain weapons and technologies, by force if necessary, without any negotiation or mutual agreement. Whereas one of the prime purposes of negotiated arms control was to avoid war, now some strategists argue that it may be desirable to use military power to enforce arms control, in particular to prevent the proliferation of **weapons of mass destruction**. The 2003 Anglo-American invasion of Iraq is an example of this new thinking about arms control being put into practice.

Further reading
Jeffrey A. Larsen, *Arms Control: Cooperative Security in a Changing Environment* (Boulder: Lynne Rienner, 2004)
Jeffrey A. Larsen and James M. Smith, *Historical Dictionary of Arms Control and Disarmament* (Lanham: Scarecrow Press, 2005)
Steve Tulliu and Thomas Schmalberger, *Coming to Terms with Security: A Lexicon for Arms Control, Disarmament and Confidence-Building*, UNIDIR/2003/22 (Geneva: UNIDIR, 2003)

ARMS RACE

An arms race exists when two or more parties rapidly increase their military capabilities, in terms of both quantity and quality, in response to similar increases in the other's capabilities. One explanation for this behaviour is that, following the dynamic of the **security dilemma**, an increase in one party's capabilities induces fear in the other, which consequently increases its own military strength. This in turn induces fear in the original party, which increases its own capacity further, and so on, in a rapidly increasing spiral. This explanation of arms races, sometimes referred to as the 'spiral model', places their causes firmly in external competition. Some analysts dispute this and argue that their real root lies in domestic politics, and that arms races happen when the interests of the **military–industrial complex** exert excessive influence within policy-making institutions. Regardless of the causes of arms races, an increase in military capacity by one state alone does not constitute one. There must be two or more parties acting and reacting in an upwards spiral for an arms race to exist.

Security experts also disagree about the consequences of arms races. Many regard them as purely negative. Arms races are said to exacerbate tensions between states, and thus to increase the likelihood of **war**. States in the midst of an arms race may choose to launch a **preventive war** if they possess some temporary advantage which will soon be lost. In addition, the existence of large military forces increases the potential for accidental war and means that if war does break out the damage may be much larger than if military capabilities were smaller. Against this, some experts argue that arms races can enhance **security** and prevent war by ensuring that each side has a credible **deterrent** against aggression by the other. An example of an arms race which allegedly contributed to the outbreak of war is the Anglo-German naval arms race prior to the First World War. An example which did not lead to war is the nuclear arms race between the United States and Soviet Union during the Cold War.

Further reading
Charles L. Glaser, 'The Causes and Consequences of Arms Races', *Annual Review of Political Science*, vol. 3, no. 1, 2000, pp. 251–276
Colin S. Gray, 'The Arms Race Phenomenon', *World Politics*, vol. 24, no. 1, October 1971, pp. 39–79
Bruno Tertrais, 'Do Arms Races Matter?', *The Washington Quarterly*, vol. 24, no. 4, Autumn 2001, pp. 123–33

ASSOCIATION OF SOUTHEAST ASIAN NATIONS (ASEAN)

The Association of Southeast Asian Nations (ASEAN) was established in 1967 by Indonesia, Malaysia, the Philippines, Singapore, and Thailand, and now has ten members following the accession of Brunei, Cambodia, Laos, Myanmar, and Vietnam. Its stated aims are to accelerate economic growth, social progress, and cultural development in the region, and to promote regional **peace** and stability. Since 2003, the association's work has officially rested on three pillars: the ASEAN Security Community (ASC); the ASEAN Economic Community; and the ASEAN Socio-Cultural Community. The ASC is based on the concept of **comprehensive security**, and has developed a plan of action based on five 'strategic thrusts', namely political development, shaping and sharing of norms, **conflict prevention**, **conflict resolution**, and post-conflict **peacebuilding**. Important steps towards the creation of the ASC include the 1976 Treaty of Amity and Cooperation in Southeast Asia (TAC), in which ASEAN members renounced the use of force against each other, and established a regional mechanism for peaceful conflict resolution (known as the High Council of the TAC), and the 1997 Treaty on the Southeast Asia Nuclear Weapon Free Zone. In 1994 ASEAN also created the ASEAN Regional Forum (ARF), which consists of ASEAN members and 15 other states with interests in the region, including Australia, China, the United Kingdom, and the United States. The ARF discusses issues such as the **proliferation** of **weapons of mass destruction**, **counter-terrorism**, transnational **organized crime**, and **intelligence** sharing. It is also active in the arena of conflict prevention with regard to issues such as territorial disputes in the South China Sea. ASEAN has deliberately chosen not to become a formal **collective defence** or **collective security** organization such as the **North Atlantic Treaty Organization**. Instead, it has worked to enhance regional **security** using an approach based on informal structures and inclusiveness. In the process, it has made substantial, but as yet incomplete, progress towards creating a new **security community** in Southeast Asia.

Further reading
ASEAN Secretariat website, www.aseansec.org/
Dominik Heller, 'The Relevance of the ASEAN Regional Forum (ARF) for Regional Security in the Asia-Pacific', *Contemporary Southeast Asia*, vol. 27, no. 1, 2005, pp. 123–45
Rodolfo C. Severino, 'Towards an ASEAN Security Community', *Trends in Southeast Asia Series*, no. 8 (Singapore: Institute of Southeast Asian Studies, 2004)

ASYMMETRIC WARFARE

Asymmetric warfare is a term used to describe a method of fighting **wars** in which the two sides use markedly different **tactics** and weapons. Normally this happens because of a decided imbalance of power between the two combatants which makes it impossible for the weaker party to fight using the methods of the stronger. Asymmetric warfare thus includes strategies such as **insurgency**, **terrorism**, **guerrilla warfare**, **information warfare**, **netwar**, and **cyberwarfare**.

In no war are the combatants ever entirely equal nor do they ever use exactly similar methods. Indeed, the pursuit of new weapons and tactics to surprise and defeat the enemy is a vital aspect of conventional, 'symmetric', war. It is necessary for the asymmetry to be very large for the term to apply. Thus, the concept lacks definitional precision, and for this reason is rejected by some commentators as unhelpful. Nevertheless, it has won common acceptance.

Further reading
Roger Barnett, *Assymetrical Warfare: Today's Challenge to US Military Power* (Washington, DC: Brassey's, 2003)
Stephen J. Blank, *Rethinking Asymmetric Threats* (Carlisle, PA: SSI, 2003)
Steven J. Lambakis, 'Reconsidering Asymmetric Warfare', *Joint Force Quarterly*, no. 36, Winter 2005, pp. 102–108
Rod Thornton, *Assymetric Warfare* (Cambridge: Polity, 2006)

AUSTRALIA GROUP

The Australia Group was founded at the initiative of the Australian government in 1985 in response to the use of **chemical weapons** in the Iran-Iraq War. It consists of 39 nation states plus the European Commission, and is an export control regime, similar to the **Missile Technology Control Regime**. Its purpose is to combat the **proliferation** of chemical and **biological weapons**. To this end, the Australia Group establishes 'control lists' of restricted items, and members are expected not to grant licences for the export of items on the list when there is a suspicion that they may be used to develop **weapons of mass destruction**. The group meets annually to coordinate members' activities. It is a voluntary and informal network which operates without any charter or constitution. Implementation of the control lists is left to the discretion of each member.

Further reading
Australia group website: www.australiagroup.net/index_en.htm

BALANCE OF POWER

A balance of power exists in international politics when no single nation or group of nations within a given region possesses sufficient power to dominate and force others in that region to obey its will. A balance of power may operate on many levels – the 'general' balance of power describing the situation in the international system as a whole, and 'local' balances of power operating at lower levels. The balance of power may exist between just two states (a 'simple' balance) or between three or more (a 'complex' one). Proponents of the theory of **Realism** maintain that states, either consciously or unconsciously, will behave in such a way as to create a balance of power. If one state acquires a preponderance of power, others will join in opposing it to restore balance. The corrupting nature of power will reinforce this tendency, as a dominant state is likely to abuse its position and so create resistance. Also, successful coalitions which have defeated their opponents will tend to fall apart because once they have achieved victory the logic behind the coalition disappears. States may not explicitly seek a balance of power (they may for instance seek a pre-dominant position), but for these reasons Realist theory suggests that their actions will tend to produce one regardless. This may not neces-sarily be the case, as shown by the continued support shown by other Western states for the United States and the **North Atlantic Treaty Organization** even after the fall of the USSR. Rather than seeking to balance the predominant power, lesser states may prefer to form an alliance with it, a process known as 'bandwagoning'. However, the development of the **Common European Security and Defence Policy** and the **Shanghai Cooperation Organization** may be early steps towards the creation of a new balance, and so the theory may yet be proven correct.

This may or may not be beneficial in terms of international **secu-rity**. Some theorists have posited that maintaining a balance of power is desirable. In its absence the dominant state will be free to coerce others, while these others will seek to challenge it, producing conflict. A balance of power ensures mutual **deterrence** and thus possibly **peace**. Against this, others point out that balances of power have in the past failed to produce peace, as proven by the outbreak of the First World War. The **Cold War**, during which there was a balance of power between the USA and USSR, saw numerous 'proxy wars' between the two. Hegemonic stability theory suggests that peace is more likely to emerge when a single power enjoys **hegemony**. Evi-dence of this is the fact that there are substantially fewer wars world-wide now that there is a single dominant power than there were during the Cold War.

Further reading
Hedley Bull, 'The Balance of Power and International Order', in Hedley Bull, *The Anarchical Society: A Study of Order in World Politics* (Basingstoke: Macmillan, 1977)

Kenneth N. Waltz, 'Anarchic Orders and Balances of Power', in Robert O. Keohane (ed.), *Neorealism and its Critics* (New York: Columbia University Press, 1986)

Martin Wight, 'The Balance of Power and International Order', in Alan James (ed.), *The Basis of International Order* (Oxford: Oxford University Press, 1973), pp. 85–115

BALLISTIC MISSILE

A ballistic missile is a type of missile which follows a ballistic trajectory for most of its flight path. Its main components are a rocket and a warhead. Once the rocket has burnt its fuel, the path of the missile cannot be altered. In some cases, the warhead will fall to earth with the rest of the missile. In other cases, the missile may release one or more 're-entry vehicles', which can be guided towards separate targets along the general trajectory of the missile. Ballistic missiles may carry conventional explosives as well as **nuclear**, **biological**, and **chemical weapons**. They are an inefficient delivery system for the latter two types of weapons, because unless the warhead is suitably insulated, the heat generated in flight will destroy most biological and chemical agents before they can reach the target.

Ballistic missiles are categorized according to their range: intercontinental ballistic missiles (ICBMs) have a range of 5,500+ kilometres; intermediate-range ballistic missiles of 3,000–5,500 kilometres; medium-range ballistic missiles of 1,000–3,000 kilometres; and short-range ballistic missiles of up to 1,000 kilometres. Ballistic missiles have a number of advantages. Most importantly, their speed of flight makes them difficult to intercept, and ballistic missile defence systems such as the American **National Missile Defence** have yet to prove their effectiveness. However, ballistic missiles also suffer from several disadvantages. Compared with **air power**, they are rarely cost effective as a means of delivering munitions. Aircraft can not only deliver a greater payload, but are also reusable. Consequently, ballistic missiles have very rarely been used during **war**, the four exceptions being the use of V2 rockets by Germany during World War Two, and the use of SCUD missiles by the Soviet Union in Afghanistan in the 1980s, by both sides in the Iran-Iraq war of 1980–88, and by Iraq during the Gulf War of 1991. While they remain useful for nuclear **deterrence**, their limitations mean that only those states which lack a powerful air force are likely to invest heavily in them as a method of delivering conventional weapons. They are one of the few means by which weaker states can inflict damage on powerful Western nations, their armed forces, and their citizens. Because of this, preventing the **proliferation** of ballistic missile technology has become a priority for many Western states, leading to counter-proliferation arrangements such as the **Missile Technology Control Regime** and the **Proliferation Security Initiative**.

Further reading
Federation of American Scientists, *Ballistic Missile Basics*, www.fas.org/nuke/intro/missile/basics.htm
Steve Fetter, 'Ballistic Missiles and Weapons of Mass Destruction: What is the Threat? What Should be Done?', *International Security*, vol. 16, no. 1, Summer 1991, pp. 5–42

BANDWAGONING, see BALANCE OF POWER

BIOLOGICAL AND TOXIN WEAPONS CONVENTION
The 'Convention on the Prohibition of the Development, Production and Stockpiling of Bacteriological (Biological) and Toxin Weapons and Their Destruction', more commonly known as the Biological and Toxin Weapons Convention, was signed on 10 April 1972 and came into force on 26 March 1975. Signatories to the convention undertake not to produce or stockpile biological agents and toxins, or weapons, equipment, and means of delivery to use such agents in a hostile manner. The prohibition of the development and stockpiling of agents and toxins is not absolute, but refers to 'quantities that have no justification for prophylactic, protective, or other peaceful purposes'. Signatories are permitted to retain and develop small quantities of agents and toxins for purposes of medical research and the development of defensive measures against biological attack. The quantities are not defined in the convention. The Biological and Toxin Weapons Convention broke new ground in the area of **arms control** by obliging its signatories not just to refrain from developing and producing **biological weapons**, but also to destroy or divert to peaceful purposes any such weapons already in their possession. The United States

confirmed that it had destroyed all such weapons by the end of 1975. After the collapse of the Soviet Union the Russian government admitted that Moscow had continued a biological weapons programme in contravention of the convention. This highlighted the need for a system of treaty **verification**. To address this issue, an international ad hoc group was established in 1994. Its efforts to produce a legally binding protocol to the convention to ensure compliance ended in failure in 2001, when the United States announced that it was unwilling to accept the verification system being proposed.

Further reading
The Biological and Toxin Weapons Convention Website: www.opbw.org/
Malcolm R. Dando, *Preventing Biological Warfare: The Failure of American Leadership* (Basingstoke: Palgrave, 2002)
Thomas Graham Jr and Damien J. LaVera, *Cornerstones of Security: Arms Control Treaties in the Nuclear Era* (Seattle: University of Washington Press, 2003)

BIOLOGICAL WEAPONS
Biological weapons consist of micro-organisms and of biologically-derived toxins which are used to cause death or harm in humans or animals. These include bacteria, viruses, rickettsiae (micro-organisms which must be grown within living cells), fungi, and toxins. Notable examples of biological weapons are the anthrax bacteria and the ricin toxin. The ability of living organisms to reproduce and spread means that biological weapons (excepting toxins) could potentially infect and kill very large numbers of people. Consequently, together with **nuclear weapons** and **chemical weapons** they are classified as **weapons of mass destruction**. However, not all biological weapons fit this classification, as only some are lethal and not all are contagious or infectious. As yet, none have been widely used in **war** or by terrorists. In large part this is because of the weapons' indiscriminate nature – there is no clear way of preventing the weapons from affecting friendly military forces and civilians as much as those of the enemy. In addition, while it is relatively easy to produce deadly biological agents, it is very difficult to disseminate them in an effective manner, and their effects are uncertain and the results delayed. The ideal dissemination method is an aerosol; other methods tend either to destroy the agent or fail to spread it over a wide area.

Nevertheless, a biological attack on a civilian target, even if it failed to kill or harm many people, could cause mass panic. Biological weapons could be attractive to some terrorist groups as much for their psychological as for their physical effects. The use of biological weapons is prohibited by the Geneva Protocol of 1925, and their production and stockpiling by the **Biological Weapons and Toxins Convention** of 1972.

Further reading
Joseph Cirincione, with Jon B. Wolfensthal and Miriam Rajkumar, *Deadly Arsenals: Tracking Weapons of Mass Destruction* (Washington, DC: Carnegie Endowment for International Peace, 2002)
Jeanne Guillemin, *Biological Weapons: From the Invention of State-Sponsored Programs to Contemporary Bioterrorism* (New York: Columbia University Press, 2005)
Steve Tulliu and Thomas Schmalberger, 'Biological Weapons', in *Coming to Terms with Security: A Lexicon for Arms Control, Disarmament and Confidence-Building*, UNIDIR/2003/22 (Geneva: UNIDIR, 2003)

BIPOLARITY, see UNIPOLARITY

C4ISR
C4ISR stands for 'Command, Control, Communications, Computers, Intelligence, Surveillance, and Reconnaissance'. Holding pride of place in the acronym soup of military jargon, C4ISR is sometimes expanded even further into C4ISTAR, the additional letters standing for 'Target Acquisition'. C4ISR is an essential component of **network-centric warfare** and the **Revolution in Military Affairs**. It describes processes and equipment through which tactical military **intelligence** from all sources is fused together and made rapidly available to those who require it to make command decisions and strike enemy targets. Its focus is on the tactical level and on military targeting, rather than on the collection, analysis and dissemination of strategic intelligence. Critics of the C4ISR approach maintain that it overemphasizes immediate targeting priorities at the expense of deeper analysis of enemy intentions and longer-term problems, and that it relies too extensively on high technology while neglecting human factors. Nevertheless, the use of C4ISR systems undoubtedly enhances combat effectiveness at the tactical level.

Further reading
John Ferris, 'Netcentric Warfare, C4ISR and Information Operations:
    Towards a Revolution in Military Intelligence?', in L.V. Scott and Peter
    Jackson (eds), *Understanding Intelligence in the Twenty-First Century*
    (London: Routledge, 2004), pp. 54–77

CENTRAL INTELLIGENCE AGENCY (CIA)

The Central Intelligence Agency (CIA) was created in 1947 to provide
the United States government with a centralized body for the analysis
of information collected from all sources within the American **intelligence** community. In addition to all-source analysis, the CIA also
carries out human intelligence collection outside the borders of the
United States, is responsible for the dissemination of intelligence to
government officials and the military, and carries out **covert action**
overseas. Until 2004, the head of the CIA was known as the Director
of Central Intelligence (DCI) and was responsible not merely for
running the CIA but also for coordinating the work of the intelligence
community as a whole. Following the intelligence failures associated
with **Al Qaeda's** attack on America on 11 September 2001 and with
Iraqi **weapons of mass destruction**, the Intelligence Reform and Terrorism Prevention Act of 2004 abolished the position of DCI, and
created a new post of Director of National Intelligence, which has
taken over the DCI's coordinating role. The head of the CIA is now
known as the Director of the Central Intelligence Agency, reflecting
the fact that his responsibilities have been reduced to leading the
work of the CIA itself.

The headquarters of the CIA are in Langley, Virginia. It is divided
into four directorates. The Directorate of Intelligence is responsible
for analysing and disseminating all-source intelligence. The Directorate of Operations carries out human intelligence gathering operations overseas and is also responsible for covert action. The Directorate
of Science and Technology carries out technical research and development, seeking ways to apply technology to intelligence problems. The
Directorate of Support provides administrative services to the CIA.
The CIA also maintains close links with foreign intelligence agencies
such as the British **Secret Intelligence Service**.

CIA activities, especially covert action, have often been controversial. In response to various scandals involving the CIA, the US Congress passed the Hughes-Ryan Amendment in 1974, obliging the
President of the United States to report all covert action undertaken

by American intelligence agencies to Congress. This requirement was strengthened by the 1980 Intelligence Oversight Act. Furthermore, in 1976 the US Senate created the Senate Intelligence Select Committee, and in 1977 the House of Representatives created the House Permanent Select Committee on Intelligence. Since then, both committees have exercised legislative oversight of the activities of the CIA.

The CIA's record is mixed. While there have been some notable intelligence successes, such as during the Cuban Missile Crisis, there have also been some notable failures, such as the failures to predict the fall of the Shah of Iran in 1979 and to foresee India's **nuclear weapons** test in 1998, and most recently the incorrect assessments that Iraq possessed weapons of mass destruction. The prestige of the CIA has suffered in some circles of the US government, and the downgrading of the role of the head of the CIA in 2004 can be interpreted as a loss of power and status for the organization. While the CIA is meant to be the sole provider of all-source intelligence analysis for the US government, agencies within the Department of Defence, most notably the Defence Intelligence Agency, have on occasions adopted a similar role, at times even competing, rather than cooperating, with the CIA for the ear of those in authority. The continued existence of a plethora of rival intelligence agencies suggests that the CIA has not provided an adequate solution for the problem for which it was created, namely the need for a single, authoritative, central intelligence agency.

Further reading
Central Intelligence Agency website: www.cia.gov/index.html
John Prados, *Safe for Democracy: The Secret Wars of the CIA* (Chicago: Ivan R. Dee, 2006)
Rhodri Jeffreys-Jones, *The CIA and American Democracy*, 3rd edn (New Haven: Yale University Press, 2003)

CERTAIN CONVENTIONAL WEAPONS CONVENTION
The 'Convention on Prohibitions or Restrictions on Use of Certain Conventional Weapons Which May be Deemed to be Excessively Injurious or to Have Indiscriminate Effects' was opened for signature on 10 April 1982 and came into force on 2 December 1982. The convention seeks to limit the use in war of conventional weapons which cause superfluous injury or unnecessary suffering.

There are five protocols to the convention, each dealing with different types of weapons. Protocols I, II and III were presented at the same time as the original convention, although Protocol II was amended and strengthened in 1996. Protocol IV was added in 1996 and Protocol V in 2003. Ninety nine states have signed one or more of the protocols, but in varying numbers for each protocol. Protocol I prohibits the use of any weapon 'the primary effect of which is to injure by fragments which in the human body escape detection by X-rays'. Protocol II restricts, but does not prohibit, the use of mines, booby-traps, and other remotely activated devices. The amended protocol stipulates that, among other things, remotely-delivered anti-personnel landmines must be fitted with self-destruction or self-deactivation mechanisms which will render the mine unusable once the mine no longer serves the military purpose for which it was laid. Anti-personnel landmines which are not remotely delivered and do not contain such mechanisms must be placed in clearly marked and monitored areas. The **Ottawa Convention** banning landmines has supplanted Protocol II, but several states which have not signed the Ottawa Convention continue to be bound by Protocol II instead. Protocol III restricts the use of incendiary weapons. These may not be dropped from the air against military targets situated among any concentration of civilians, nor may they be used against military targets by means of delivery other than the air unless the target is clearly separated from concentrations of civilians and all feasible measures have been taken to minimize incidental loss of civilian life. Protocol IV prohibits the use of laser weapons specifically designed as their sole combat function or one of their combat functions to cause permanent blindness. Protocol V places on contracting parties an obligation upon the cessation of hostilities to mark, clear, remove, or destroy all explosive remnants of war, such as unexploded shells, in the territories that they control.

Further reading
US delegation to the Convention on Certain Conventional Weapons: www. ccwtreaty.com/

Arms Control Association, *Convention on Certain Conventional Weapons at a Glance*: www.armscontrol.org/factsheets/CCW.asp

Thomas Graham Jr and Damien J. LaVera, *Cornerstones of Security: Arms Control Treaties in the Nuclear Era* (Seattle: University of Washington Press, 2003)

CHEMICAL, BIOLOGICAL, RADIOLOGICAL, AND NUCLEAR WEAPONS (CBRN), see WEAPONS OF MASS DESTRUCTION (WMD)

CHEMICAL WEAPONS

Chemical weapons are defined by the **Chemical Weapons Convention** as toxic chemicals and their precursors, and munitions and devices designed specifically to cause harm or death through the toxic properties of those chemicals. Together with **nuclear weapons** and **biological weapons** they are classified as **weapons of mass destruction**. They are generally divided into four types: choking agents, such as phosgene and chlorine, which cause the lungs to fill up with liquid and thus cause death by asphyxiation; blister agents, such as mustard gas, which burn and blister any body parts, external or internal, which they come into contact with; blood agents, such as cyanide, which react with blood and prevent it from distributing oxygen to the body; and nerve agents, such as sarin, tabun and VX, which attack the nervous system. In addition, there are incapacitating and harassing agents, which do not cause death or permanent injury but do temporarily reduce a person's ability to function. Chemical weapons may be delivered as gas, aerosol, or liquid. The former two are more likely to kill, but disperse more rapidly than liquids, which can be used to contaminate areas and so to inhibit movement.

Chemical weapons suffer from several disadvantages which cast some doubt upon their classification as weapons of mass destruction. First, very large quantities are needed to cause mass death. Second, adverse meteorological conditions, such as wind or rain, disperse chemical weapons and reduce their effectiveness. Third, military forces can easily protect themselves against chemical weapons through the use of gas masks and protective clothing. From a military point of view, their main effect against a modern, well-defended army would probably be to reduce its operational efficiency by forcing its members to take protective measures rather than to cause mass casualties. The relative ease with which chemical agents can be produced could make them an attractive weapon for a terrorist organization. Civilian targets lack the means to protect themselves from chemical attack, and terrorists could in theory kill hundreds of civilians through the use of chemical weapons. However, it is sufficiently difficult to spread chemical weapons in such a manner as to contaminate a wide area that this might be beyond the capability of terrorists.

The use of chemical weapons is prohibited by the Geneva Protocol of 1925. In addition, the Chemical Weapons Convention of 1997 prohibits signatories from developing, producing, stockpiling or retaining chemical weapons, or transferring them to another party.

Further reading
Steve Tulliu and Thomas Schmalberger, 'Chemical Weapons', in *Coming to Terms with Security: A Lexicon for Arms Control, Disarmament and Confidence-Building*, UNIDIR/2003/22 (Geneva: UNIDIR, 2003)
Michael L. Moodie, 'The Chemical Weapons Threat', in Sidney D. Drell, Abraham D. Sofaer, and George D. Wilson, *The New Terror: Facing the Threat of Biological and Chemical Weapons* (Stanford: Hoover Institution Press, 1999), pp. 5–38

CHEMICAL WEAPONS CONVENTION

The 'Convention on the Prohibition of the Development, Production, Stockpiling and Use of Chemical Weapons and on their Destruction' was signed in Paris on 13 January 1993, and now has 180 signatories. It came into force on 29 April 1997. Parties to the convention have agreed to never under any circumstances use **chemical weapons**, nor to develop, produce, stockpile or retain chemical weapons, nor to transfer them to another party. In addition, parties to the convention are obliged upon signing the treaty to submit a list of all such weapons and production facilities which they possess and to destroy all of these within ten years of the treaty coming into effect (i.e. by 29 April 2007). For technical and financial reasons, progress in meeting this deadline has been slow, especially in Russia, and it seems certain that neither the United States nor Russia will succeed in destroying all stockpiles by April 2007 as required. An independent body known as the Organization for the Prohibition of Chemical Weapons (OPCW), based in The Hague, Netherlands, is responsible for verifying compliance with the convention. Any state party is entitled to demand a challenge inspection by the OPCW of any site where it suspects prohibited activities may be taking place. The creation of the OPCW and of such an intrusive on-site inspection system provides the convention with a particularly robust **verification** regime, and in this way distinguishes it from the **Biological and Toxin Weapons Convention**, which lacks similar verification measures.

Further reading

Thomas Graham Jr and Damien J. LaVera, Cornerstones of Security: Arms Control Treaties in the Nuclear Era (Seattle: University of Washington Press, 2003)

Organization for the Prevention of Chemical Weapons website: http://www.opcw.org/

Ramesh Thakur and Ere Haru, *The Chemical Weapons Convention: Implementation, Challenges and Opportunities* (Tokyo: United Nations University Press, 2006)

CIVIL WAR

Civil wars are internal conflicts considered to be in some sense different from other forms of internal conflict, such as an **insurgency** against an indigenous government. Three possible criteria can be considered in defining this distinction: the type of violence; the aims of the violence; and the scale of the violence. First, some commentators prefer to use the term only for those internal struggles which involve conventional **war** between well-organized armed forces, such as for instance the war between the forces of the King and Parliament in the English Civil War or between the armies of the Union and the Confederacy in the American Civil War. Second, other commentators prefer to use criteria describing the aim of the violence. The term 'civil war' may most accurately refer to struggles within a state to control that state. This would mean that wars of secession are not in truth civil wars. If this line of thinking is followed, the fact that a conflict is concerned with contesting control of the state may be more important in defining a civil war than whether the combatants use conventional military means. This would rule out sectarian violence, however widespread, if it is not directed at some higher political goal. However, not all struggles to control the state can be considered civil war, for simple reasons of scale. A minor guerrilla or terrorist campaign can hardly be credited with the appellation of civil war. The third criterion, that of scale, is thus also important. The use of the term implies a certain level of violence which raises the situation above mere instability or insurgency into something more serious. Some definitions of civil war place the bar at 1,000 deaths per annum, but this number is rather arbitrary, and defining civil war in purely quantitative terms misses the qualitative aspects which differentiate it from other forms of internal conflict. Rather unsatisfactorily, therefore, we are left in a position where no definition is entirely suitable.

Further reading
Paul Collier and Anke Hoeffler, *Data Issues in the Study of Conflict*, paper
    prepared for the conference on 'Data Collection on Armed Conflict',
    Uppsala, 8–9 June 2001. Available online at: http://www.csae.ox.ac.uk/
    econdata/pdfs/edds2002-01.pdf
Paul Collier and Nicholas Sambanis, 'Understanding Civil War: a New
    Agenda', *The Journal of Conflict Resolution*, vol. 46, no. 1, February 2002,
    pp. 3–12

COLD WAR

The term 'Cold War' refers to the period of heightened political and
ideological tension which existed from 1945 to 1991 between the
democratic, capitalist states of Western Europe and North America,
led by the United States and bound together in the **North Atlantic
Treaty Organization (NATO)**, and the communist states of Eastern
Europe, led by the Soviet Union and bound together in the Warsaw
Pact. It is called a 'cold' war because despite the tensions the two
blocs never directly fought one another. Historians disagree about its
causes. Some consider the basic cause to have been incompatible
political and economic ideologies. Others see the roots of the Cold
War as lying in Soviet expansionism and the forcible imposition of
communist government on Eastern Europe in the late 1940s. Still
others regard Soviet actions as having been primarily defensive in
nature, based on a desire to create a buffer zone to prevent another
invasion of the USSR, and so interpret the Cold War as a product of
mutual misperceptions.

Regardless of the Cold War's causes, its practical consequence was
to establish a bipolar international **security** system centred on the two
main protagonists, the USA and the USSR. As tensions between the
two rose, they engaged in an **arms race** but avoided **war** through the
workings of nuclear **deterrence**. This brought **peace** between the two
blocs and a degree of certainty in international relations, but although
NATO and the Warsaw Pact never fought each other directly, they
did do so indirectly. The Cold War was not a peaceful era. Each bloc
sought to expand its worldwide influence by forming alliances with
Third World states and arming them to defend themselves against
internal and external enemies, while at the same time seeking to
overthrow the allies of the other bloc through **revolution, coup d'état,
insurgency** and **guerrilla warfare**. In this way, the two sides combated

each other via proxies in a phenomenon known as 'proxy wars'. The result was an ever-increasing incidence of violent conflict worldwide. This increase continued right up to the end of the Cold War, with international conflict reaching a peak of intensity in 1992. Since then, the number of wars throughout the world has declined significantly. In light of this evidence and the nuclear risks of the era, the current tendency in some circles to look back at the Cold War with nostalgia as a period of peace and stability displays a certain amount of historical forgetfulness.

Further reading
Michael L. Dockrill and Michael F. Hopkins, *The Cold War, 1945–1991* (Basingstoke: Palgrave Macmillan, 2006)
Saki R. Dockrill and Geraint Hughes (eds), *Palgrave Advances in Cold War History* (Basingstoke: Palgrave Macmillan, 2006)
John Lewis Gaddis, *The Cold War: a New History* (London: Allen Lane, 2006)

COLLECTIVE DEFENCE

The guiding principles of collective defence are that an attack on one member of a group should be considered an attack on all, and that all members of the group should come to each other's defence if such an attack should occur. In some instances these principles may be formalized in a treaty and the creation of an alliance. A prime example of a collective defence organization bound by treaty is the **North Atlantic Treaty Organization (NATO)**. The knowledge that all the members of the alliance will come to one another's aid should in theory provide **deterrence** against attack, as well as greater strength should deterrence fail. Collective defence differs from **collective security**, which is more universal in its application, in that it imposes no obligation to protect others outside the group in question.

Further reading
Yoram Dinstein, 'Collective Self-defence' in Yoram Dimstein, *War, Aggression and Self-Defence*, 3rd edn (Cambridge: Cambridge University Press, 2001), pp. 222–245
Richard Myers, 'Collective Defence in the 21st Century', *RUSI Journal*, vol. 150, no. 5, October 2005, pp. 12–15

COLLECTIVE SECURITY

Collective security rests on the assumptions that **security** is indivisible and that an act of aggression against any member of the international community is an attack on all, obliging them to take action to defeat it. In this way it is similar to, but not synonymous with, **collective defence**. The members of a collective defence system such as the **North Atlantic Treaty Organization (NATO)** pledge to defend each other against any **threat** coming from outside the group. Collective security, by contrast, is a more universal concept. Thus, while NATO for most of its history can be seen as primarily a collective defence organization, the **United Nations**, like the League of Nations and the nineteenth-century Concert of Europe before it, can be seen as an effort to establish a system of collective security.

The existence of a collective security system should in theory act as a **deterrent** against aggression, and if that fails, as a means of reversing aggressive acts. In most circumstances collective security systems lack credibility as there exists no means of binding members to their obligation to defend others, and they will probably avoid acting unless vital **national interests** are at stake. Potential aggressors can reasonably expect that they will be able to escape unpunished. Collective security is likely to work only when the national interests of the most important members of the system happen to coincide with one another. In this way a collective security system may inadvertently become a tool for cementing the power of the powerful rather than for protecting the security of the community as a whole. Successful examples of collective security in action are the military operations undertaken by the United Nations to defend South Korea from North Korea from 1950 to 1953 and to drive Iraq from Kuwait in 1991, but these are exceptional cases. The United Nations action against Iraq in 1991 created hopes in some circles that a 'New World Order' would follow the **Cold War** and that the world's leading nations would finally take the concept of collective security seriously. On the contrary, collective security remains more of an aspiration than a reality.

Further reading

Yoram Dinstein, 'Collective Security' in Yoram Dimstein, *War, Aggression and Self-Defence*, 3rd edn (Cambridge: Cambridge University Press, 2001), pp. 246–282

Marina S. Finkelstein and Lawrence S. Finkelstein (eds), *Collective Security* (San Francisco: Chandler Publishing Company, 1966)

Lynn H. Miller, 'The Idea and the Reality of Collective Security', *Global Governance*, vol. 5, no. 3, July–September 1999, pp. 303–332

COMMON EUROPEAN SECURITY AND DEFENCE POLICY (CESDP)

The Common European Security and Defence Policy (CESDP) is the name given to efforts by the European Union (EU) in the past fifteen years to become an autonomous actor in the realms of **security** and defence. These efforts began with the Maastricht Treaty of 1992, in which EU leaders agreed to launch a Common Foreign and Security Policy (CFSP) and to create a European Security and Defence Identity (ESDI). Subsequent events, in particular the **wars** in the former Yugoslavia, served to convince many that the EU's ability to cope with international crises was insufficient. Consequently, the Amsterdam Treaty of 1999 committed the EU to creating a CESDP to carry out the so-called 'Petersberg Tasks' (named after the Petersberg Hotel near Bonn where EU leaders announced the tasks), namely humanitarian operations, **peacekeeping**, crisis management, and **peacemaking**. To this end, the EU established a position of High Representative of Common Foreign and Security Policy, responsible for both the EU's common foreign policy and the CESDP. The objective of the CESDP is to create the ability for the EU to carry out the Petersberg tasks without the support of the United States or the **North Atlantic Treaty Organization (NATO)** in the event that those others choose not to act.

In 1999 the EU committed itself to establishing a European Rapid Reaction Force (ERRF) of 60,000 troops, capable of being deployed within 60 days and of carrying out operations for at least a year. The ERRF is not a standing force. Troops remain under the control of national governments, and the latter commit themselves to providing certain forces in the event that they are needed.

Overall responsibility for CESDP lies with the European Council, operating through the Political and Security Committee of the EU. This consists of ambassador-level representatives from each member state, who determine the EU's response to a given crisis. The PSC is aided by the EU Military Committee, which is composed of the Chiefs of Defence of the member states. In addition, a small EU Military Staff has been established to plan and support EU military operations.

Military and police forces have been deployed under the rubric of the CESDP to Bosnia, Congo and Macedonia. The EU is also providing support to the Palestinian Authority to help it manage the Rafah border crossing between the Gaza Strip and Egypt. These have been fairly modest operations, and the ability of the EU to carry out something on a larger scale without US or NATO support remains unproven. The potential exists for CESDP to eventually supplant NATO, but this will not be possible for many years, if ever, and so far the EU has stressed the requirement for CESDP to complement and support NATO, rather than duplicate or rival it. Meanwhile, the failure of EU members to ratify the proposed EU Constitution is likely to stall further institutional reform for some time. CESDP is very much a work in progress and its final shape remains uncertain.

Further reading
Fraser Cameron, 'The Future of the Common Foreign and Security Policy', *The Brown Journal of World Affairs*, vol. 9, no. 2, Spring 2003, pp. 115–124
Andrea Ellner, 'The European Security Strategy: Multilateral Security with Teeth?', *Defense and Security Analysis*, vol. 21, no. 3, September 2005, pp. 223–242
Neil Winn, 'Towards a Common European Security and Defence Policy', *Geopolitics*, vol. 8, no. 2, Summer 2003, pp. 47–68

COMMONWEALTH OF INDEPENDENT STATES (CIS)

The Commonwealth of Independent States (CIS) was formed in December 1991 and consists of 12 of the 15 former republics of the Soviet Union (the absentees being the three Baltic states). Its creation was an attempt to preserve some form of association among the republics as the Soviet Union fell apart. The association is very loose, and as the CIS's title suggests, all the members retain full **sovereignty** and independence. In May 1992, six CIS members, Armenia, Kazakhstan, Kyrgyzstan, Russia, Tajikistan and Uzbekistan, signed the CIS Collective Security Treaty (CST), which formed a Collective Security Council to coordinate **security** activities. The treaty came into effect for a five year period in April 1994, after Azerbaijan, Belarus, and Georgia also signed. The treaty was renewed in 1999, but at that point Azerbaijan, Georgia and Uzbekistan withdrew from it. The remaining six signatories formed the Collective Security Treaty Organization in 2002. The one major achievement of the CST was the creation of a CIS joint air defence system in 1995. There is also some coordination among members on issues such as **terrorism**, **organized crime** (including drug trafficking and human trafficking), illegal **migration**, and **proliferation** of both conventional weapons and **weapons of mass destruction**. Much of this is on a bilateral rather than CIS-wide level, and members remain wary of giving too much authority to an organization which will inevitably be dominated by the Russian Federation. The CIS has as yet made little progress towards integrating security measures among its members.

Further reading

P. N. Andreyev, 'Military–Political Cooperation of CIS Countries: Stages and Main Areas', *Military Thought*, vol. 9, no. 4, 2000, pp. 30–40

Ye. Belov and O. Putintsev, 'CIS: Countering Threats to Security and Stability', *International Affairs: a Russian Journal of World Politics, Diplomacy, and International Relations*, vol. 51, no. 1, 2005, pp. 95–105

Artem Mal'gin, 'The Commonwealth of Independent States: Summary of a Decade', *Russian Politics and Law*, vol. 40, no. 5, September–October 2002, pp. 43–54

COMMUNICATIONS SECURITY, see INFORMATION SECURITY

COMPLEX EMERGENCIES

Complex emergencies, often referred to as 'complex humanitarian emergencies', are major humanitarian crises distinguishable from purely natural disasters because they are both a product of human conflict and political in origin. In this sense, a refugee crisis which results from **civil war** is a complex emergency whereas one which results from, say, an earthquake is not. Complex emergencies involve a combination of armed conflict, movements of peoples, shortages of food, and possibly also the spread of disease, resulting in large-scale mortality. The United Nations Office for the Coordination of Humanitarian Affairs (OCHA) states that they are characterized first by 'extensive violence and loss of life; massive displacements of people; widespread damage to societies and economies'; second by 'the need for large-scale multifaceted humanitarian assistance'; third by 'the hindrance or prevention of humanitarian assistance by political and military constraints'; and fourth by the existence of 'significant security risks for humanitarian relief workers in some areas'. Some commentators also associate complex emergencies with collapses in state authority, and thus with **failed states**. This need not be the case and, indeed, in some instances, such as the **genocide** in Rwanda in 1994, the problem was not state failure, but rather the ruthless and brutal exercise of power by the state.

The term 'complex emergencies' first came into use in Africa in the late 1980s. It reflects a growing recognition of the complex links between man-made conflict and natural disaster, such as famine. It also reflects the fact that many contemporary conflicts are not clear, simple **wars** between two clearly delineated parties, but more confusing struggles, often involving numerous competing factions. These factors, coupled with the difficulties of providing humanitarian assistance in such circumstances, means that resolving complex emergencies may be considerably more difficult than traditional **war termination.**

Further reading
Jose Miguel Albala-Bertrand, *What is a Complex Humanitarian Emergency? An Analytical Essay*, Working Paper no. 420 (London: Queen Mary University, 2000)
David Keen, *Complex Emergencies* (Cambridge: Polity, 2007)

COMPREHENSIVE NUCLEAR TEST BAN TREATY (CTBT)
The Comprehensive Nuclear Test Ban Treaty (CTBT) was opened for signature on 24 September 1996. It will come into force when ratified by all of the 44 states listed in Annex 2 to the treaty, which are those states who possessed nuclear power or research reactors at the time the treaty was written. To date, 135 states, but only 34 of those listed in Annex 2, have ratified the treaty, and so the treaty has not yet entered into force. The most notable state not to have ratified the CTBT is the United States, the US Senate having rejected ratification in a vote in October 1999.

If it came into force, the CTBT would prohibit all signatories from carrying out any explosions of **nuclear weapons** or any other nuclear explosions at locations under their jurisdiction. It would therefore supplant the **Partial Test Ban Treaty**, which had permitted underground explosions. The treaty would also establish an organization known as the Comprehensive Nuclear Test Ban Treaty Organization (CTBTO) to help ensure implementation of its provisions, and to provide a forum for consultation and cooperation among the state parties. If created, the CTBTO will implement and monitor the treaty's **verification** measures, including exchanges of data and on-site inspections. Pending the entry into force of the treaty, a Preparatory Commission for the CTBTO has been created, with the two tasks of developing a verification regime and promoting treaty ratification. The prospects of the remaining necessary states ratifying the CTBT are currently not good, and it is possible that the treaty will never enter into force at all.

Further reading
Preparatory Commission for the Comprehensive Nuclear Test Ban Treaty Organization website, www.ctbto.org/
Thanos P. Dokos, *Negotiations for a CTBT, 1958–1994: Analysis and Evaluation of American Policy* (Lanham: University Press of America, 1995)
Thomas Graham Jr and Damien J. LaVera, *Cornerstones of Security: Arms Control Treaties in the Nuclear Era* (Seattle: University of Washington Press, 2003)

COMPREHENSIVE SECURITY

Japanese Prime Minister Masayoshi Ohira was the first to coin the term 'comprehensive security', in 1980. It represents an approach to **security** policy which takes a comprehensive view of the subject and which reflects current discussions about the need to broaden and deepen the concept of security. Although it does not ignore the requirement for military defence, it insists that analyses of **national security** must include all relevant issues, including **economic security**, **energy security**, **environmental security**, **human security**, and **societal security**. This approach encourages cooperation among states on issues such as the environment, while at the same time looking beyond the state as the sole referent object in international security. While it is most often used in discussions of security in East Asia, where it has gained some influence, it has universal applicability. The European Union's **Common European Security and Defence Policy**, for instance, can be seen as being influenced by comprehensive security thinking.

Further reading
Tsuneo Akaha, 'Japan's Comprehensive Security Policy: a New East Asian Environment', *Asian Survey*, vol. 31, no. 4, April 1991, pp. 324–340
James C. Hsiung, *Comprehensive Security: Challenge for Pacific Asia* (Indianapolis: University of Indianapolis Press, 2004)

COMPUTER SECURITY, see INFORMATION SECURITY

CONFIDENCE AND SECURITY BUILDING MEASURES (CSBMs)

Confidence and Security Building Measures (CSBMs) are a form of **arms control**, and consist of measures undertaken by states to reduce the likelihood of **war** by dispelling mistrust. CSBMs are based on the belief that war can be the result of states misperceiving other states' motives. By making military preparations more open, CSBMs reassure states that those are not hostile or a prelude to surprise attack. In this way, they seek to overcome the problem of the **security dilemma**.

CSBMs can be divided into three types: information and communication measures; inspection measures; and military constraints. Information measures include exchanges of information about armed forces and providing advance notice of military exercises. Communication measures include the establishment of hotlines to enable leaders to communicate in times of crisis. Inspection measures include on-site **verification** of compliance with arms control treaties, and the sending of observers to monitor military exercises. Military constraints seek to limit the possibilities for surprise attack by placing numerical and geographical restrictions on the deployment of armed forces.

Notable examples of confidence and security building measures are the Stockholm Agreement of 1986 and the Vienna Documents of 1990, 1992, 1994 and 1999. These oblige members of the **Organization on Security and Cooperation in Europe (OSCE)** to notify each other of major military exercises and permit observation of them. Other examples of CSBMs are: the **Cold War** hotline agreements between the USA and USSR; the **Open Skies Treaty**; the **Conventional Forces in Europe Treaty**; and the United Nations Register of Conventional Arms.

Further reading

R. B. Byers. F. Stephen Larrabee, and Allen Lynch, *Confidence-Building Measures and International Security* (New York: Institute for East–West Security Studies, 1987)

Wojciech Multan, 'The Role of Confidence-Building Measures in the Prevention and Resolution of Conflicts', in *Conflict Resolution: New Approaches and Methods* (Paris: UNESCO, 2000), pp. 85–111

Steve Tulliu and Thomas Schmalberger, *Coming to Terms with Security: A Lexicon for Arms Control, Disarmament and Confidence-Building,*

UNIDIR/2003/22 (Geneva: UNIDIR, 2003), Chapter 8 'Confidence- and Security-Building Measures', pp. 135–164

CONFLICT PREVENTION

Conflict prevention consists of actions undertaken to prevent tensions between and within states from escalating into violence. The term refers both to actions intended to resolve immediate crises (sometimes referred to as 'operational' prevention), and to those (sometimes referred to as 'structural' prevention) intended to eliminate the underlying causes of conflict and thereby to create the conditions for longer-term stability and **peace**, so that tensions which might lead to **war** do not appear in the first place. A third category of conflict prevention, known as 'systemic prevention', refers to measures that address global challenges. Operational prevention requires **intelligence** and early warning of potential conflicts, and makes use of measures such as fact-finding and monitoring missions, the creation of channels of communication between disputing parties, negotiation, mediation, preventive deployments of armed forces, and **confidence and security building measures**. It may also involve the threat of force to deter potential combatants, thus overlapping to some extent with **peace enforcement**. Structural and systemic prevention involve enhancing **human security** at national, regional, and global levels through economic development and the promotion of democracy and human rights, as well as measures to enhance the capacity of multilateral institutions.

Since the end of the **Cold War**, both states and international organizations have put increasing emphasis on conflict prevention, reflecting a widely held belief that their previous policies had focused too much on reacting after conflicts began rather than on stopping them from beginning. To this end, organizations such as the European Union and the **Organization for Security and Cooperation in Europe (OSCE)** have begun to institutionalize conflict prevention policies and practices, creating new bodies such as the OSCE's Conflict Prevention Centre to provide a permanent capacity to deal with these issues. Determining the success of conflict prevention measures is difficult. The number of armed conflicts worldwide has declined significantly in the past fifteen years and some commentators believe that this is related to enhanced conflict prevention activity, although some others believe that it is caused by unrelated factors, such as the end of the Cold War.

Further reading
Alice Ackerman, 'The Idea and Practice of Conflict Prevention', *The Journal of Peace Research*, vol. 40, no. 3, May 2003, pp. 339–347
David Carment and Albrecht Schnabel (eds), *Conflict Prevention: Path to Peace or Grand Illusion?* (Tokyo: United Nations University Press, 2003)
T. David Mason and James D. Meernik (eds), *Conflict Prevention and Peacebuilding in Post-War Societies* (London: Routledge, 2006)

CONFLICT RESOLUTION

Conflict resolution refers to the process of finding a long-term solution to conflicts. In the sphere of international **security**, this is generally interpreted in terms of resolving violent conflict between and within states. Conflict resolution is different from **war termination**, as it seeks to achieve more than bringing a **war** to an end. Rather, it seeks to address the deeper causes of conflict to prevent its recurrence and establish a positive **peace**. It has a role to play not only in bringing fighting to an end, but also in the process of **peacebuilding** after fighting has stopped. Practitioners and theorists are also increasingly focusing on using conflict resolution techniques to prevent violence from erupting in the first place.

Warring parties may undertake to resolve their conflicts through direct negotiation. Often, though, the intervention and assistance of a third party will be necessary to help negotiations succeed. The third party may do this through either mediation or arbitration. In the case of mediation, the third party can assist communication between the parties, and can also make suggestions of possible solutions, although the parties are not obliged to accept these suggestions. Mediators may choose to bring some influence of their own to the negotiating table in the form of coercive power or bribes, in order to encourage agreement. Alternatively, they may act as 'powerless' negotiators whose role is limited to communication and facilitation. The mediator aims to change the parties' perception of their interests, and in particular to take a longer-term view of what these interests may be. In the case of arbitration, the conflicting parties agree in advance to abide by the terms of the settlement proposed by the mutually-accepted arbitrator. It is not always possible, however, for the arbitrator to enforce this undertaking.

Third parties in conflict resolution processes may be states, international organizations, non-governmental organizations, or individuals. Negotiations between representatives of states is often referred to as Track I diplomacy, while negotiations between individuals from the conflicting groups who do not officially represent the state are referred to as Track II. The latter suffer from the disadvantage that those participating lack the power to make decisions. However, Track II diplomacy may help conflict resolution in the long term by building constituencies for peace within civil societies and slowly dismantling patterns of mistrust between people in opposing groups.

Further reading
David P. Barash and Charles P. Webel, 'Diplomacy, Negotiations, and Conflict Resolution', in David P. Barash and Charles P. Webel, *Peace and Conflict Studies* (Thousand Oaks: Sage, 2002), pp. 267–290
Hugh Miall, Oliver Ramsbotham, and Tom Woodhouse, *Contemporary Conflict Resolution*, 2nd edn (Cambridge: Polity, 2005)
Peter Wallensteen, *Understanding Conflict Resolution* (London: Sage, 2006)

CONTAINMENT
Containment is a **strategy** by which states protect their **national security** from external **threat** not by aggressive action to eliminate the threat but by a more patient effort to contain its influence and prevent its spread, while waiting for the superiority of their internal political and economic systems to eventually overcome it by peaceful means. The concept of containment was first proposed by the US diplomat George Kennan in 1947, and thereafter became the basis of US national security strategy vis-à-vis the Soviet Union. It can be contrasted with the alternative strategy of 'rollback', which called for the United States to take active measures to overthrow communism where it already existed. Containment instead called for the USA merely to oppose further communist expansion. This in turn implied some form of accommodation with the Soviet Union and recognition that peaceful coexistence was desirable. Advocates of containment were confident that in the long term, the internal failings of the communist system, combined with the exercise of American **soft power**, would cause communism to collapse from within. According to Kennan, his original conception of containment was purely political, but others interpreted it also in a military sense, and the policy thus provided a basis for actions such as US military intervention to prevent a communist takeover in South Vietnam.

Since the end of the **Cold War**, debates concerning how to deal with the threats posed by alleged **rogue states** such as North Korea,

Iran, and Iraq have involved contrasting concepts of containment and **preventive war**. Supporters of containment argue that it proved highly successful during the Cold War, and can be applied to other situations. Opponents argue that rogue states and terrorists are irrational actors who cannot be contained, and that whereas Soviet **nuclear weapons** made a more aggressive strategy too dangerous during the Cold War, a similar deterrent against preventive action no longer exists. Military action, they argue, can be undertaken at relatively little **risk**. These debates indicate that while containment is most commonly associated with US strategy during the Cold War, it retains contemporary relevance.

Further reading
John Lewis Gaddis, *Strategies of Containment: a Critical Appraisal of American National Security Policy during the Cold War*, revised and expanded edition (New York: Oxford University Press, 2005)
Charles Gati, 'What Containment Meant', *Foreign Policy*, no. 7, Summer 1972, pp. 22–40
Fredrik Logevall, 'Bernath Lecture: a Critique of Containment', *Diplomatic History*, vol. 28, no. 4, September 2004, pp. 473–499
Chalmers M. Roberts, W. Averell Harriman, Arthur Krock, and Dean Acheson, 'How Containment Worked', *Foreign Policy*, no. 7, Summer 1972, pp. 41–53

CONTRACTORS, see PRIVATE MILITARY COMPANIES (PMCs)

CONVENTIONAL FORCES IN EUROPE (CFE) TREATY
The 'Treaty on Conventional Armed Forces in Europe', commonly known as the Conventional Forces in Europe (CFE) Treaty, was signed on 19 November 1990 by the then members of the **North Atlantic Treaty Organization (NATO)** and NATO's communist equivalent, the Warsaw Pact. The treaty aimed to reduce the number of conventional weapons in Europe, defined as the area between the Atlantic Ocean and the Ural mountains. To this end, it divided Europe into four zones and one 'flank zone', and restricted the numbers of weapons which each alliance was permitted in each zone. In all five zones together, the two alliances were limited to 20,000 battle tanks (defined as tanks weighing at least 16.5 metric tons and armed with a gun of at least 75 mm calibre), 20,000 artillery pieces of 100 mm calibre or higher, 30,000 armoured combat vehicles (defined as those

designed to carry a squad of infantry and bearing a cannon of at least 20 mm calibre), 6,800 combat aircraft, and 2,000 attack helicopters. In addition, limits were placed on how many weapons could be held by each individual state (following the breakup of the USSR and Czechoslovakia, the totals allotted to those countries were redivided among their successor states). A subsequent 'Concluding Act of the Negotiation on Personnel Strength of Conventional Armed Forces in Europe' (the so-called CFE 1-A agreement), signed in July 1992, placed limits on the numbers of military personnel.

The CFE Treaty contains detailed **verification** provisions. Each state party to the treaty is obliged to provide the other parties with details of all its treaty-limited equipment, its numbers, types, and location. States may carry out a limited number of challenge inspections of declared sites per year to verify that the numbers declared are correct. These inspections are supervised by a Joint Consultative Group, based in Vienna.

Following the collapse of the Warsaw Pact and the USSR, the state parties agreed on 1 December 1996 to revise the treaty. In November 1999 an 'Agreement on the Adaptation of the CFE Treaty' was signed. This eliminated the group totals previously applied to NATO and the Warsaw Pact as blocs, and replaced them with limits for each state. Russia also affirmed its commitment to reduce its forces in the flank zone as required by the original treaty. This has not happened, largely because of the war in Chechnya. Moreover, Russia continues to maintain military forces in Georgia and Transdnestr. Because of these facts, several other states, including the USA, have refused as yet to ratify the adapted treaty. The original treaty remains in force, although in July 2007 Russia suspended its participation in protest against an American decision to deploy anti-**ballistic missile** defence systems in the Czech Republic.

Further reading

Treaty on Conventional Forces in Europe, http://www.fas.org/nuke/control/cfe/index.html

Richard A. Falkenrath, *Shaping Europe's Military Order: the Origins and Consequences of the CFE Treaty* (Cambridge, MA: MIT Press, 1995)

Thomas Graham Jr and Damien J. LaVera, *Cornerstones of Security: Arms Control Treaties in the Nuclear Era* (Seattle: University of Washington Press, 2003)

Jeffrey A, Larsen and Gregory J. Rattray (eds), *Arms Control Toward the 21st Century* (Boulder: Lynne Rienner, 1996)

COOPERATIVE SECURITY

Cooperative security is activity undertaken by states in cooperation with one another to reduce the likelihood of **war**, or to reduce the damage caused by war should it occur. Unlike **collective security**, which involves states taking combined action against a specific state which threatens international **security**, cooperative security is not necessarily directed against a specific target. Rather, it more often involves improving the environment within which states operate, through activities such as **disarmament**, **arms control**, **confidence and security building measures**, defence diplomacy (e.g. **Partnership for Peace**), economic development, **peace operations**, and countering the **proliferation** of weapons. Together these are meant to enhance international stability and mitigate problems associated with the **security dilemma**, thus helping to maintain **peace**. The most notable cooperative security organization is the **Organization of Security and Cooperation in Europe**. Many other institutions, while being originally designed for the purposes of **collective defence** or **collective security**, have also taken on a cooperative security role in recent years. The **United Nations** and the **North Atlantic Treaty Organization** are examples.

Further reading

Richard Cohen and Michael Mihalka, *Cooperative Security: New Horizons for International Order*, Marshall Center Papers, no. 3 (Garmisch-Partenkirchen: George C. Marshall European Center for Security Studies, 2001)

Michael Mihalka, 'Cooperative Security in the 21st Century', *Connections: The Quarterly Journal*, vol. 4, no. 4, Winter 2005, pp. 113–122

COUNTER-INSURGENCY (COIN)

Counter-insurgency is defined as being the actions of a government and its security forces to combat efforts to overthrow the government by force and to prevent that **threat** from recurring. Numerous communist and nationalist uprisings in colonial possessions gave this matter a particular significance for Western powers after the Second World War, although by the end of the twentieth century it had declined somewhat in significance. In the last few years, counter-insurgency has once again risen to prominence, largely because of the US-led campaigns in Iraq and Afghanistan. It is now the primary military task of many Western armed forces. The central problem in counter-insurgency is how to identify the insurgents and kill, capture, or neutralize them, without in the process harming the civilian population and thereby encouraging it to support the **insurgency**. One solution, as formulated in the counter-insurgency doctrine developed by Sir Robert Thompson during the Malayan Emergency, is to pursue a political strategy which splits the people from the insurgents, and then use minimum force, abide by the law, and subordinate all military activity to the political strategy. The success of this British approach in Malaya is often contrasted with the failure of the more military-oriented strategy adopted by the Americans in Vietnam and initially in Iraq following the invasion of 2003, although the differing circumstances of each example makes such comparisons problematic. Many of the principles of counter-insurgency strategy can also be applied to **counter-terrorism**.

Further reading
Ian Beckett and John Pimlott (eds), *Armed Forces and Modern Counter Insurgency*, (London: Croom Helm, 1985)
Anthony James Joes, *Resisting Rebellion: the History and Politics of Counterinsurgency* (Lexington: University of Kentucky Press, 2004)
Robert Thompson, *Defeating Communist Insurgency: Experiences from Malaya and Vietnam* (London: Chatto and Windus, 1967)

COUNTER-TERRORISM
Counter-terrorism refers to strategies and policies designed to limit, and if possible eliminate, **terrorism**. Two primary models of counterterrorist strategy exist. These are the 'war model' and the 'criminal justice model'. The war model views the campaign against terrorism as being akin to **war**. The **'global war on terrorism'** proclaimed by the US government in 2001 is in line with this model. It sees terrorists as people who must be fought with military force, and with whom no negotiation is possible. There are serious flaws in this model. First, it legitimizes the terrorists' struggle as war rather than crime. Secondly, it overlooks the fact that many terrorist groups, while using illegitimate means, do represent people with legitimate grievances. In such instances, military reprisals do nothing to produce a lasting solution.

The criminal justice model considers terrorism to be an illegitimate expression of potentially legitimate political views. The solution to terrorism is seen as political rather than military. Governments should seek to undermine popular support for the terrorists by addressing the grievances which led to violence. In the meantime, they deal with terrorist violence in the same manner as with any **organized crime**. The lead in the campaign is taken by the police, not the armed services, and those involved abide strictly by the rules of criminal justice. If found, suspected terrorists are arrested, not killed, and are put on trial like any other accused persons. Supporters of this approach would deny that terrorism can be solved by purely military methods. Indeed, they would argue that the use of excessive violence against terrorists plays into their hands, by breeding more discontent and thus more terrorism, and that it taints the very character of the state to use illegal methods to defend itself.

In practice, most counter-terrorist campaigns combine the two models, and the approach adopted in any particular scenario will in large part depend on circumstances. In liberal democracies the great challenge is to combat terrorism effectively without undermining the principles and liberties being defended. Major terrorist incidents often result in new anti-terrorist legislation, an example being the 2002 Patriot Act in the USA. Such legislation gives rise to fears that basic rights are being undermined in the vain pursuit of perfect **security**.

Further reading
Yonah Alexander, *Combating Terrorism: Strategies of Ten Countries* (Ann Arbor: University of Michigan Press, 2002)
Russell D. Howard and Reid L. Sawyer, *Terrorism and Counterrorism: Understanding the New Security Environment* (Guildford, CT: McGraw-Hill, 2002)
Paul Wilkinson, *Terrorism versus Democracy: The Liberal State Response*, revised edition (London: Routledge, 2006)

COUP D'ÉTAT

A *coup d'état* is a sudden and unconstitutional overthrow of a national government and its replacement by another. Most often, the *coup* is mounted by a part of the state apparatus, usually the armed forces, but it can also be undertaken by outside forces, such as foreign **mercenaries**. It differs from a **revolution** in that it does not involve mass popular participation and seeks merely to replace those at the top of the state system rather than to fundamentally restructure that system, although it could be the first step on the road towards such a restructuring.

Those carrying out a *coup* aim to rapidly seize the main levers of state power. As a first step, those parts of the armed forces and internal **security** services which may be opposed to the *coup* must be neutralized. Thereafter, the participants in the *coup* seek to quickly kill, arrest, or expel senior members of the previous government, to occupy government offices, and to take control of the means of communication, including the broadcast media. This may be accomplished without bloodshed, but only if success is rapid. If a *coup* is only partially successful, **civil war** may result. *Coups* may happen for a variety of reasons: personal ambition; to eliminate incompetent, brutal, or corrupt state leaders; to defend institutional interests, particularly when the armed forces feel threatened by government policy; and for ideological purposes. Those mounting the *coup* may either take power themselves or put somebody else in power. To succeed, a *coup* does not need the active support of the population or of the state bureaucracy, but the passive acquiescence of most is highly desirable. Worldwide there have been over 300 *coup* attempts over the past fifty years, nearly 200 of which have been successful, but their incidence has decreased since the end of the **Cold War**. *Coups* have been most common in Africa, Latin America, and South-East Asia.

Further reading
Eric Carlton, *The State against the State: the Theory and Practice of the Coup d'Etat* (Aldershot: Scolar, 1997)
Bruce W. Farcau, *The Coup: Tactics in the Seizure of Power* (Westport: Praeger, 1994)
Edward Luttwak, *The Coup d'Etat: a Practical Handbook* (Cambridge, MA: Harvard University Press, 1979)

COVERT ACTION

Covert action refers to activities undertaken overseas by government agencies which the said government wishes to keep secret. These include activities such as the secret provision of aid to political supporters in foreign countries, disinformation, black **propaganda** and other forms of **psychological operations**, provocation, sabotage, subversion, assassination, and support for **insurgencies, coups**, and **terrorism**. The need for secrecy means that responsibility for covert action is often given to **intelligence** agencies, but despite this connection it is a separate activity from intelligence. An example of a successful covert operation (at least in terms of achievement of its immediate objectives) was the American provision of military aid to the Afghan mujahideen during the 1980s, which assisted the latter in defeating the Soviets. Covert action often backfires, and when details become public the political damage may be considerable. It is, therefore, a very risky activity. Various scandals concerning covert action by American intelligence agencies in the 1970s and 1980s led the US Congress to stipulate that it must be informed before any covert actions are undertaken. It is alleged that during the **Global War on Terrorism** the Bush administration has been able to circumvent this requirement to some extent by giving responsibility for covert actions to military special forces and redesignating them as military operations rather than covert action.

Further reading
Mark M. Lowenthal, *Intelligence: From Secrets to Policy*, 3rd edn (Washington, DC: CQ Press, 2006)
John Prados, *Safe for Democracy: The Secret Wars of the CIA* (Chicago: Ivan R. Dee, 2006)
Len Scott, 'Secret Intelligence, Covert Action, and Clandestine Diplomacy', in L.V. Scott and Peter Jackson (eds), *Understanding Intelligence in the Twenty-First Century* (London: Routledge, 2004), pp. 162–179

CRITICAL SECURITY STUDIES
Critical security studies are an approach to the study of **security** with growing influence in the corridors of academia. They can be divided into two streams: the first includes any writings that can be considered critical of the dominant modes of thought in security studies; the second, which is the sense in which the term is more normally used, is associated with a particular, emancipatory, political agenda. This second stream draws its inspiration to a large degree from Marxist thought filtered through the Frankfurt School of critical theory, although there are also other influences. Critical security studies of this kind gain much of their energy from an intense dislike of **Realism**. They reject the idea that one can have an objective knowledge of the world ('positivism' in short), and claim that perceptions of facts are inevitably shaped by values. Realism's positivist message merely masks the fact that it is driven by concealed values which it

perpetuates by claiming that they represent truth. In the eyes of students of critical security theory, the values of Realism are statist, militarist, masculinist, and elitist. Critical security studies aim to expose these underlying values, and show how they contribute to the oppression of the weak.

Critical security theorists reject the idea that their role should be to describe objectively how international society works, as they deem that impossible. Rather, they see their role as being to change the world. Critical security studies are, therefore, quite openly political, and are moreover associated with a particular political agenda which identifies with the weak and oppressed and calls for their **emancipation** from traditional statist structures and concepts of security. Critical security theorists accordingly welcome the broadening and deepening of definitions of security to include the concerns of ordinary people. Critics consider critical security studies tainted by political bias, while the revolutionary agenda potentially alienates those with the power to make security policy. In addition, the dense theoretical discussions which characterize much of critical security studies render them inaccessible to many readers. For these reasons, as well as the fact that the emphasis of the school has to date been more on criticism than on the production of pragmatic security policies, one must doubt the practical significance of critical security studies. They can play a useful role, however, by forcing people to admit the hidden assumptions and interests behind security policies.

Further reading
Ken Booth (ed.), *Critical Security Studies and World Politics* (Boulder: Lynne Rienner, 2005)
Karin Fierke, *Critical Approaches to International Security* (Cambridge: Polity, 2007)
Keith Krause and Michael C. Williams (eds), *Critical Security Studies: Concepts and Cases* (London and New York: Routledge, 2003)
Richard Wyn Jones (ed.), *Critical Theory and World Politics* (Boulder: Lynne Rienner, 2001)

CRUISE MISSILE

A cruise missile is an unmanned self-guided warhead-delivery vehicle which flies under power using air for lift and for its engines; in essence a flying bomb. The first cruise missile used in **war** was the German V-1 during the Second World War. This was very inaccurate.

The development of terrain contour matching technology in the 1970s, and more recently of the Global Positioning System, has overcome this problem, enabling modern cruise missiles to strike targets with very great accuracy. Other advantages of cruise missiles are that they are cheaper and easier to construct than aircraft and do not need expensive-to-train pilots. They are also small, which means that large numbers can be carried on platforms such as bomber aircraft and submarines, and they can in some cases avoid detection by radar. On the other hand, they are relatively slow, especially compared with **ballistic missiles**, and so can be shot down. Cruise missiles can be used to carry both conventional and **nuclear weapons**. The US armed forces used them extensively in the former configuration during both the Gulf War of 1991 and the invasion of Iraq in 2003.

Further reading

Richard K. Betts (ed.), *Cruise Missiles: Technology, Strategy, Politics* (Washington, DC: Brookings, 1981)

Cruise Missiles: Background, Technology, Verification (Ottawa. Department of External Affairs, 1987)

Kenneth P. Werrell, 'The Weapon the Military Did Not Want: the Modern Strategic Cruise Missile', *The Journal of Military History*, vol. 53, no. 4, October 1989, pp. 419–438

CYBERWARFARE

Cyberwarfare is warfare waged via computers and the internet. It includes both offensive measures designed to damage opponents' information systems and defensive measures to protect one's own systems from hostile attack. Confusingly, the term has also been used to describe military operations using information-based techniques, thus conflating it with **information warfare** and **network-centric warfare**. Modern states and their armed forces are increasingly dependent on computers. Attacks on these computers may be as damaging as traditional military attack. Cyberwarfare has a number of aims: to exploit others' information for oneself (in other words, espionage); to deceive opponents; to disrupt enemy information systems or temporarily deny enemies the use of them; and to destroy these systems. Methods include: data attacks, such as spamming, which can overload a computer system and cause it to fail; hacking into computers in order to extract information; software attacks, such as viruses, worms, and logic bombs; and physical attacks on computers or the communications systems which link them. Such attacks may be conducted both by states and by non-state actors such as terrorists. Some commentators fear that a future **war** will begin with an 'electronic Pearl Harbor', which will deliver a sudden and catastrophic blow to friendly computer systems. The need to protect against such an attack makes **information security** a vital priority for all modern states.

Further reading
John Arquilla and David Ronfeldt, 'Cyberwar is Coming', *Comparative Strategy*, vol. 12, no. 2, Spring 1993, pp. 141–165
John V. Blane (ed.), *Cyberwarfare: Terror at a Click* (Huntington: Novinka, 2001)
Global Organized Crime Project, *Cybercrime, Cyberterrorism, Cyberwarfare: Averting an Electronic Waterloo* (Washington, DC: CSIS Press, 1998)

DEMOCRATIC PEACE THEORY

Democratic **Peace** Theory posits that established liberal democratic states rarely, if ever, wage **war** against one another. Proponents of the theory argue that this is as close to an absolute rule as it is possible to find in the fields of international relations and **security** studies. Democratic states are also often portrayed as more peaceable than non-democratic states. The theory suggests that if liberal democracy spreads, the incidence of inter-state war should decline. There is considerable evidence in favour of the theory, but it overlooks some points. First, while it is true that liberal democratic states have rarely waged war against one another, it is not true that they do not wage war significantly less than other types of states. In fact, liberal democracies regularly wage war against non-democracies. Of the five states who have fought the most inter-state wars since 1945, four (the UK, France, USA and Australia) have liberal democratic political systems. In addition, studies suggest that states in the process of democratizing are the most likely to wage war: promoting democracy may in the long term reduce war, but in the short term is more likely to produce it. It is also argued that while liberal democratic states *rarely* fight each other, it is untrue that they *never* fight each other. Much depends on how one defines an established liberal democracy. Supporters of democratic peace theory tend to argue that exceptions to the theory are not really exceptions because one of the states involved was either not a *liberal* democracy, or was not an *established* one. The problem is that until 1945 there were very few *established liberal* democracies, and for most of the time since then those few were forced to ally with one another in defence against communism. There have not been a sufficient number of liberal democracies over a sufficient length of time to thoroughly test the theory. In addition, rules may be established suggesting that other like-minded groups rarely fight one another – indeed this holds true for communist states as much as democratic ones. The region where there were the fewest inter-state wars in the twentieth century, Latin America, was not noted in that timespan for liberal democratic government.

Even if democratic peace theory is correct, it is unclear why this phenomenon exists. One argument is that ordinary citizens bear the brunt of the costs of war, and are more likely to oppose it than the ruling elites. It follows that because democracy gives power to ordinary people, it makes war less likely. This does not seem an adequate explanation. First, given that most democratic states now have professional armies and fight mainly **limited wars** far from home against enemies which are generally much weaker than they are, ordinary citizens are largely isolated from the costs of war. Second, if true, this explanation would suggest that democracies would be unlikely to wage war at all. But as shown above, this is not true. Democracies often wage war, just not often against each other. Other theorists suggest either that the rarity of inter-democracy war is a product of shared values, so that democracies form a **security community**, in which it is assumed that conflicts will be resolved peacefully, or that it is a product of the particular nature of democratic institutions. These institutions and their decisions, such as that to wage war, are relatively transparent and so the distrust which leads to war is reduced. An alternative theory maintains that democratic peace has been a product not of any special feature of democracy but rather of first the communist threat during the **Cold War** and then of US **hegemony** after it. Whether the democratic peace will continue in the long term remains to be seen.

Further reading
Charles Lipson, *Reliable Partners: How Democracies Have Made a Separate Peace* (Princeton: Princeton University Press, 2003)
Karen Rasler and William R. Thompson, *Puzzles of the Democratic Peace Theory, Geopolitics and the Transformation of World Politics* (Basingstoke: Palgrave, 2005)

Jack Snyder and Edward Mansfield, *Electing to Fight: Why Emerging Democracies Go To War* (Boston, MA: MIT Press, 2005)

DETERRENCE

Deterrence is a psychological strategy designed to dissuade a second party from undertaking a certain action by persuading it that the costs of the action will outweigh the benefits. It involves the **threat** of harm rather than its application. Once it becomes necessary to carry out the threatened response, deterrence has failed.

Deterrence will only work if certain conditions exist. First, those making the threat must be able to communicate it effectively to their adversaries. This means making it clear what actions are prohibited and exactly what costs will ensue if the prohibited actions are undertaken. Second, those making the threat must actually possess the capability to carry it out. Third, the threat must be believable. This is a matter of credibility. If the threat is massively disproportionate to the prohibited action, the person being deterred will be unlikely to believe that the threatening state will act, even if it has the ability to do so. Similarly, if the threatening state has previously shown itself to be weak and unwilling to **risk** conflict, its threats will lack credibility. Deterrence is thus linked to reputation. Finally, deterrence assumes some degree of rationality in those being deterred. To succeed, those doing the deterring need to understand the values of their adversaries and how they measure costs and benefits.

The strategy of deterrence gained prominence during the **Cold War**, particularly with regard to nuclear deterrence. The US policy of **Mutually Assured Destruction (MAD)** sought to deter a Soviet attack on Europe by threatening the annihilation of the USSR should such an attack take place. Fearing that a surprise first strike could destroy their ability to respond, American nuclear strategists also determined that nuclear deterrence was dependent on the possession of a sufficiently large nuclear force to strike back even if much of the force was destroyed in the initial enemy attack. This is known as an 'invulnerable second strike capability'. The USA and USSR sought to create this capability by building up a very large number of **nuclear weapons** and placing them on a variety of land, sea and air-based platforms (those three being known as the 'nuclear triad') in order to reduce vulnerability. They also negotiated the **Anti-Ballistic Missile Treaty** in 1972, further enhancing deterrence by preventing either side from being able to protect itself from nuclear retaliation.

'Extended deterrence' refers to extending one's deterrent to cover allies. So, for instance, the United States threatened to retaliate against the Soviets should they launch a nuclear attack against a fellow member of the **North Atlantic Treaty Organization**. Extended deterrence is not entirely credible in a nuclear context, as it is reasonable to assume that a nuclear state will not risk its own destruction by retaliating on behalf of an ally when it itself has not yet been attacked. Lack of faith in extended deterrence contributed to British and French decisions to maintain an independent nuclear deterrent throughout the Cold War.

The language of deterrence has declined in popularity since the end of the Cold War. Many commentators believe that contemporary threats to **security**, such as **terrorism** and **rogue states**, are immune to deterrence, although this may not necessarily be true. Deterrence also has no obvious role to play in areas such as **environmental, societal**, and **human security**.

Further reading
Phil Williams, 'Deterrence', in John Baylis, Ken Booth, John Garnett, and Phil Williams, *Contemporary Strategy: Theories and Policies* (New York: Holmes and Meier, 1975)
Patrick Morgan, *Deterrence Now* (Cambridge: Cambridge University Press, 2003)
Keith B. Payne and C. Dale Walton, 'Deterrence in the Post-Cold War World', in John Baylis, James Wirtz, Eliot Cohen, and Colin S. Gray (eds), *Strategy in the Contemporary World: An Introduction to Strategic Studies* (Oxford: Oxford University Press, 2002), pp. 161–182

DIRECTION GÉNÉRALE DE LA SÉCURITÉ EXTÉRIEURE (DGSE)

The Direction Générale de la Sécurité Extérieure (DGSE) is the foreign **intelligence** service of France. Its headquarters on Boulevard Mortier in Paris are often referred to as 'la piscine' on account of the nearby swimming pool in the Rue de Tourelle. The DGSE was created in 1982, replacing the Service de Documentation Extérieure et de Contre-Espionage (SDECE). The organization is subordinated to the Ministry of Defence, and is believed to have about 4,000 employees. It carries out the collection and analysis of human, signals, and imagery intelligence on political, military, and economic matters, but is best known not for its intelligence gathering activities but for its **covert action**. In particular, DGSE acquired international notoriety when two of its agents sank the Greenpeace ship *Rainbow Warrior* off New Zealand in 1985.

Further reading
Claude Silberzahn, *Au Coeur du Secret: 1500 Jours aux Commandes de la DGSE, 1989–1993* (Paris: Fayard, 1995)
Nigel West, 'La Piscine', in Nigel West, *Games of Intelligence: The Classified Conflict of International Espionage* (New York: Crown, 1989), pp. 154–170

DIRECTION DE LA SURVEILLANCE DU TERRITOIRE (DST)

The Direction de la Surveillance du Territoire (DST) is the internal **security intelligence** agency of France. The DST was created in 1944 to combat espionage and the influence of foreign powers on French territory. Part of the Ministry of the Interior, the DST is nowadays responsible for **counter-terrorism**, counter-espionage, and the protection of France's economic and scientific infrastructure, including the protection of French technology. In recent years, the main priority of the DST has been the threat from Islamic **terrorism**, particularly that emanating from North Africa. The DST works closely with the French foreign intelligence service, the **Direction Générale de la Securité Exterieure (DGSE)**, and with the French police through France's Anti-Terrorism Coordination Unit (Unité de Coordination de la Lutte Anti-Terroriste). The DST is highly secretive and not subject to any form of parliamentary oversight.

Further reading
Peter Chalk and William Rosenau, *Confronting the Enemy 'Within': Security Intelligence, the Police, and Counterterrorism in Four Democracies* (Santa Monica: RAND, 2004)
Ministère de l'Intérieure, 'La Direction de la Surveillance du Territoire', http://www.interieur.gouv.fr/sections/a_l_interieur/la_police_nationale/organization/dst

DIRTY BOMB, see RADIOLOGICAL WEAPON

DISARMAMENT

Disarmament involves the reduction or elimination of military capabilities. This may be carried out unilaterally, bilaterally, or multilaterally. Unilateral disarmament may be voluntary, when a state chooses of its own volition to reduce its armaments, or may be imposed, normally when a state or non-state actor is defeated in **war**. Examples of enforced disarmament are the arms reductions and restrictions imposed on Germany after the First World War and on Iraq after the Gulf War of 1991. Bilateral and multilateral disarmament result from negotiation and treaties. They are intended to reduce tension and the dangers involved in the **security dilemma** and **arms races** by reducing the numbers of weapons held by each side. Disarmament of this sort is based on the principle that the existence of weapons is as much a cause as a symptom of conflict, and that a world with fewer weapons will be one with fewer tensions and less likelihood of war. Histori-cally, however, disarmament treaties have had little success in reduc-ing levels of armaments in the long term and in preventing war. The failure of disarmament agreements, such as the Washington Naval Treaty of 1922 and the London Treaty of 1930, to prevent the rearma-ment of Germany and Japan and the outbreak of the Second World War led to disillusionment and a belief that disarmament could even be counterproductive. During the Cold War period the emphasis shifted towards a broader concept of **arms control**, although disarma-ment returned to the international agenda at the end of the 1980s with the signing of treaties such as the **Conventional Forces in Europe Treaty**, the **Intermediate-Range Nuclear Forces Treaty**, and the **Stra-tegic Arms Reduction Treaties**.

Further reading
David Barash and Charles P. Webel, 'Disarmament and Arms Control', in David Barash and Charles P. Webel, *Peace and Conflict Studies* (Thousand Oaks: Sage, 2002), pp. 315–343
Ken Booth, 'Disarmament and Arms Control', in John Baylis, Ken Booth, John Garnett, and Phil Williams, *Contemporary Strategy: Theories and Policies* (New York: Holmes and Meier, 1975), pp. 89–113
Steve Tulliu and Thomas Schmalberger, *Coming to Terms with Security: A Lexicon for Arms Control, Disarmament and Confidence-Building*, UNIDIR/2003/22 (Geneva: UNIDIR, 2003)

DISEASE, see PANDEMIC

ECONOMIC COMMUNITY OF WEST AFRICAN STATES (ECOWAS)

The Economic Community of West African States (ECOWAS) is an international organization consisting of 16 states in West Africa. Founded in 1975, ECOWAS's original purpose was to promote economic integration and development among its members, but it has since acquired a more active role in **security** affairs. ECOWAS members agreed security protocols in 1978 and 1981. These had little significance until 1990, when ECOWAS formed a **peacekeeping** force known as the ECOWAS Monitoring Group (ECOMOG), which deployed into Liberia during the **civil war** in that country. ECOMOG troops subsequently also intervened in Sierra Leone and Guinea-Bissau. Some observers regard these missions as a model of how regional organizations could take responsibility for **peace operations** in the future. Others, by contrast, have criticized ECOMOG's performance, and have even argued that its intervention prolonged the civil war in Liberia. Nevertheless, building on that experience, in 1999 ECOWAS heads of government endorsed a new **collective security** regime known as the Mechanism for Conflict Prevention, Management and Resolution, Peacekeeping, and Security. As part of this mechanism, ECOWAS now possesses a Department of Defence and Security, responsible for planning and managing peace operations and supporting a standby force to carry out such missions.

Further reading
Seth Appiah-Mensah, 'Security is Like Oxygen: a Regional Security Mechanism for West Africa', *Naval War College Review*, vol. 54, no. 3, Summer 2001, pp. 52–62
Economic Community of West African States website, http://www.ecowas.int
Herbert Howe, 'Lessons of Liberia: ECOMOG and Regional Peacekeeping', *International Security*, vol. 21, no. 3, Winter 1996/97, pp. 145–176

ECONOMIC SANCTIONS

Economic sanctions consist of economic penalties imposed on a country in order to coerce its government into changing its policies. An alternative objective is to impoverish the people of the country in question, in the hope that this will lead to political discontent and the overthrow of the government. Sanctions may also be used in order to show resolve and to create a precedent that undesirable behaviour is punished, thus strengthening **deterrence**, and to satisfy domestic political demands. In the latter case, the real purpose of sanctions may be more symbolic than practical; their objective is to demonstrate that the home government is 'doing something', rather than to change the policies of the target country.

Sanctions are of three main sorts: restrictions on imports of that country's goods and services, making it harder for it to earn foreign currency; restrictions on exports to that country, making it harder for it to obtain the goods and services it needs for its economy to function properly; and restrictions on its access to international finance. Sanctions may be applied by a single country or by many, and may seek to damage the entire economy of the target or may be limited to just one sector. At one point, theorists suggested that to be effective, sanctions needed to be comprehensive and fully enforced. In other words, multilateral sanctions which harm the entire economy of the target are more likely to be successful than unilateral sanctions which are less universally applied. During the 1990s, experience of the effects of such sanctions on countries like Iraq created a view that they impose intolerable humanitarian costs for limited political benefit. In recent years there has been a shift towards more targeted sanctions, including so-called 'smart sanctions'. Instead of seeking to reduce the wealth and quality of life of ordinary people, these are aimed more directly at political decision-makers, by, for instance, freezing the bank accounts of important persons and refusing them entry into other countries.

Experts disagree as to whether economic sanctions are an effective tool of foreign and **security** policy. One study conducted in the 1980s maintained that sanctions achieve their stated objectives in about one-third of all cases. Other experts dispute this claim and suggest that the success rate of sanctions is much lower. Sanctions have proved popular because they are seen as a more humane way of coercing others than **war**. This perception has also been challenged recently, and it has been suggested that in some instances the opposite may be the case. For instance, it is alleged that sanctions were responsible for over 500,000 excess deaths in Iraq during the 1990s. These statistics are also disputed, and thus the debates about the efficacity and morality of economic sanctions remain unresolved.

Further reading

David Cortright and George A. Lopez (eds), *Economic Sanctions: Panacea or Peacebuilding in a Post-Cold War World?* (Boulder: Westview, 1995)

Gary Clyde Hufbauer, Jeffrey J. Schott, and Kimberly Ann Elliott, *Economic Sanctions Reconsidered: History and Current Policy* (Washington, DC.: Institute for International Economics, 1985)

Robert A. Pape, 'Why Economic Sanctions Do Not Work', *International Security*, vol. 22, no. 2, August 1997, pp. 90–136

ECONOMIC SECURITY

Like many terms in the field of **security** studies, 'economic security' lacks a clearly agreed definition. It may be viewed at both the individual and the state level. In the former case, economic security at its most basic implies freedom from poverty, but it is generally seen as going beyond that to include the possession of sufficient economic resources to participate with dignity in society, as well as to have some protection against uncertainty and **risk**. Economic security may encompass aspects such as employment security (in other words some form of legal protection against arbitrary dismissal), income security (for instance, minimum wages), and unemployment insurance.

At the level of the state, economic security implies maximizing the state's relative economic strength, on the grounds first that economic strength is desirable in and of itself and second that **national power**, including military power, is ultimately dependent on economic power. Economic security also means reducing the state's vulnerability to external economic shocks, as well as to the use of economic weapons such as **economic sanctions**. This means that economic security can be defined in terms of 'security of supply', for instance having a safe and reliable supply of weapons, energy, and essential raw materials, such as oil, gas, and minerals. Economic security in this context is bound up with **energy security**. Historically speaking, states have often sought economic security of this kind by attempting to make themselves self-sufficient in terms of raw materials and military production, and on occasion even by waging **war** to guarantee supply. Critics of such policies argue that economic well-being is better served by free trade and international cooperation than by the pursuit of self-sufficiency. Economic problems, it is argued, require economic solutions, not political or military ones. For this reason, while some commentators consider that the pursuit of economic security ought to be a primary component of **national security** policy, others disagree.

Further reading
Vincent Cable, 'What is International Economic Security?', *International Affairs*, vol. 71, no. 2, 1995, pp. 305–324
ILO Socio-Economic Security Programme, *Economic Security for a Better World* (Geneva: International Labour Organization, 2004)
Helen E. S. Nesadurai, 'Introduction: Economic Security, Globalization and Governance', *The Pacific Review*, vol. 17, no. 4, 2004, pp. 459–484

Ejercito de Liberacion Nacional (ELN),
see Fuerzas Armadas Revolucionarios de Colombia (FARC)

EMANCIPATION

Emancipation is a key concept in the school of **critical security studies**, and attitudes towards it divide followers of the school into two camps. Theorists in the first camp see critical security studies as a generic term for work of all sorts which challenges traditional **security** assumptions; those in the second (associated with the Frankfurt School of critical theory) believe that critical security studies should be devoted to a specific emancipatory political agenda. These latter see states often not as providers of security but as the main threat to **human security**. Security consists of emancipating individuals from such oppressive structures, so that they can live their lives in the way they wish. This implies freeing them from the **threats** of **war**, poverty, ill-health, social and economic discrimination, and political oppression. Emancipation, it is argued, leads to more stable societies. Such societies are less prone to internal conflict, and, as suggested by **democratic peace theory**, are less likely to wage **war** against one another. Whereas traditional, military-orientated views of security focus on the task of preserving 'negative' **peace**, emancipation will lay the ground for a truer, and more stable, 'positive' peace. Emancipation and security are thus inextricably linked, and in the eyes of some critical security theorists are in fact identical.

Critics argue that emancipation covers such a broad spectrum of issues as to become meaningless. Another criticism is that emancipation and security are not in fact synonymous; emancipation does not necessarily bring security, and in fact may bring insecurity. The critical security theorists' assumption that people need to be liberated from oppressive states is also open to challenge. While this may be true for some, for many the greatest problem may in fact be the absence of strong states capable of providing them with security. State building, rather than emancipation, may be the key to security. The goals of emancipation are laudable, but the concept will require further refinement and clearer definition if it is to have genuine and lasting influence.

Further reading
Ken Booth, 'Security and Emancipation', *Review of International Studies*, vol. 17, no. 4, October 1991, pp. 313–326

Ken Booth (ed.), *Critical Security Studies and World Politics* (Boulder: Lynne Rienner, 2005)

Mohammed Ayoob, 'Defining Security: A Subaltern Realist Perspective', in Keith Krause and Michael C. Williams (eds), *Critical Security Studies: Concepts and Cases* (London and New York: Routledge, 2003), pp. 121–146

ENERGY SECURITY

Energy security implies guaranteed access to a reliable supply of energy (e.g. oil, gas, coal, and nuclear fuels) at a reasonable price. Given the importance of energy to a modern economy, energy security is a vital **national interest** as well as an essential component of **economic security**. Energy security may be threatened in a number of ways. First, those who control the energy sources may cut off the supply or raise prices sharply as a form of economic and political blackmail. Second, energy production facilities may be destroyed as a result of **war** or sabotage. Third, the transport of energy supplies may be interrupted, for instance as an indirect consequence of war.

One means of protecting against these **threats** is to gain physical control of the energy supply. This involves serious political, economic, and military costs, and so in the modern era states prefer instead to ally themselves with energy-producing countries. If they have the means, they may also wish to develop an off-shore military intervention capability which can move quickly to protect supply if it is ever threatened. Further measures to enhance energy security include: reducing one's dependence on foreign sources of energy by developing domestic supplies; ensuring that one is not overly dependent on a single supplier for any particular form of energy; diversifying the forms of fuels on which one depends; stockpiling fuel; and finally, reducing energy consumption by means of conservation measures and financial incentives.

Further reading

David A. Deese and Joseph S. Nye, *Energy and Security* (Cambridge, MA: Ballinger, 1981)

Jan H. Kalicki and David L. Goldwyn, *Energy and Security: Toward a New Foreign Policy Strategy* (Washington, DC: Woodrow Wilson Center Press, 2005)

Ian Rutledge, *Addicted to Oil: America's Relentless Drive for Energy Security* (London: I.B. Tauris, 2005)

ENGAGEMENT

Engagement is a **national security strategy** with a variety of different meanings. In its first sense, it can be seen as being opposed to the policy of isolationism. Whereas the isolationist state stands aside from problems elsewhere in the world until such time as they pose a direct **threat** to its national security, the state practising a strategy of engagement adopts a more interventionist approach. In this way, engagement is a proactive rather than a reactive strategy. By becoming engaged in international problems, states hope to be able to ameliorate them before they turn into crises or, even worse, **war**, and should that not be possible, to prevent the negative consequences of conflict from spreading too widely. Engagement therefore implies a commitment to **conflict prevention** and **conflict resolution**, as well as **peace operations**.

Engagement also implies operating in conjunction with others, and thus also the creation and maintenance of alliances, and a preference for **multilateralism** versus unilateralism. The decision by the United States to remain engaged in Europe throughout the **Cold War** through the mechanism of the **North Atlantic Treaty Organization (NATO)** is an example of this sort of engagement. Some American commentators also speak of 'deep engagement'. As in the case of NATO, this involves the long-term deployment of armed forces into areas where vital **national interests** are believed to be at stake, and the formation of military alliances with regional states. According to critics of such policies, the term 'engagement' has thereby been distorted to become synonymous with military imperialism.

In a final sense, engagement describes a strategy of seeking to change the politics of other states by non-confrontational means. It may also be contrasted with the policy of **containment**. Faced by another state which is a potential adversary or which is believed to be acting in a undesirable manner (by, for instance, abusing human rights), those following a strategy of engagement will not seek to contain it by forging military and political alliances against it, nor to change its politics through coercive measures such as **economic sanctions**. Instead they will enter into dialogue with it, and maintain trade and cultural relations with it, in the hope of thereby gaining some moral influence over it. The United States, for instance, practised a strategy of 'constructive engagement' towards South Africa during the apartheid era, resisting efforts to completely isolate the South African regime, on the grounds that it could exert more influence over the South Africans by engaging positively with them. Engagement of this sort is subject to the criticism that it may be indistinguishable from **appeasement**.

Further reading

Robert J. Art, 'Geopolitics Updated: the Strategy of Selective Engagement', *International Security*, vol. 23, no. 3, Winter 1998–99, pp. 79–113

Michael Mastanduno, 'Preserving the Unipolar Moment: Realist Theories and U.S. Grand Strategy after the Cold War', *International Security*, vol. 21, no. 4, Spring 1997, pp. 49–88

ENVIRONMENTAL MODIFICATION CONVENTION

The 'Convention on the Prohibition of Military or Any Other Hostile Use of Environmental Modification Techniques' was signed in Geneva on 18 May 1977 and came into force on 5 October 1978. Parties to the convention undertake 'not to engage in military or any other hostile use of environmental modification techniques which have widespread, long-lasting or severe effects as the means of destruction, damage or injury to any other state party'. The phrase 'environmental modification techniques' refers to techniques for changing the dynamics, composition or structure of the Earth through the deliberate manipulation of natural processes. This includes manipulation of the weather. Although the ability of states to modify the environment in such a way as to use it as a weapon of **war** remains extremely limited, the convention recognized that technological advances might make such activities possible in the future and sought to pre-empt this.

Further reading

www.fas.org/nuke/control/enmod/text/environ2.htm

Colonel Tamzy J. House et al., 'Weather as a Force Multiplier: Owning the Weather in 2025', *Air Force 2025*, http://www.fas.org/spp/military/docops/usaf/2025/v3c15/v3c15-1.htm

Thomas Graham Jr and Damien J. LaVera, *Cornerstones of Security: Arms Control Treaties in the Nuclear Era* (Seattle: University of Washington Press, 2003)

ENVIRONMENTAL SECURITY

Environmental security implies protecting humans against harm caused by deterioration of the natural environment. This in turn implies protecting the environment from man-made damage, so as to reduce the likelihood of humans suffering directly and indirectly from such damage. There are two sorts of environmental **threats** to **human security**: natural disasters, such as earthquakes; and man-made problems, such as global warming, deforestation, and ozone depletion. The term 'environmental security' is most often used to refer to protection from the second of these, on the grounds that earthquakes, hurricanes and so forth are not caused by human action and cannot be prevented (although some action can be taken to reduce their harmful effects).

The environment can be seen as a **security** issue for simple existential reasons – people require food, water, fuel and other resources in order to survive. Pollution and depletion of these resources directly threaten life. Protecting the environment is a matter of the greatest importance for national and human security. Another reason for considering the environment a security issue is that damage to the environment may contribute to violent conflict. Shortages of natural resources may result in '**resource conflicts**' as groups or states fight to gain control of those things which are scarce, such as water. Alternatively, environmental degradation may produce conflict within states, as damage to the natural environment forces populations to move from the countryside into the cities, creating social dislocation and eventually violence. Authors such as Robert Kaplan and Thomas Homer-Dixon have argued that as the human population grows and increases its consumption, resource scarcity will become more common, and conflicts of this sort will increase. This is seen as being a particularly serious problem for the Third World. Others, though, argue that resource scarcity is exaggerated and that such conflicts are less likely than is claimed.

The exact link between environmental degradation and violent conflict is in any case uncertain. There are few examples so far of resource **wars**, and other factors appear to be far more important in determining whether groups fight one another. For this and other reasons, commentators are divided as to whether the environment should be considered a security issue. There is general agreement that environmental problems cannot be solved by individual nations, as they cross borders. Promoting the environment as a security issue implies adopting a new form of **cooperative security** which transcends the traditional state-centred security model.

Further reading

Jon Barnett, *The Meaning of Environmental Security* (London: Zed, 2001)

Paul F. Diehl and Nils Petter Gleditsch, *Environmental Conflict* (Boulder: Westview, 2001)

Simon Dalby, *Environmental Security* (Minneapolis: University of Minnesota Press, 2002)

Marc A. Levy, 'Is the Environment a Security Issue?', *International Security*, vol. 20, no. 2, Fall 1995, pp. 35–62

ESCALATION

Most, if not all, **wars** are **limited wars**. There exist explicit or tacit understandings among the belligerents as to the acceptable limits of the use of force. These limits govern the non-use of certain types of weapons, the immunity of certain types of target, geographical restrictions concerning the deployment of forces, and so on. Escalation is the process by which these limits on the waging of war are breached. This separates an escalation from the mere invention of a new tactic or weapon or a mere increase in the level of resources committed to the conflict, although the term is sometimes used with reference to the latter.

Escalation may happen in one large step, or in many small ones. Herman Kahn identified 44 steps on the 'ladder of escalation' from 'ostensible crisis' to 'spasm or insensate war' in which 'all the buttons are pressed'. Along the ladder, Kahn identified six thresholds, steps which represent particularly sharp changes in the character of the escalation (for instance, from no nuclear use to nuclear use, and from nuclear strikes on military targets to nuclear strikes on cities). It is possible to de-escalate, as well as to escalate, but in general this is considered much more difficult. Once limits are broken it is hard to re-establish them.

Belligerents may escalate for a number of reasons. The first is to gain some advantage over their enemy, be it temporary or decisive. A second is to avoid defeat – when facing the prospect of defeat the incentive to abide by legal, moral or other limits to war inevitably declines. A third is that once war has begun, the stakes increase. Faced by the knowledge that one's side has already suffered substantial losses, anything less than decisive victory becomes less acceptable, and means previously considered off limits no longer appear so unthinkable.

The tendency towards escalation is present in all wars. As Carl von Clausewitz pointed out, each side in a conflict tries to outdo the other, setting up what he referred to as an 'interaction'. Once one side escalates, the other may retaliate, either by an equal escalation of its own, or by an even larger counter-escalation, designed to compensate for the lost advantage or to deter further escalation. This counter-escalation may in turn be met by another escalation, and so forth until a state of total or **absolute war** is reached. At this point, as Clausewitz pointed out, the action ceases to be proportionate to the political purpose of the war.

A spiral of escalation of this sort is particularly likely to occur when an escalation threatens a vital **national interest** of the enemy, but not all escalations are met by counter-escalations. Combatants may be aware of the dangers and restrain themselves. The extent to which conflicts escalate varies substantially and is largely contingent on situation-specific factors.

Further reading

Carl von Clausewitz, *On War*, edited and translated by Michael Howard and Peter Paret (Princeton: Princeton University Press, 1976), Chapter 3.B

Herman Kahn, *On Escalation: Metaphors and Scenarios* (New York: Praeger, 1965)

Richard Smoke, *War: Controlling Escalation* (Cambridge, MA: Harvard University Press, 1977)

ESSENTIALLY CONTESTED CONCEPT

Many theorists, especially those associated with **critical security studies**, opine that **security** is an 'essentially contested concept', an idea introduced by W.B. Gallie in 1956. An essentially contested concept is different from one which is merely vague or confused, containing a variety of possible meanings. The term implies that people agree that there is a single core concept, such as 'security', but also that this is so 'value-laden' that they cannot, and never will, reach agreement on what it means.

Gallie stated that seven criteria apply to essentially contested concepts. First, they have an 'appraisive character', that is to say that they signify 'some kind of valued achievement'. Second, they are internally complex. Third, different people may describe their meaning in different ways. Fourth, they are 'open' concepts; that is to say that they can be revised in the light of new circumstances, 'the accredited achievement must be of a kind that admits of considerable modification in the light of changing circumstances'. Fifth, there is reciprocal recognition among the parties contending the meaning of the concept that it is indeed contested. Sixth, the core concept rests on an original 'exemplar', which ensures that competing parties are in fact contesting the same concept. And finally, continued debates over the meaning should lead to greater coherence of conceptual usage.

The idea of the essentially contested concept is not universally accepted. Some commentators maintain that theories of 'essentially contestedness' are 'incoherent'. If this is indeed the case, then the assertion that security is such a concept is of no value. Assuming, however, that the theory has some validity, it is not clear whether the concept of security fits the criteria listed by Gallie. Certainly, there is agreement that there is a central core concept – security – and considerable disagreement as to its exact meaning. It is apparently internally complex, and it is also described by different people in different ways. However, it is not obvious that security is an 'appraisive' concept, nor even that it is open. Arguably, the basic definition of security as 'freedom from **threat**' is remarkably constant. Debates focus on issues such as which threats and whose security should take priority, but the core concept remains unaltered. In addition, Gallie drew a distinction between 'contestable' and 'contested' concepts. Security, according to some commentators, does not really fit the latter description, because those who take different views of the meaning of security do not actually contest their views with each other; instead they largely ignore one another. Followers of **Realism** and critical security studies operate in academic realms which are widely separated from each other. There is no reciprocal recognition that the concept is contested. Security may, therefore, be not so much 'essentially contested' as 'confused or inadequately explicated'.

If one nevertheless accepts the classification of security as essentially contested, it is not clear what the practical implications of this are. For some, it may provide an excuse to redefine security in whatever way they please, to suit their own political agenda. This perhaps explains the idea's popularity. For others, it may lead to a decision to avoid trying to define security at all. This, however, makes the concept of security rather worthless. One may conclude that the idea that security is an essentially contested concept is itself contestable and, even if it is true, it may not be very helpful.

Further reading
David A. Baldwin, 'The Concept of Security', in Paul F. Diehl (ed.), *War*, vol. 1 (London: Sage, 2005), pp. 1–24
David Collier, Fernando Daniel Hidalgo, and Andra Olivia Maciuceanu, 'Essentially Contested Concepts: Debates and Applications', *Journal of Political Ideologies*, vol. 11, no. 3, October 2006, pp. 211–246
W. B. Gallie, 'Essentially Contested Concepts', *Proceedings of the Aristotelian Society*, vol. 56, 1956, pp. 167–198

ETHNIC CLEANSING

The term 'ethnic cleansing' came into use in the early 1990s during the **wars** in the former Yugoslavia. It refers to a policy of eliminating all members of a certain ethnic group from a given territory. Members of the targeted group may be killed, in which case ethnic cleansing amounts to **genocide**, may be expelled by force from the land being 'cleansed', or may be encouraged to leave of their own accord by means of discriminatory policies, harassment, and intimidation. Although the term 'ethnic cleansing' is relatively new, the practice is not. Examples outside Yugoslavia include the expulsion of Jews and Muslims from Spain at the end of the 15th century, the forcible relocation of many native Americans from their homelands by the United States in the nineteenth century, the expulsion of Germans from parts of Eastern Europe at the end of the Second World War, and the mass displacement of both Hindus and Muslims during the partition of India in 1947.

Analysts disagree as to the primary motives for ethnic cleansing. Some seem them as economic: those carrying out the cleansing are able to seize the land and property of those cleansed. Others see them as being rooted in ancient ethnic hatreds. Yet others see the motives as primarily military, being to defeat an **insurgency** by removing the population which supports it. These are not mutually incompatible, and many examples of ethnic cleansing may include some combination of all three.

Further reading
Andrew Bell-Fialkoff, 'A Brief History of Ethnic Cleansing', *Foreign Affairs*, vol. 72, no. 3, Summer 1993, pp. 110–121
Michael Mann, *The Dark Side of Democracy: Explaining Ethnic Cleansing* (Cambridge: Cambridge University Press, 2005)

Drazen Petrovic, 'Ethnic Cleansing: an Attempt at Methodology', *European Journal of International Law*, vol. 5, no. 3, 1994, pp. 342–359

ETHNIC CONFLICT

Ethnic conflict refers to violent conflict between opposing ethnic groups within a state. Because there are no firm, objective criteria for determining what constitutes an ethnic group, it is inevitably difficult to determine which conflicts deserve the appellation 'ethnic'. Generally, these can be seen to be conflicts in which questions of group identity and recognition, rather than material concerns, play a central role. Members of the competing sides identify themselves as being members of separate ethnicities due to differing cultures, languages, religions, and so forth. They also see the others as a threat to their identity. Alternatively, they may consider that their group has been given insufficient status and recognition by the others. They wish to reduce the influence of those others, which they do by trying to physically eliminate or expel them or by trying to create their own independent state. Ethnic conflicts are often **wars** of secession, and may be accompanied by **genocide** and **ethnic cleansing**. In the early 1990s, a series of particularly bitter wars, such as those in the former Yugoslavia and Rwanda, led many observers to speak of a resurgence of ethnic conflicts and to believe that these would constitute the main threat to international order in the post-**Cold War** world. In fact, the incidence of ethnic conflict has declined since the early 1990s and the threat from it appears to be rather less than originally feared.

Further reading
Milton Esman, *An Introduction to Ethnic Conflict* (Cambridge: Polity, 2004)
Rajat Ganguly and Ray Taras, *Understanding Ethnic Conflict: The International Dimension* (New York: Longman, 1998)
Ted Robert Gurr, 'Ethnic Warfare on the Wane', *Foreign Affairs*, vol. 79, no. 3, May/June 2000, pp. 52–64
David A. Lake and Donald Rothchild, 'Containing Fear: The Origins and Management of Ethnic Conflict', *International Security*, vol. 21, no. 2, Autumn 1996, pp. 41–75

EURO-ATLANTIC PARTNERSHIP COUNCIL (EAPC),
see PARTNERSHIP FOR PEACE

EUROPEAN RAPID REACTION FORCE (ERRF), see COMMON EUROPEAN SECURITY AND DEFENCE POLICY (CESDP)

EUROPEAN SECURITY AND DEFENCE IDENTITY (ESDI), see COMMON EUROPEAN SECURITY AND DEFENCE POLICY (CESDP)

EUSKADITA TA ASKATASUNA (ETA)

Euskadita ta Askatasuna (ETA) is a terrorist organization dedicated to winning independence from Spain for the Basque people. ETA was founded in 1959 in response to the suppression of Basque language and culture by the Spanish dictator, General Franco. Since then the organization has killed over 700 people, including a number of government officials. Most notably, in 1973 ETA assassinated Franco's chosen successor, Admiral Luis Carrero Blanco. During the 1980s, government security services engaged in an illegal campaign of assassination of suspected ETA members and their supporters. Revelations concerning this led to the conviction of several officials in the late 1990s. In recent years ETA's activities have diminished considerably. In 1998 the organization declared a ceasefire and entered into dialogue with the government, but it resumed its campaign of violence in 2000, accusing the government of not being interested in negotiation. The attacks on America by **Al Qaeda** on 11 September 2001, and the 11 March 2004 train bombings in Madrid by Islamic terrorists, reduced support for terrorist attacks generally, and have made it harder for ETA to operate. ETA has been unable to regain its former strength, and it has not killed anybody since 2003. The arrest of scores of suspected members in France and Spain in 2004 further weakened the group. In March 2006, ETA declared a permanent ceasefire, but in September 2006 it undermined this by stating that it would after all continue its armed struggle. It has since resumed attacks. The political wing of ETA, *Herri Batasuna*, was banned in 2002.

Further reading
Edward V. Linden (ed.), *Foreign Terrorist Organizations: History, Tactics, and Connections* (New York: Nova Science, 2004)

William S. Shepard, 'The ETA: Spain Fights Europe's Last Active Terrorist Group', *Mediterranean Quarterly*, vol. 13, no. 1, Winter 2002, pp. 54–68

EXTRAORDINARY RENDITION, see RENDITION

FAILED STATES

Failed states are countries in which the state has lost, or never had, control of its territory or of the monopoly of the use of force. Failed states are generally unable to collect taxes, enforce law and order, or provide public services. During the **Cold War**, little attention was paid to the phenomenon of failed states, but this has changed in recent years and especially since the terrorist attacks of 11 September 2001, which were planned in a country considered by most observers to be a failed state, namely Afghanistan. Along with **rogue states**, with whom they are sometimes mistakenly conflated, failed states are increasingly being regarded as a major source of global instability and conflict.

The disintegration of state authority tends to create disorder, violence, and economic collapse, and thus causes humanitarian crises. This in turn may lead to refugees fleeing into neighbouring states, with destabilizing consequences. State arsenals may be seized, and weapons may fall into the hands of criminals and warlords. Terrorists may also find safe haven within failed states from which to launch attacks on other countries. As a result, state failure is not merely a concern for those living within the borders of the country concerned but may also sometimes pose a major **threat** to international **security**. Examples of failed states since the end of the Cold War include Haiti, Somalia, Yugoslavia, Albania, Afghanistan, and Iraq post-2003. Despite the prominence of such examples, the frequency of state failure has actually decreased in the past fifteen years. Commentators differ as to how significant the phenomenon actually is.

Further reading
Rosa Ehrenreich Brooks, 'Failed States or the State as Failure?', *The University of Chicago Law Review*, vol. 72, no. 4, Fall 2005, pp. 1159–1196
'The Failed States Index', *Foreign Policy*, no. 149, July/August 2005, pp. 56–65
Susan L. Woodward, '*Failed States*', *Naval War College Review*, vol. 52, no. 2, Spring 1999, pp. 55–68

FATAH

Founded by Yasser Arafat in 1958, Fatah is a secular political movement dedicated to the creation of an independent Palestinian state.
From 1969 onwards, it has been the dominant force within the **Palestine Liberation Organization (PLO)**. For many years Fatah engaged
in guerrilla and terrorist actions against Israel, but since 1993 it has
officially been committed to a peaceful settlement of the Palestinian-
Israeli dispute and to recognizing Israel's right to exist within secure
borders. Nevertheless, elements associated with Fatah, most notably
the **Al Aqsa Martyrs Brigade**, have continued to commit acts of **terrorism** against Israeli targets. In the past few years, Fatah's popularity
among Palestinians has declined considerably, and the movement
has lost ground to Islamic groups, especially **Hamas**, which defeated
Fatah in the 2006 elections to the Palestinian parliament.

Further reading
Anat N. Kurz, *Fatah and the Politics of Violence: The Institutionalisation of a
    Popular Struggle* (Brighton: Sussex Academic Press, 2005)
Yonah Alexander, *Palestinian Secular Terrorism* (Ardsley: Transnational
    Publishers, 2003)

FEDERAL BUREAU OF INVESTIGATION (FBI)

Established in 1908, the Federal Bureau of Investigation (FBI) is the
law enforcement agency of the US government, with responsibility
for investigating cases falling within federal, rather than state, jurisdiction. These include transnational **organized crime** (such as drug
trafficking), public corruption, white-collar crime, cyber-crime, and
significant violent crime. The FBI is also responsible for internal
security intelligence. In this capacity, it carries out both counter-
espionage and **counter-terrorism** activities. The discovery in 2001 that
an important member of the FBI's counter-intelligence division,
Robert Hanssen, was a Russian spy, and revelations of mistakes by
the FBI prior to the terrorist attacks of 11 September 2001, have led
to major criticism of the agency. A particular complaint is that the
FBI has concentrated too much on investigating crimes after they
have happened rather than on trying to prevent them. In response,
in 2005 the FBI created a new National Security Branch (NSB), with
responsibility for counter-intelligence, counter-terrorism, and combatting the **proliferation** of **weapons of mass destruction**. The NSB
has shifted the FBI towards a more preventive approach, gathering

intelligence in order to detect and disrupt terrorist groups before they can act. At present the FBI employs approximately 30,000 people. The overwhelming majority are situated within the USA, but the FBI also maintains over 50 offices in US embassies overseas in order to liaise with foreign law enforcement and intelligence agencies.

Further reading
Edward V. Peykar (ed.), *The FBI: Past, Present and Future* (Hauppage: Nova Science, 2005)
Richard Gid Powers, *Broken: The Troubled Past and Uncertain Future of the FBI* (New York: Free Press, 2004)
Theoharis, Athan G., *The FBI and American Democracy: a Brief Critical History* (Lawrence: University of Kansas Press, 2004)

FEDERAL'NAIA SLUZHBA BEZOPASTNOSTI (FSB)

The Federal'naia Sluzhba Bezopastnosti (Federal Security Service, FSB) is Russia's internal **security intelligence** service. It is responsible for counter-espionage, **counter-terrorism**, border security, and the fight against **organized crime**. In 1991, the Soviet **intelligence** service, the KGB, which had previously carried out both internal **security** and foreign intelligence roles, was split into several sections, including a new foreign intelligence service, the **Sluzhba Vnezhnei Razvedki** (Foreign Intelligence Service – SVR), a signals intelligence service, the Federal'noe Agentsvo Pravitel'stvennoi Sviazi i Informatsii (Federal Agency of Government Communications and Information – FAPSI), and a domestic security agency, the Federal'naia Sluzhba Kontrrazvedki (Federal Counterintelligence Service – FSK). In 1995, the FSK was reorganized and became the FSB. Furthermore, in 2003, the FSB absorbed FAPSI, and has thus now gained responsibility for the collection, analysis and dissemination of signals intelligence. The President of the Russian Federation directs the work of the FSB, which has acquired considerable investigative powers. Several former members of the FSB have acquired positions of importance within the Russian government, most notably Vladimir Putin, who was head of the FSB until becoming Prime Minister, and later President, in 1999.

Further reading
Amy Knight, *Spies without Cloaks: the KGB's Successors* (Princeton: Princeton University Press, 1996)
Agentura website, *Federal Security Service, FSB*, http://www.agentura.ru/english/dosie/fsb

FOOD SECURITY

Food security is a condition in which people live free from hunger and malnourishment and free from the fear of hunger and malnourishment. It operates at numerous levels – individual, household, national, regional and global. The United Nations Food and Agriculture Organization (UNFAO) divides it into four components: *availability* – there must be sufficient food for all people at all times; *accessibility* – all people must have access to that food; *acceptability* – the food to which people have access must be culturally acceptable to them; and *adequacy* – the food must be healthy and safe, and adequate measures must be in place to ensure that the food is being produced in a sustainable manner which does not threaten production for future generations. Food security is a fundamental human need. However, UNFAO assesses that some 840 million people worldwide suffer from chronic undernourishment. This is primarily a problem in the developing world, but even in the richest countries there are persons who are dependent on welfare and charity programmes for their survival. According to UNFAO, 11 million of those suffering chronic undernourishment live in the industrialized world. The Rome Declaration on Food Security adopted by the World Food Summit in 1996 set world leaders the task of halving the numbers who suffer from hunger worldwide by 2015. Achieving this target will be difficult. Even with continued improvements in agriculture, **war**, environmental degradation, and other problems will threaten mankind's ability to increase food production to match population growth and to distribute that food equitably.

Further reading
M. Koc, R. McRae, L. Mougeot, and J. Welsh, 'Introduction: Food Security is a Global Concern', in M. Koc et al. (eds.), *For Hunger Proof Cities: Sustainable Urban Food Systems* (Ottawa: International Development Research Centre), pp. 1–7
Kirstin Mechlem, 'Food Security and the Right to Food in the Discourse of the United Nations', *European Law Journal*, vol. 10, no. 5, September 2004, pp. 631–648
'The Quest for Food Security in the Twenty-First Century', *Canadian Journal of Development Studies*, vol. 19, Special Issue, 1998

FOURTH GENERATION WAR

Fourth Generation War (4GW) is a term used by some American military theorists to describe the type of **asymmetric warfare** which dominates contemporary international conflict. According to the proponents of 4GW, modern **war** has passed through three previous generations. In the first generation, which lasted from 1648 to about 1860, armies fought each other in organized lines. The bases of military activity were order and discipline. In the second generation, which is associated most commonly with the First World War, armies saw the key to victory as lying in the use of massive firepower. The third generation was characterized by manoeuvre warfare, which was non-linear and in which combatants sought to get behind enemy lines and cause their opponents to collapse without having to destroy them. Third generation war placed more emphasis on initiative than obedience and thus moved away from the previous stress on order. Fourth Generation War has moved further in the direction of disorder and decentralization. The state has lost its monopoly on war and wars are now fought between states and non-state actors. There are also no front lines. Victory is won on the moral plane, and in this battle the tools of the previous generations, such as massed firepower, are not merely redundant but perhaps even counterproductive. The continued reliance of states on these outdated practices means that 4GW allows the weak to defeat the strong.

Proponents of the concept of 4GW argue that states need to completely reconsider the manner in which they fight wars and the structure of their armed forces. Some critics reject the entire concept of 4GW, arguing that struggles between states and non-state actors are nothing new, and that traditional armies can still triumph against insurgents, guerrillas, and terrorists. Supporters of the concept counter that 4GW is more than just **insurgency**. Those who wage 4GW fight not just on the battlefield but across the political, economic and social spectra, including in areas such as ideology, **propaganda**, and **netwar**. This, they argue, makes 4GW something entirely distinct.

Further reading

Antulio J. Echevarria II, *Fourth-Generation War and Other Myths* (Carlisle, PA: SSI, 2005)

William S. Lind, 'Understanding Fourth Generation War', *Military Review*, September–October 2004, pp. 12–16

Tom Hammes, *The Sling and the Stone: On War in the 21ˢᵗ Century* (St Paul: Zenith, 2004)

FUERZAS ARMADAS REVOLUCIONARIOS DE COLOMBIA (FARC)

The Revolutionary Armed Forces of Colombia (Fuerzas Armadas Revolucionarios de Colombia, FARC) is a guerrilla organization which claims to represent the rural poor, and has been carrying out an armed **insurgency** against the Colombian government since 1964. It is the larger of the two insurgent groups in Colombia, the other being the Ejercito de Liberacion Nacional (ELN). Notionally Marxist in ideology, FARC controls substantial areas of the Colombian countryside, and is financed by kidnapping, extortion and narcotics trafficking. This has enabled FARC to become probably the best financed insurgent group worldwide, but to some extent the organization's battles have over the years become as much about controlling the trade in cocaine as about overthrowing the Colombian government. In November 1998, President Andres Pastrana granted FARC a safe haven in central Colombia in an effort to kickstart **peace** negotiations. In 2002 Pastrana's successor, President Alvaro Uribe, declared an end to the ceasefire and ordered the Colombian army to recapture the demilitarized zone. Since then government forces have enjoyed some success but FARC remains undefeated.

Further reading
Mark Peceny and Michael Durnan, 'The FARC's Best Friend: US Antidrug Policies and the Deepening of Colombia's Civil War in the 1990s', *Latin American Politics and Society*, vol. 48, no. 2, Summer 2006, pp. 95–116
Philippe Serres, 'The FARC and Democracy in Columbia in the 1990s', *Democratization*, vol. 7, no. 4, 2000, pp. 191–218

GENEVA CONVENTIONS

The Geneva Conventions are international treaties governing the rules of **war**. The original Geneva Convention was signed in 1864. After the Second World War, this was revised, and on 12 August 1949 four new conventions were signed to replace it. Subsequently, two additional protocols were agreed in 1977, and a third in 2005. The conventions of 1949 cover the following subjects: Convention I, the amelioration of the condition of the wounded and sick in armed forces in the field; Convention II, the amelioration of the condition of wounded, sick, and shipwrecked members of armed forces at sea; Convention III, the treatment of prisoners of war; and Convention IV, the protection of civilian persons in time of war. The three additional protocols cover the following: Protocol I, the protection of victims of international armed conflicts; Protocol II, the protection of victims of non-international armed conflicts; and Protocol III, the adoption of an additional distinctive emblem, sometimes referred to as the 'red crystal', to supplement the existing emblems, namely the red cross and red crescent, used to mark medical and other facilities which are immune from attack.

The Geneva Conventions aim to mitigate the harm caused by war. The first two conventions establish the principle that members of armed forces who have laid down their arms or become incapacitated due to wounds or sickness should be immune from further acts of violence and from humiliating and degrading treatment. Chaplains and medical personnel, as well as medical facilities and transports, should also be respected and protected in all circumstances. Convention III determines who should be considered a prisoner of war, and stipulates that prisoners of war must be humanely treated at all times. The convention provides considerable detail about the obligations of those who hold prisoners. Convention IV similarly lays out the obligations of warring parties towards civilians, as well as the obligations of occupying powers towards the population of such foreign territories as they occupy. Among other things, the convention prohibits pillage, reprisals, and the taking of hostages.

Feeling that the Geneva Conventions of 1949 were inadequate to deal with the complications of modern war, in particular the growing incidence of **civil war**, the International Committee of the Red Cross led the drive to agree the additional protocols of 1977. Significant amendments introduced in the additional protocols include a prohibition on the use of weapons which 'cause superfluous injury or unnecessary suffering', and a broadening of the definition of who may be considered a 'combatant' and as such be entitled to the rights of a prisoner of war if captured. The protocols sought in this way to bring within the bounds of the convention many of those participating in **guerrilla warfare** who had previously stood outside it. However, at the same time, it stated that **mercenaries** should not have the rights of prisoners of war. The protocols also prohibit indiscriminate attacks on civilian targets, protect cultural objects, and outlaw the use of starvation as a weapon of war. In these ways, Protocols I and II significantly strengthen the protections previously provided by the Geneva Conventions.

One hundred and ninety four countries have ratified the four Geneva Conventions, but only 166 have ratified Protocol I, and 162

Protocol II. Ratification of Protocol III is ongoing. To date, 75 countries have signed Protocol III, and nine have ratified it. Among the
countries which have refused to ratify Protocols I and II is the United
States. In part this helps to explain the differences between the USA
and other countries regarding the status of prisoners captured during
the **Global War on Terrorism** and held at Guantanamo Bay and
elsewhere.

Further reading
Basic Rules of the Geneva Conventions and Their Protocols (Geneva: International Committee for the Red Cross, 1983)
Francois Bugnion, 'The Geneva Conventions of 12 August 1949: From the
1949 Diplomatic Conference to the Dawn of the New Millenium', *International Affairs*, vol. 76, no. 1, January 2000, pp. 41–50

GENOCIDE
According to the Genocide Convention of 1948, genocide is the 'intent
to destroy, in whole or in part, a national, ethnic, racial or religious
group as such'. This may be done by killing, by causing serious bodily
or mental harm to group members, by deliberately inflicting conditions of life on the group calculated to bring about its physical destruction in whole or in part, by imposing measures intended to prevent
births within the group, or by forcibly transferring children of the
group to another's custody. This legal definition poses some problems. Proving that some person or organization not only committed
mass murder, but did so with the specific intention of destroying the
target group as such, is extremely difficult. In addition, it is unclear
what is meant by destroying a group 'in part'. The International
Criminal Tribunal for the former Yugoslavia has defined this as being
a 'substantial part', significant enough to have an impact on the group
as a whole. This judgement clarifies the issue to some extent, but still
leaves scope for interpretation.

Examples of genocide include the Second World War Holocaust
of Jewish people, the **ethnic cleansing** of Bosnians in the early 1990s,
and the massacres carried out in Rwanda in 1994. The Genocide
Convention defines genocide as an international crime and imposes
an obligation on signatories to punish those who carry it out or con-
spire or incite others to do so. Until recently, this obligation was not
met, and acts of genocide went unpunished. This began to change in

the 1990s with the institution of international courts to try cases of genocide in Rwanda and the former Yugoslavia, and with the creation of the **International Criminal Court**. In addition, a number of Western states have now enacted legislation giving their domestic courts jurisdiction over acts of genocide regardless of where they are committed. The desire to prevent genocide also played a significant role in the 1990s in legitimizing in many circles the principles of military **humanitarian intervention** and the **responsibility to protect**.

Further reading

George J. Andreopoulos (ed.), *Genocide: Conceptual and Historical Dimensions* (Philadelphia: University of Pennsylvania Press, 1994)

Alexander Laban Hinton (ed.), *Genocide: an Anthropological Reader* (Oxford: Blackwell, 2002)

Adam Jones, *Genocide: a Comprehensive Introduction* (London: Routledge, 2006)

Martin Shaw, *What is Genocide?* (Cambridge: Polity, 2007)

GLAVNOE RAZVEDYVATEL'NOE UPRAVLENIE (GRU)

The Glavnoe Razvedyvatel'noe Upravlenie General'nogo Shtaba (Main Intelligence Directorate of the General Staff – GRU) is the military **intelligence** service of the Russian Federation and previously of the Soviet Union. The GRU is responsible for the collection and analysis of both tactical and strategic military intelligence. It makes extensive use of human espionage overseas, and also maintains a capability in the areas of signals and imagery intelligence. The GRU has shown special interest in the military planning of foreign states and in the acquisition of secret military technology, with an increasing emphasis on the latter since the collapse of the Soviet Union. Unlike the Soviet civilian intelligence service, the KGB, the GRU survived the end of communism without having to undergo significant reform, in large part because, as a specifically military agency focused on gathering information about foreign powers, it had never been closely associated with internal political repression.

Further reading

Federation of American Scientists webpage, *Main Intelligence Directorate*, http://www.fas.org/irp/world/russia/gru/index.html

Viktor Suvorov, *Soviet Military Intelligence* (London: Grafton, 1986)

GLOBAL WAR ON TERRORISM (GWOT)

In the aftermath of the terrorist attacks on the United States on 11 September 2001, US President George W. Bush and other administration officials declared a 'global war on terrorism' (GWOT), sometimes also referred to as the 'global war on terror' or more simply the 'war on terror'. The parameters of the GWOT are ill-defined. Interpreted narrowly, it can be seen as being focused against extremist Islamic **terrorism**, especially the **Al Qaeda** terrorist group. Interpreted more broadly, it implies waging **war** against terrorism of every sort wherever it appears worldwide. Furthermore, the government of the United States has also included within the scope of the GWOT action to prevent **rogue states** from providing safe havens or **weapons of mass destruction** to terrorist organizations, as well as action to promote democracy in the Middle East so as to address the political grievances which some commentators posit are the root causes of most contemporary terrorism directed against the United States. In this sense, the invasion of Iraq in 2003 and the continuing US **counter-insurgency** campaign in that country, as well as broader efforts to combat the **proliferation** of weapons of mass destruction, can also be seen as part of the GWOT.

The term 'global war on terrorism' has proven to be extremely controversial. In the first place, the use of the word 'war' suggests an adherence to the war model of **counter-terrorism** operations. This implies seeking predominantly military solutions to the problem of terrorism, an approach rejected by many counter-terrorism specialists. Second, critics argue that the language of the GWOT conflates too many issues, which are not necessarily connected, and are best dealt with separately, such as terrorism, rogue states, democratization, and proliferation. Third, some argue that it is futile to wage war on 'terror' in the broader sense: terrorism is a **strategy** not an entity, and as such cannot be defeated. It would make more sense to talk of a war against Al Qaeda. Against this, US officials argue that the terminology of the GWOT expresses a truth that the United States is engaged in a war against global extremism, and also point out that the strategy of the GWOT is not restricted to the use of military means. Rather, it encompasses a whole set of military, diplomatic, financial, internal **security**, **intelligence**, and humanitarian activities, designed to tackle the problem of terrorism on multiple levels.

Key aspects of the GWOT have included: the invasions of Afghanistan and Iraq to remove the regimes of the **Taliban** and Saddam Hussein, and to deny Al Qaeda safe havens; continued efforts to combat **insurgency** and develop democratic government in those states, as well as the provision of humanitarian and financial aid to rebuild their economies; international efforts to eliminate the sources of terrorist financing; enhancing internal security through tighter border controls and legislation to strengthen the power of the state vis-à-vis terrorist suspects, as well as the capture, arrest, and occasional **rendition** of such suspects; and reform of intelligence agencies and an expansion in intelligence gathering activities and intelligence sharing among the allies of the United States.

Further reading
Jeffrey Record, *Bounding the Global War on Terrorism* (Carlisle, PA.: Strategic Studies Institute, 2003)
The White House, *Progress Report on the Global War on Terrorism* (Washington, DC: The White House, 2003)

GOVERNMENT COMMUNICATIONS HEADQUARTERS (GCHQ)

Government Communications Headquarters (GCHQ) is the British organization responsible for signals **intelligence** and **information security**. Based in Cheltenham, Gloucestershire, in a building popularly known as 'The Doughnut', GCHQ was founded in 1946 as the successor to the wartime Government Code and Cipher School, famous for its work at Bletchley Park deciphering the German Enigma code. The director of GCHQ reports to the Foreign and Commonwealth Secretary and the organization is bound by the terms of the Intelligence Services Act 1994 and the Regulation of Investigatory Powers Act 2000. GCHQ intercepts, decrypts and analyses electronic communications, and shares information with foreign signals intelligence organizations such as the American **National Security Agency**. Through its 'information assurance' agency, the Communications Electronic Security Group (CESG), GCHQ also helps protect government communications and information systems against hackers and other **cyberwarfare** threats.

Further reading
Government Communications Headquarters website, http://www.gchq.gov.uk/
Nigel West, *GCHQ: The Secret Wireless War, 1900–1986* (London: Weidenfeld and Nicolson, 1986)

GUERRILLA WARFARE

Guerrilla warfare is a form of **irregular warfare** and is often an important aspect of **insurgency**. The term 'guerrilla' first came into use during Napoleon's struggle against the irregular forces of the Spanish from 1808 to 1814, and means 'little war'. However, the practices of guerrilla warfare long predate the use of the term. Guerrilla warfare is a **strategy** used by weak military forces to defeat stronger ones by avoiding conventional combat and by using hit-and-run tactics. On occasion, guerrilla warfare may even be combined with conventional military action to force the enemy to fight on several fronts – examples being the parallel guerrilla and conventional military operations undertaken by the North Vietnamese against the United States during the Vietnam War, and the partisan operations carried out behind German lines by Soviet guerrillas in the Second World War.

The Chinese communist leader Mao Tse Tung developed one of the most influential models of guerrilla warfare. In this Mao divided guerrilla campaigns into three phases. In the initial mobilization phase, the guerrillas seek to win the support of the population by means of **propaganda** and efforts to undermine the government. In the second phase, that most usually associated with guerrilla warfare, the guerrillas carry out a protracted **war** against the government and its **security** forces, attacking and destroying military, political and economic targets wherever possible, but avoiding pitched battle. Finally, in the third and decisive phase, when the guerrillas have become sufficiently strong, they abandon guerrilla tactics and adopt the methods of conventional warfare to overthrow the government and seize power.

The point of main effort in Mao's model of guerrilla warfare was operations among the rural peasantry. While this idea made sense in early twentieth-century China, it is of limited use in more urbanized societies, where power, wealth, and most of the population are in the cities. In the 1960s, therefore, the Brazilian revolutionary Carlos Marighela adapted Mao's thought to create a model for urban guerrilla warfare. According to this the guerrillas should launch a crime wave which will drive the government into repressive measures, which in turn will drive the population to support the guerrillas. This strategy subsequently proved popular with urban terrorist organizations, and thus somewhat blurred the distinction between guerrilla warfare and **terrorism**. Similarly, the terms 'guerrilla warfare' and insurgency are often used without distinction, although strictly speaking the latter may include many tactics other than those of guerrilla warfare.

Further reading
Walter Laqueur (ed.), *The Guerrilla Reader: a Historical Anthology* (Philadelphia: Temple University Press, 1977)
Sam C. Sarkesian (ed.), *Revolutionary Guerrilla War* (Chicago: Precedent, 1975)

Gulf Cooperation Council (GCC)

The Gulf Cooperation Council (GCC) is an international organization consisting of six countries, namely Bahrain, Kuwait, Oman, Qatar, Saudi Arabia, and the United Arab Emirates. Founded in 1981, the GCC aims to deepen and strengthen the relationships among its members in all areas, including **security**. GCC states have undertaken some measures to unify military operational procedures, training, and curricula, and to ensure that their military systems are compatible, but much more remains to be done in these areas. They also conduct joint military exercises, and have established a 5,000-strong Peninsula Shield rapid deployment force and a joint early warning and air defence system. Overall, however, the military integration of the GCC states remains limited. Their capacity to defend themselves against external threats was shown to be insufficient when Iraq invaded Kuwait in 1990, and little has been done since then to reduce their dependence on outside powers, in particular the USA. Despite the region's strategic significance and the wealth of its members, the GCC at present remains a relatively minor player in the world of international security.

Further reading
Ed Blanche, 'GCC Security: New Alliances in the Making?', *Middle East*, no. 312, May 2001, pp. 4–8
Gulf Cooperation Council website: http://www.gcc-sg.org/home_e.htm

Guojia Anquan Bu

The Ministry of State Security, Guojia Anquan Bu, is China's **intelligence** and **security** service. It has responsibility for both foreign intelligence and domestic **security intelligence**. The service is divided into ten bureaux, the most important being the Second Bureau, which is responsible for collection of intelligence overseas, the Fourth Bureau, which is responsible for technology, and the Sixth Bureau, which deals with counter-intelligence. Guojia Anquan Bu has a large network of spies operating outside China, with a particular interest in gathering economic and technological secrets, especially in the United States. Some experts believe that the Chinese may have several hundred agents operating within the United States, and that they have had considerable success in obtaining military and economic secrets, including nuclear technology. Guojia Anquan Bu also operates signals intelligence facilities within China and is believed to be developing an imagery satellite capability.

Further reading
Nicholas Eftimiades, *Chinese Intelligence Operations* (Annapolis: Naval Institute Press, 1994)
Federation of American Scientists, 'Ministry of State Security', www. fas.org/irp/world/china/mss/index.html

HAMAS

Hamas (the Islamic Resistance Movement) is a militant Palestinian Islamic organization with various wings involved in political, terrorist, and social activities. Hamas was created in 1987 with the aim of destroying the state of Israel and establishing an Islamic state throughout the territory of historic Palestine. Its members have carried out numerous terrorist attacks against Israeli targets, including acts of **suicide terrorism** and the launching of rockets from the Gaza Strip into Israel. Hamas has won considerable support among Palestinians through the social services its organization has provided, including schools and clinics. Benefiting from this and the perceived corruption and incompetence of the **Fatah**-led Palestinian Authority (PA), in 2006 Hamas won a majority in elections to the Palestinian parliament, and formed a government under Prime Minister Ismail Haniya. Many Western states then cut off financial support to the PA, demanding that Hamas recognize Israel's right to exist. Hamas declared a truce with Israel in 2004, but has not yet been willing to meet this further demand. Armed clashes between Israel and Hamas were renewed in June 2006, when Israel detained two Hamas members in the Gaza Strip. In response, Hamas kidnapped an Israeli soldier, which in turn led to an armed Israeli incursion into Gaza and the arrests of many Hamas members of parliament. In late 2006, Hamas members were also involved in armed clashes with supporters of

Fatah. Of late the internal struggles with Fatah have taken precedence over the external battle against Israel, and Hamas's future will depend not merely on its terrorist activities but also on how it is seen to perform as a governing party.

Further reading
Matthew Levitt, *Hamas: Politics, Charity and Terrorism in the Service of Jihad* (New Haven: Yale University Press, 2006)
James P. Wooten, 'Hamas: The Organization, Goals and Tactics of a Militant Palestinian Organization', in Edward V. Linden (ed.), *Foreign Terrorist Organizations: History, Tactics, and Connections* (New York: Nova Science, 2004)

HARD POWER, see SOFT POWER

HEGEMONY
Hegemony describes a situation in which a single state or group of states exercises sufficient dominance over others to be able to shape the rules and norms of the international system to its own advantage. Other states have to accept, or at least adapt to, the demands of the hegemonic power. Hegemony may be worldwide or regional. In the former sense, it is commonly associated with **unipolarity**. Examples of historic hegemony are British dominance of the international scene in the nineteenth century, and American dominance in the late twentieth and early twenty-first century, although in both cases it is possible to question how hegemonic this dominance truly was or is.

Specialists in the theory of international relations disagree as to whether hegemony enhances international stability and thus **security**. Hegemonic stability theory suggests that the dominant power can establish and also enforce norms of international behaviour, thus ensuring stability. **Realism**, by contrast, suggests that other states will inevitably act so as to restore a **balance of power** and re-create a multipolar system.

Realism sees hegemony as primarily a product of **hard power**, especially economic and financial power. Internal cohesion within the hegemonic society is also a vital precondition for external hegemony. The hegemon imposes its rules and norms by means of threats and bribes. This interpretation of hegemony sees it as largely coercive, and views it in terms of dominance of the weak by the strong. The Italian Marxist Antonio Gramsci offered an alternative analysis based on consent. From the Gramscian perspective, hegemony rests on moral and intellectual leadership and on the dominance of ideas and values. In this sense, **soft power** is more important. Through globalized economics, relationships among the social classes of different countries, and international institutions, the ideas of the hegemonic power come to exert such dominance that, as long as minor concessions are made, consent is assured, and coercion is not required. Looking at the current world order, US, or probably more accurately Western, hegemony can thus be seen as resting as much on the spread of ideas of democracy, human rights, and economic liberalism, as on economic and military might. If it is based primarily on economic and military power, Western hegemony seems likely to vanish in due course as Asian states such as China and India acquire greater wealth. If the Gramscian view is correct, and it is based more on moral and intellectual leadership, it may prove to be longer lasting.

Further reading
Robert W. Cox, 'Gramsci, Hegemony and International Relations: an Essay in Method', in Stephen Gill (ed.), *Gramsci, Historical Materialism and International Relations* (Cambridge: Cambridge University Press, 1993), pp. 49–66
Joseph S. Nye Jr, *Soft Power: The Means to Success in World Politics* (New York: Public Affairs, 2004)
George Sorense, 'Hegemony and World Orders', *Cooperation and Conflict*, vol. 36, no. 3, 2001, pp. 306–311

HEZBOLLAH, see HIZBALLAH

HIZBALLAH

Hizballah (the Party of God) was created in 1982 in response to the Israeli invasion of Lebanon. Like **Hamas**, it is a multifaceted Islamic organization, whose various wings engage in military, political, and social activities. It draws its support from the Shia element of the population in southern Lebanon, Beirut, and the Bekaa valley, and its ideological inspiration from the Iranian Islamic revolution of 1979. Politically it supports the establishment of an Islamic state in Lebanon and opposes the existence of the state of Israel. Since 1992, it has participated in Lebanese general elections, and 14 Hizballah members sit in parliament. Hizballah receives substantial financial and military support from Iran and Syria.

Hizballah's military wing, the Islamic Resistance, first gained prominence for its campaign to drive the Israel Defence Forces (IDF) out of Lebanon after Israel's 1982 invasion. The resistance carried out a prolonged **insurgency** against the IDF in southern Lebanon, which eventually resulted in an Israeli withdrawal in 2000. This victory provided a substantial boost to Hizballah's reputation. Hizballah has also carried out numerous acts of **terrorism**. It is blamed for the bombing of the US Marine barracks in Beirut in October 1983, which killed over 200 American Marines. It has also been implicated in the bombing of the Israeli embassy in Argentina in 1992, although its involvement in this operation has not been confirmed.

Following the Israeli withdrawal from Lebanon, Hizballah continued its campaign against Israel, on the basis that the latter continued to occupy an area of Lebanese territory, known as the Shebaa Farms. From 2000 to 2006 Hizballah regularly launched rockets attacks against Israel. In summer 2006, Hizballah fighters kidnapped two Israeli soldiers. A massive Israeli armed response followed, and the IDF once again advanced into southern Lebanon. In the ensuing fighting, the Islamic Resistance surprised the Israelis with the sophistication of its defences and weaponry. It fired several thousand rockets into Israel and engaged in pitched battles with the IDF in southern Lebanon, frustrating Israeli efforts to destroy it. Once the Israelis withdrew, Hizballah refused to disarm in accordance with the terms of the ceasefire resolution. Although Hizballah suffered heavy casualties during the 2006 war, its popularity and that of its leader Sheikh Hassan Nasrallah among the Shia population of Lebanon appear if anything to have been enhanced.

Further reading
Judith P. Hark, *Hezbollah: the Changing Face of Terrorism* (London: I. B. Tauris, 2004)
Hala Jaber, *Hezbollah: Born with a Vengeance* (London: Fourth Estate, 1997)

HIV, see PANDEMIC

HOMELAND SECURITY

The modern term 'homeland **security**' came into use in the United States following the terrorist attacks of 11 September 2001 and the subsequent creation in the USA of a Department of Homeland Security. Homeland security refers to efforts to prevent terrorist attacks within one's own borders and to mitigate the harm done by such attacks should they occur. It involves both civilian and military measures, although the USA prefers to name the military aspect 'homeland defence'. Activities included within the scope of homeland security include **intelligence**, border security, protection of critical infrastructure, and emergency response. Homeland security may also include warning of, and response to, natural disasters, such as earthquakes and hurricanes. The US Department of Homeland Security combines many agencies which were previously separate, in an effort to improve coordination, but certain key actors, including the **Federal Bureau of Investigation** and the Department of Defence, remain distinct.

Further reading
Howard Ball, *US Homeland Security: a Reference Handbook* (Santa Barbara: ABC-CLIO, 2005)
Adrian A. Erckenbrack and Aaron Scholer, 'The DoD Role in Homeland Security', *Joint Force Quarterly*, no. 35, Autumn 2004, pp. 34–41
US Department of Homeland Security website: http://www.dhs.gov/dhspublic/

HUMAN SECURITY

Whereas the focus of international **security** has generally been on the security of states, human security concentrates on individuals. First promoted by the United Nations Development Program in its 1993 Development Report, the concept of human security came to the fore shortly thereafter when adopted by several mid-ranking Western states, most notably Canada and Norway. The basic contentions are that individuals, not states, should be the focus of attention and that the security of all people is inter-connected. Oppressive governments, poverty, and injustice can lead to **terrorism, migration,** and other threats to international security.

Human security thus means the protection of individuals against both violent and non-violent threats. The 2003 report of the Commission on Human Security defined it as protecting 'the vital core of all human lives in ways that enhance human freedoms and human fulfillment'. This implies guaranteeing fundamental human rights, economic development, social justice, education, and healthcare. The difficulty with this definition is that it is so broad as to be potentially meaningless, since almost everything can be included within it. It provides little guidance for practical action. Consequently, states promoting the human security agenda have tended to concentrate their efforts more narrowly on reducing the harm to civilians caused by armed conflict. The most notable achievement in this regard was the **Ottawa Convention** banning landmines.

Human security implies also that one makes some effort to hold to account those who violate human rights, even if this means violating state **sovereignty**. Human security can involve the use of **hard power** and **war** to protect individuals deemed to be suffering from oppressive governments. The concept provides important philosophical underpinnings to the ideas of **humanitarian intervention** and the **responsibility to protect**, as well as to the creation of the **International Criminal Court**.

Further reading
Commission on Human Security, *Human Security Now* (New York: Commission on Human Security, 2003)
Mary Kaldor, *Human Security* (Cambridge: Polity, 2007)
Rob McRae and Don Hubert (eds), *Human Security and the New Diplomacy: Protecting People, Promoting Peace* (Montreal and Kingston: McGill-Queen's University Press, 2001)
Roland Paris, 'Human Security: Paradigm Shift or Hot Air?', *International Security*, vol. 26, no. 2, Autumn 2001, pp. 87–102

HUMANITARIAN INTERVENTION

Humanitarian intervention is the use of force to intervene in the internal affairs of another country without its permission, for humanitarian purposes. These include preventing grave violations of human rights or providing relief from famine. The key element is that of intention. A **war** fought for entirely selfish purposes, to seize territory or resources for instance, which happened incidentally to serve a humanitarian purpose, would not constitute a humanitarian intervention. While it is true that no state ever acts for entirely altruistic purposes, and that issues of **national interest** always play some role in decision-making, an intervention may still be considered 'humanitarian' provided that the humanitarian motive is the primary one. It is extremely difficult to ascertain whether this is the case, and it is easy for states to claim a primary humanitarian motive when in practice they are pursuing naked interests. Consequently, the concept of humanitarian intervention is open to significant abuse.

In recognition of this fact, international law had until recently given short shrift to the idea that humanitarian intervention could be legitimate. While there had been many examples of humanitarian intervention prior to 1945, as well as some support in **just war theory** for the concept, the growing destructiveness of modern weaponry and the experiences of the two world wars instilled a strong desire for a firm presumption against war. The international community reached a broad consensus after the Second World War that the only just cause for war was self-defence, a principle which was enshrined in the Charter of the **United Nations**. Thus in 1949, the **International Court of Justice** ruled that 'The court can only regard the alleged right of intervention as a manifestation of a policy of force, such as has, in the past, given rise to the most serious abuses, and such as cannot . . . find a place in **international law**', and similarly ruled in 1986 that 'intervention is wrong when it uses methods of coercion'.

Despite this, the concept that states have a right, even an obligation, to engage in humanitarian intervention in the face of gross abuses of human rights has acquired increasing support since the failure of the international community to intervene to prevent the **genocide** in Rwanda in 1994. The intervention by the **North Atlantic Treaty Organization (NATO)** in Kosovo in 1999 is seen by many as establishing a new legal norm in favour of humanitarian intervention. The establishment of the principle of a **'responsibility to protect'** has further reinforced this norm. The shift in international opinion on this subject reflects both changing moral attitudes and changes in the **balance of power**. Public opinion finds it increasingly unacceptable when state leaders hide behind state **sovereignty** to abuse human rights. At the same time, the collapse of the Soviet Union and the end of the **Cold War** has reduced the possibility that humanitarian interventions will lead to a broader international conflict. Western states feel that they can use force with relative impunity and so they wish to remove the legal constraints which prevent them from so doing. This, though, once again raises the danger that the concept of humanitarian intervention may be abused for the pursuit of power.

Further reading
J. L. Holzgrefe and Robert O. Keohane (eds), *Humanitarian Intervention: Ethical, Legal, and Political Dilemmas* (Cambridge: Cambridge University Press, 2003)
Richard Norman and Alexander Moseley (eds), *Human Rights and Military Intervention* (Aldershot: Ashgate, 2002)
Wing Commander J. E. Linter, 'Humanitarian Intervention: Legitimising the Illegal?', *Defence Studies*, vol. 5, no. 2, June 2005, pp. 271–294
Thomas Weiss, *Humanitarian Intervention* (Cambridge: Polity, 2007)

INFORMATION SECURITY

Information security refers to activities undertaken to prevent secret information from falling into hostile hands, as well as to activities to protect information systems, such as computers, from attack. There are various aspects of information security: physical security, which involves the construction and maintenance of physical structures to protect documents, computers and personnel and to prevent others from stealing or physically attacking them; document security, which involves the creation of special regulations pertaining to the handling of sensitive printed material; personnel security, which includes procedures such as the vetting of intelligence officials and others with access to confidential information to ensure that they do not have habits and weaknesses which might make them liable to betray secrets to others; communications security, which reduces the likelihood of communications being intercepted or illicitly read by reducing electronic emissions and encrypting data; computer security, which protects computers against hacking, viruses, and other forms of **cyberwarfare**; deception, which protects the truth by encouraging others to believe untruths; and counter-intelligence, which consists of more active measures to eliminate, damage, or hinder hostile **intelligence** gathering activities. The massive expansion in the use of information technology in the past two decades has provided numerous opportunities for those wishing to steal confidential information or sabotage information systems. As a result, information security has become increasingly important for both governments and private corporations.

Further reading
Michael Herman, *Intelligence Power in Peace and War* (Cambridge: Cambridge University Press, 1996)
Mark M. Lowenthal, *Intelligence: From Secrets to Policy*, 3rd edn (Washington, DC: CQ Press, 2006)
Global Organized Crime Project, *Cybercrime, Cyberterrorism, Cyberwarfare: Averting an Electronic Waterloo* (Washington, DC: CSIS Press, 1998)

INFORMATION WARFARE (IW)

The term 'information warfare' (IW) refers to a variety of subjects and is used in several different ways, leading to a certain degree of definitional confusion. On the one hand, many use the phrase when discussing the use of modern information technology in warfare, and thus link IW with concepts such as **Network-centric Warfare** and the **Revolution in Military Affairs**. On the other hand, IW can also refer to broader political and **propaganda** battles to control the flow and interpretation of information and to gain victory through superior manipulation of national and international public opinion, in which sense it is similar to **psychological operations**. The term is also sometimes used when discussing **cyberwarfare** and the possibility of attacks by hostile elements on information systems. In all of these respects, the use of the term reflects a common belief that the key to success in contemporary warfare lies as much in the amassing and use of information as it does in firepower.

Further reading
John Arquilla and David Ronfeldt (eds), *In Athena's Camp: Preparing for Conflict in the Information Age* (Santa Monica: RAND, 1997)
E. Anders Eriksson, 'Information Warfare: Hype or Reality', *The Non-Proliferation Review*, Spring–Summer 1999, pp. 57–64

INSURGENCY

Insurgency is a form of **asymmetric warfare** fought within the boundaries of a state. The aims of insurgency are to overthrow the existing government or to expel a foreign occupier. The insurgents' military weakness relative to their opponents usually forces them to adopt non-conventional methods of struggle. These include **propaganda**, subversion, **guerrilla warfare** and **terrorism**, and also, according to some theorists, the methods of **netwar** and **Fourth Generation Warfare**. The insurgents aim to gradually wear down the state's will to fight, and also to persuade the civil population to switch support to them from the government. They may hope to provoke government forces into overreacting and enacting repressive measures, which will drive the population into their arms. The struggle with insurgents is thus as much political as it is military, and much **counter-insurgency** theory stresses the need to separate the insurgents from the civil population and to win the hearts and minds of the latter. If the insurgency gains sufficient strength, it may morph into conventional **war**, but often the government collapses or the occupiers withdraw before this point is reached. Insurgencies are frequently protracted, lasting many years, even decades. Defeating them requires a long-term commitment. During the **Cold War**, insurgency was often referred to as 'revolutionary war', given that it was most often practised by Marxist revolutionaries, but the term has now largely dropped out of use.

Further reading
Bernard B. Fall, 'The Theory and Practice of Insurgency and Counterinsurgency', *Naval War College Review*, vol. 51, no. 1, Winter 1998, pp. 46–57
John A. Nagl, *Learning to Eat Soup with a Knife: Counterinsurgency Lessons from Malaya and Vietnam* (Chicago: University of Chicago Press, 2002)

INTELLIGENCE

Intelligence is processed information provided to, and used by, political and military leaders to help them make decisions on the basis of informed analysis rather than instinct. Most experts differentiate between information and intelligence: the former being unanalysed data, the latter being the product which results from the analysis and combining of pieces of information. This reflects the fact that what matters is the interpretation of the information, rather than the raw data itself.

The word 'intelligence' is often used to mean secret information. This need not be the case. So-called 'open-source' intelligence (OSINT), gathered from sources which are open to anybody (such as newspapers, the internet, television, and academic journals) is still intelligence. Secret intelligence is usually divided into three main types: signals intelligence (SIGINT), which is derived from the interception and interpretation of communications and of electronic emissions; imagery intelligence (IMINT), sometimes also referred to as photographic intelligence; and human intelligence (HUMINT), which is derived from human sources, such as spies.

The process by which intelligence is produced is referred to as the 'intelligence cycle'. This consists of four stages: direction, in which those in authority task the intelligence agencies, telling them what questions they want answered (known as 'intelligence requirements'); collection, in which the agencies collect the information needed to answer the questions; analysis, in which the agencies collate, evaluate, and interpret the information; and dissemination, in which they report to those who tasked them on their conclusions. Intelligence failure may occur at any stage of the cycle: because the wrong questions have been asked, because insufficient or inaccurate information has been collected, because the information has been incorrectly analysed (perhaps due to intellectual biases), or because the correct answer has been found but has not been disseminated to those in authority (perhaps out of fear of giving bad news to superiors).

Most modern states invest heavily in intelligence agencies, both for internal security and to gather information about foreign targets. Tactical support to military operations absorbs the great majority of the intelligence budget in many countries, such as the United States. Strategic-level intelligence on political, military and economic affairs is also important. Intelligence plays an important role in the **verification** of **arms control** agreements, and in this way contributes to maintenance of international stability.

The scale of the intelligence community in larger countries is such that managing and coordinating the various agencies is extremely difficult. The secrecy which surrounds intelligence also creates problems of accountability and democratic oversight. Recent prominent intelligence failures, such as the flawed assessments concerning Iraq's **weapons of mass destruction** programmes prior to the March 2003 invasion of Iraq, suggest that adequate solutions to these problems have not yet been found.

Further reading
Peter Gill and Mark Phythian, *Intelligence in an Insecure World* (Cambridge: Polity 2006)
Michael Herman, *Intelligence Power in Peace and War* (Cambridge: Cambridge University Press, 1996)
Mark M. Lowenthal, *Intelligence: From Secrets to Policy*, 3rd edition (Washington, DC: CQ Press, 2006)

INTERMEDIATE-RANGE NUCLEAR FORCES (INF) TREATY

The 'Treaty between the United States and the Union of Soviet Socialist Republics on the Elimination of Their Intermediate-Range and Shorter-Range Missiles', more commonly referred to as the Intermediate-Range Nuclear Forces (INF) Treaty, was signed on 8 December 1987 and came into force on 1 June 1988. The treaty obliged the two parties to eliminate all missiles with a range of between 500 and 5,500 kilometres by 1 June 1991. The treaty broke new ground with the scope of its verification provisions. It allowed both sides to conduct on-site inspections at missile operating bases, support facilities and production facilities. They could also carry out inspections to confirm the destruction of missiles and associated equipment, and to carry out continuous monitoring at missile production facilities in Magna, Utah, and Votkinsk, Russia. Almost 2,700 missiles were destroyed as a result of the treaty.

Further reading

Federation of American Scientists, *Intermediate-Range Nuclear Forces (INF) Texts*, http://www.fas.org/nuke/control/inf/text/index.html

Thomas Graham Jr and Damien J. LaVera, *Cornerstones of Security: Arms Control Treaties in the Nuclear Era* (Seattle: University of Washington Press, 2003)

INTERNATIONAL ATOMIC ENERGY AUTHORITY (IAEA)

The International Atomic Energy Authority (IAEA) is an agency of the **United Nations (UN)** and reports to the UN Security Council and General Assembly. Established in 1957 and headquartered in Vienna, Austria, its role is to guarantee the safe, secure, and peaceful use of nuclear technology. It divides its mission into three pillars: safety and security; science and technology; and safeguards and **verification**. In the first pillar, the IAEA helps countries to upgrade their nuclear safety and security, promoting the maintenance of international safety standards in nuclear installations and for the disposal of nuclear waste. It also helps countries to prepare for and respond to emergencies. In the second pillar, the IAEA provides expert services, specialized equipment, training, and other types of support for the peaceful use of nuclear technology in developing countries. It also supports research and development. The third pillar – safeguards and verification – is the one which attracts the most public attention. States who have signed the **Non-Proliferation Treaty** are obliged to conclude agreements with the IAEA to implement safeguards to ensure their compliance with the treaty. The IAEA then carries out inspections of their nuclear facilities to ensure that they are abiding by the terms of their safeguards agreement.

In the event that IAEA inspectors find evidence that a state is in breach of its safeguards agreement, they refer the matter to the organization's Board of Governors. The Board in turn may elect to refer the matter to the UN Security Council for action. This happened in 2006 when the Board referred Iran's nuclear programme to the Security Council, as a result of which the Council imposed limited **economic sanctions** on Iran. In 2005, the IAEA, together with its Director General, Mohammed ElBaradei, was awarded the Nobel Peace Prize.

Further reading
David Fischer, *The History of the International Atomic Energy Authority: the First Forty Years* (Vienna: IAEA, 1997)
International Atomic Energy Authority website, http://www.iaea.org

INTERNATIONAL COURT OF JUSTICE (ICJ)

The International Court of Justice (ICJ), known colloquially as the 'World Court', is the principal judicial organ of the **United Nations**. Established in 1946 and based in The Hague, the court consists of 15 judges elected by the United Nations General Assembly and Security Council for nine-year terms of office. It hears only cases involving states; individuals and non-state organizations may not bring complaints or be subject to complaints brought before the ICJ. The court's purpose is to help states resolve disputes peacefully, and its jurisdiction rests on the consent of the states involved. Jurisdiction is bestowed in a number of ways. First, the court will hear cases where both parties agree to its arbitration. Second, numerous international treaties confer jurisdiction on the court to resolve disputes related to the terms and fulfillment of the treaties. Third, states may make a unilateral declaration to accept the court's 'compulsory jurisdiction' on all legal questions relating to treaties and **international law**. Any state which has taken up this option has the right to bring a complaint to the court about any other state which has similarly exercised the option. Often such declarations are subject to reservations, excluding certain specific issues from the court's jurisdiction.

Decisions of the ICJ are binding and final, but the ICJ lacks a powerful mechanism to enforce its judgements. If a state fails to abide by a decision of the ICJ, it may be referred to the United Nations Security Council for enforcement action. There is, however, no guarantee that the Security Council will take the necessary action, especially if the judgement adversely affects the **national interests** of one of the council's permanent members. In a famous example, in 1986 the ICJ found that the United States had violated international law by placing mines in Nicaraguan harbours, but the United States refused to pay the fine imposed by the ICJ and subsequently withdrew its acceptance of the court's compulsory jurisdiction. In other instances, though, the court has been able to successfully arbitrate disputes, settling for instance various arguments over the delimitation of national boundaries.

Further reading
The International Court of Justice (The Hague: ICJ, 1983)
International Court of Justice website, http://www.icj-cij.org/
Robert Y. Jennings, 'The United Nations at Fifty: the International Court of Justice after Fifty Years', *The American Journal of International Law*, vol. 89, no. 3, 1995, pp. 493–505
Shabtai Rosenne, *The World Court: What It Is and How It Works*, 5th revised edn (Dordrecht: Martinus Nijhoff, 1995)

INTERNATIONAL CRIMINAL COURT (ICC)

Based in The Hague, the International Criminal Court (ICC) was established by the Rome Statute of 17 July 1998, the provisions of which came into effect on 1 July 2002. It is the world's first permanent court dedicated to the prosecution of serious international crimes by individuals. This differentiates it from the **International Court of Justice**, which settles disputes between states. The creation of the ICC built on the precedent of the International Military Tribunal at Nuremburg which tried Nazi leaders after the Second World War and of courts established by the **United Nations** in the 1990s to prosecute cases of **war** crimes in Sierra Leone, Rwanda, and the former Yugoslavia. It reflected a growing sense in the international community that existing national mechanisms for bringing those responsible for the most serious crimes against humanity were insufficient.

Unlike previous international courts the ICC is a permanent institution. It has jurisdiction to prosecute the 'most serious crimes of concern to the international community as a whole', namely **genocide**, crimes against humanity, and war crimes when these are 'part of a plan or policy or as part of a large-scale commission of such crimes'. The ICC also in theory has the right to prosecute people for the crime of aggression (i.e., the waging of aggressive war), but as yet the term 'aggression' has not been defined, and the court's jurisdiction over this crime will only come into effect once agreement on the definition is reached.

Primary responsibility for the prosecution of the crimes above continues to rest with national courts. The ICC only acquires jurisdiction when the courts of the country in which the crime allegedly took place, or whose national was accused, are unable or unwilling to prosecute. Cases may be referred to the court for investigation by a state party to the treaty or by the United Nations Security Council, and may also be initiated by the ICC prosecutor. The decision to prosecute rests with the ICC prosecutor, not the state party or the Security Council. This reflects the fact that the court is designed to be independent of both nation states and the United Nations. Its 18 judges serve for nine years, and are elected by an assembly of all state parties, each of which may nominate one judge for election. Despite the court's independence, some commentators complain that it remains susceptible to political pressure, and the United States has refused to ratify its founding statute, citing fears that US soldiers could be subjected to politically-motivated prosecutions.

Supporters of the ICC believe that it will enable major criminals to be brought to justice and will act as a deterrent to future large-scale breaches of human rights. Against this, critics argue that fear of prosecution by the ICC may encourage those engaged in war to continue fighting rather than surrender, and that the court will therefore complicate **war termination** and **conflict resolution**. In January 2007, the ICC began its first trial, that of Thomas Lubanga, accused of recruiting child soldiers during the **civil war** in the Democratic Republic of Congo.

Further reading

Jennifer Elsea, *International Criminal Court: Overview and Selected Legal Issues* (New York: Novinka, 2003)

Guilio M. Gallarotti and Arik Y. Preis, 'Towards Universal Human Rights and the Rule of Law: the Permanent International Criminal Court', *Australian Journal of International Affairs*, vol. 53, no. 1, 1999, pp. 95–111

International Criminal Court website, www.icc-cpi.int/
Robert W. Tucker, 'The International Criminal Court Controversy', *World Policy Journal*, vol. 18, no. 2, Summer 2001, pp. 71–81

INTERNATIONAL LAW

International law consists of the rules and principles which govern the behaviour of nation states and other actors towards one another at the international level. It is normally divided into two parts: public international law, which governs the relations of states, and private international law, which deals with individual persons and corporations when they cross national borders. Much of the latter focuses on disputes concerning jurisdiction and the competing claims of different legal systems (for instance, over the terms of an international sales contract). In recent years, the distinction between public and private international law has become increasingly blurred, but from the point of view of international **security**, it is primarily the former which is of concern.

International law derives from three sources: formal agreements between states, such as treaties; general and consistent practices among states (known as 'customary international law') even when these practices have not been formalized in treaty; and general principles common to the major legal systems, even if not incorporated in customary law or international agreements. As such, some form of international law has existed for millennia, states having always regulated their relations through custom and treaty. In the twentieth century, the body of international law expanded rapidly as did its scope, increasingly encompassing not just nation states but also regional organizations and individual persons.

Critics of international law argue that it is not really law. There are relatively few enforcement mechanisms: no world government or international police exist, and there are few effective international legal institutions. States, they maintain, comply with international law only when they find it convenient, ignoring it when it is not. This allegedly makes it qualitatively different from domestic law. Others disagree. While it is true that laws such as those prohibiting the waging of aggressive **war** have not entirely achieved their aims, domestic laws are also routinely disobeyed, and in fact most states abide by international law most of the time. Some formal enforcement mechanisms do exist: states with legal disputes may request adjudication from the **International Court of Justice**, and in extreme circumstances the **United Nations** may take action to ensure

collective security. Individual states or groups of states may also take unilateral action to punish those who transgress established norms, as in the case of the **North Atlantic Treaty Organization's** attack on Yugoslavia in 1999. These enforcement mechanisms are relatively weak compared to those available to domestic government. Self-interest, based on the principle of reciprocity, is a more powerful reason for states' compliance with their obligations: they fear that if they break their agreements others will reciprocate, so harming their interests. They may also seek the stability of a world governed by law, and believe in the legitimacy of the norms thus established.

In recent years, there has been some progress in strengthening international legal institutions, a prime example being the creation of the **International Criminal Court**. In addition, the development of the European Court of Human Rights and the European Court of Justice has created within the European Union a uniquely powerful system of international law. Some states have also incorporated aspects of international law within domestic law, giving domestic courts the power to try those charged with international crimes, most notably **genocide**. Commentators disagree about how far this determines the behaviour of states and other international actors. What is clear is that reference to international law has become commonplace in discussions about foreign and **security** policy, helping to frame the terms of debate, and thereby influencing the outcome.

Further reading

Barry E. Carter, Phillip R. Trimble, and Curtis A. Bradley, *International Law*, 4th edn (New York: Aspen, 2003)

William A. Cohn, 'The Rising Clout of International Law', *The New Presence*, vol. 8, no. 2, Summer 2006, pp. 36–39

Gerry Simpson (ed.), *The Nature of International Law* (Aldershot: Ashgate, 2001)

INVULNERABLE SECOND STRIKE CAPABILITY, see DETERRENCE

IRISH REPUBLICAN ARMY (IRA)

The Irish Republican Army (IRA) fought a prolonged campaign of **terrorism** against the the British government with the aim of persuading the British to withdraw from Northern Ireland, thereby re-uniting all the counties of Ireland under Irish rule. The IRA came into existence during the Anglo-Irish war of 1919–1921 which led to Irish independence. It opposed the treaty which divided Ireland into two, but was defeated in the subsequent Irish Civil War. Thereafter the IRA carried out sporadic, but rather ineffective, terrorist attacks against the British for several decades until 1969. Civil strife in Northern Ireland in that year provided the impetus to convert the IRA's efforts into something more substantial, and IRA activity peaked in the years 1969–1999. In 1969, the IRA also split into two – the Official IRA and the Provisional IRA (PIRA). The latter rapidly came to dominate, and it expanded terrorist operations substantially. In thirty years, PIRA killed 1,800 people, one third of them civilians, in a series of attacks in Northern Ireland, mainland Britain and Germany (the latter against personnel of the British army). Targets struck by PIRA varied widely. Particularly famous incidents were pub bombings in England in 1974, the murders of Lord Mountbatten and two British members of Parliament, Airey Neave and Ian Gow, the bombing of the Grand Hotel in Brighton in an effort to assassinate Prime Minister Margaret Thatcher and the British cabinet in 1984, and the bombing of a Remembrance Day Commemoration in Enniskillen in 1987.

PIRA declared a ceasefire in 1994, but, dissatisfied with the pace of negotiations for a political settlement, renewed its campaign of violence in February 1996. A second ceasefire was declared in July 1997, since which PIRA has refrained from terrorist action. Attention has shifted instead to political activity, led by PIRA's political wing, Sinn Fein. In July 2005, PIRA announced a permanent end to its campaign of violence and stated that it would put all its weapons out of use. Canadian General John de Chastelain, head of an international group tasked with overseeing the decommissioning of terrorist arms, confirmed in September 2005 that PIRA's entire arsenal had been destroyed, and in late 2006 stated that PIRA should no longer be considered a **threat**. There are accusations, however, that PIRA remains involved in **organized crime**. In addition, some hardline members, disgruntled with the ceasefire, left to form two new terrorist organizations, the Real IRA and Continuity IRA, and pledged to continue the armed struggle. In August 1998, the Real IRA exploded a bomb in Omagh marketplace in Northern Ireland, killing 29 people. Continuity and Real IRA have not won any significant support and since 2002 have conducted very few actions. While a return to large-scale violence cannot be entirely ruled out, there are good grounds for believing that Irish republican terrorism may finally be coming to an end.

Further reading
Tim Pat Coogan, *The IRA* (London: HarperCollins, 2000)
Peter Taylor, *The Provos: IRA and Sinn Fein* (London: Bloomsbury, 1998)
Richard English, *Armed Struggle: a History of the IRA* (London: Macmillan, 2003)

IRREGULAR WARFARE

Irregular warfare is a catch-all phrase which includes all forms of armed conflict which are not fought between the organized military forces (armies, navies, and air forces) of nation states. It thus includes **terrorism, insurgency, guerrilla warfare, netwar, cyberwarfare**, and **fourth generation war**. Irregular warfare generally takes place when one of the combatants is significantly weaker in a conventional military sense than the other, and thus chooses to avoid direct battle and to exploit alternative avenues of attack. In the past few decades this form of warfare has been much more common than conventional war, a trend which seems likely to continue for the foreseeable future. The term 'irregular warfare' has largely fallen out of use in recent years, having been replaced by '**asymmetric warfare**', with which it is to all intents and purposes synonymous.

Further reading
James D. Kiras, 'Terrorism and Irregular Warfare', in John Baylis, James Wirtz, Eliot Cohen, and Colin S. Gray (eds), *Strategy in the Contemporary World: An Introduction to Strategic Studies* (Oxford: Oxford University Press, 2002), pp. 208–32
Martin van Creveld, *The Transformation of War* (New York: Free Press, 1991)

ISLAMIC JIHAD, see PALESTINIAN ISLAMIC JIHAD

ISLAMIC MOVEMENT OF TURKESTAN, see ISLAMIC MOVEMENT OF UZBEKISTAN

ISLAMIC MOVEMENT OF UZBEKISTAN

Led by Tohir Yoldashev, the Islamic Movement of Uzbekistan (IMU) is a terrorist organization originally devoted to the overthrow of the regime of President Islam Karimov in Uzbekistan, but now holding the broader aim of the creation of an Islamic state throughout Central Asia. For this reason the IMU is now sometimes referred to instead as the Islamic Movement of Turkestan. The IMU was founded in the late 1990s, and initially focused on targets in Uzbekistan. It was soon driven out of the country by the regime's **security** forces and took refuge in Afghanistan, where it allied with **Al Qaeda** and the **Taliban**. Many of IMU's leaders and members were then killed or dispersed during the fighting which led to the collapse of the Taliban in 2001. Since then, a weakened IMU has operated primarily in Tajikistan and Kyrgyzstan, in both of which it has carried out terrorist attacks.

Further reading

Edward V. Linden (ed.), *Foreign Terrorist Organizations: History, Tactics, and Connections* (New York: Nova Science, 2004)

Anna Sabasteanski (ed.), *Patterns of Global Terrorism 1985–2005: US State Department Reports with Supplementary Documents and Statistics* (Great Barrington: Berkshire Publishing Group, 2005)

Russel D. Howard and Reid L. Sawyer, *Terrorism and Counterrorism: Understanding the New Security Environment* (Guildford, CT: McGraw-Hill, 2002)

ISLAMIC REVOLUTIONARY GUARDS CORPS, see PASDARAN

JIHAD

Often translated as 'holy **war**', *jihad* is an Arabic word meaning struggle, striving, or exertion, which has particular significance for Muslims, often being seen as a central element of Islam. Scholars disagree about exactly what constitutes *jihad*, under what circumstances it is permitted, and what obligations it imposes.

Historically, *jihad* has often been associated with violent struggle to spread or defend the religion of Islam. This use of the term is sometimes referred to as the 'lesser *jihad*', to distinguish it from the 'greater *jihad*', which is of a non-violent nature, and which involves striving towards some praiseworthy aim, such as overcoming one's own evil inclinations or exerting oneself to improve Islamic society. Some scholars maintain that the greater *jihad* is more important than the lesser. Others argue that the more peaceful interpretation of *jihad* is a later invention, and that the violent version of *jihad* has always been more important. In any case, statements by some Islamic extremists that their campaigns of violence constitute a *jihad* mean that from the point of view of international **security**, it is the violent version which is the more significant.

The concept of *jihad* derives from the *Koran* and from the recorded sayings and deeds of the Prophet Mohammed, known as the *hadith*. One aim of *jihad* is to spread Islam throughout the entire world. In this sense, *jihad* can arguably be envisioned as inherently offensive. Offensive *jihad* to spread the boundaries of Islam is a collective duty, *fard kifaya*, considered fulfilled for the entire community if a sufficient number of its members carry it out. It is permitted only under certain circumstances, lest ambitious individuals use the cover of holy war to justify acts of aggression. In particular, offensive *jihad* may only be declared by a legitimate religious leader, a Caliph or Imam.

Defensive *jihad*, fought when Islam is under attack, is not a collective, but an individual duty, *fard 'ayn*, obligatory for each and every able-bodied, adult, sane Muslim. Modern Islamic radicals reject the distinction between defensive and offensive *jihad*, saying that Islam is under attack from Western crusaders, and it is the individual obligation of every Muslim to take up arms against the enemy.

According to most scholars, *jihad* imposes restrictions on the use of force. In this sense, it is similar in some respects to Christian **just war theory**. In particular, Islam forbids Muslims from attacking women, children, the aged, and places of worship. A few commentators disagree, noting that, historically, Sunni jurists placed few if any limits on the means of war and did not recognize any concept of non-combatant immunity. They claimed that the innocent are those who support an Islamic order, and those who oppose such an order are guilty. If women and children are killed in *jihad*, that is the fault of their leaders, not of the Muslims who are fighting them. This line of thinking is not accepted by most contemporary Muslims, but has powerful precedent in Islamic tradition, and thus helps terrorist groups such as **Al Qaeda** to justify their attacks on civilian targets.

From the point of view of Shia Muslims, offensive *jihad* is difficult if not impossible, since to the Shias there is but one last Imam who is being awaited, and thus legitimate authority for declaring offensive *jihad* rests with no-one. In the Sunni tradition, it is possible for any individuals to proclaim themselves religious authorities entitled to declare *jihad*. The squabble between Shias and Sunnis over the context and rationale of *jihad* remains unsettled to this day.

Further reading
David Cook, *Understanding Jihad* (Berkeley: University of California Press, 2005)
James Turner Johnson and John Kelsay (eds), *Cross, Crescent, and Sword: the Justification and Limitation of War in Western and Islamic Tradition* (New York: Greenwood, 1990)
Rudolph Peters, *Jihad in Classical and Modern Islam: a Reader* (Princeton: Markus Wiener Publishers, 1996)
Jalil Roshandel and Sharon Chadha, *Jihad and International Security* (Basingstoke: Palgrave Macmillan, 2006)

JOINT INTELLIGENCE COMMITTEE (JIC)

The Joint Intelligence Committee (JIC) is the primary coordinating agency within the British **intelligence** system. It is part of the Cabinet Office and consists of senior officials of the Foreign and Commonwealth Office, the Home Office, the Ministry of Defence, the Department of Trade and Industry, the Department for International Development, the Treasury, and the Cabinet Office, as well as the heads of the **Secret Intelligence Service**, the **Security Service**, and the **Government Communications Headquarters**.

The JIC is responsible each year for setting the priorities of the British intelligence community, and for tasking the relevant agencies and monitoring their work. In addition to this role in direction, it acts as the central all-source intelligence analysis agency for key strategic issues. It is helped in this task by the JIC Assessments Staff, a small group of individuals seconded from various departments of government and intelligence agencies. The workings of the JIC were brought under close public scrutiny following the publication of a JIC dossier in 2002 which claimed that Iraq continued to possess and develop **weapons of mass destruction**, and following later allegations that the JIC had altered its analysis to suit the policies of the government of Prime Minister Tony Blair. Two enquiries, led by Lords Hutton and Butler, rejected these allegations, but the previously high reputation of the JIC has nonetheless been damaged.

Further reading
Percy Cradock, *Know Your Enemy: How the Joint Intelligence Committee Saw the World* (London: John Murray, 2002)
National Intelligence Machinery (London: The Stationery Office, 2006)

JUST WAR THEORY

Just war theory refers to the body of thought which addresses the question of when **war** may be considered not merely justifiable but also morally 'just'. Nearly all cultures and civilizations have developed some opinions on this issue, but the term 'just war theory' refers purely to that body of thought which has emerged from the western Christian, primarily Catholic, tradition. St Augustine and Thomas Aquinas are usually considered the founding fathers of just war theory, with other writers such as Hugo Grotius having an important role in secularizing the theory over the centuries.

Just war theory is generally divided into two aspects: *jus ad bellum*, which lays out the criteria which determine whether it is just to wage war at all; and *jus in bello*, which stipulates what actions are permissible during war. Some commentators add a third aspect, *jus post bellum*, which addresses how people should behave in the aftermath of war.

Different theorists provide slightly different lists of criteria for *jus in bello*, but most give between five and seven, all of which must be met for a war to be considered just. The first criteria is just cause. This is variously defined – for some the only just cause is self-defence, for others it may include defence of the innocent against armed attack, retaking property, or the punishment of evil. The second is legitimate or proper authority – not everybody has the right to wage war. The third is right intention – one should fight not for selfish interests but for the sake of justice. The fourth is proportionality of ends – the good achieved by war must exceed the harm done. The fifth is last resort – one may only resort to war after having exhausted all reasonable alternatives. The sixth is reasonable hope of success – no matter how just the cause, to wage war if defeat is likely is to cause harm for no benefit. And the seventh is the aim of **peace** – the purpose of war should be to create a better peace than that which preceded it. Generally speaking, debates over just war theory centre less on the validity of these criteria than on their interpretation. There are great disagreements on what constitutes just cause and legitimate authority, for instance.

Jus in bello is guided by two principles – discrimination (sometimes referred to as non-combatant immunity) and proportionality of means. The former stipulates that one may not deliberately target the innocent, usually defined as non-combatants. This does not mean that one may not undertake any action in which innocents are hurt – if one attacks a legitimate target and innocents are hurt as an unintended by-product of the attack, it may be permissible. In this case, the action is guided by the principle of proportionality. It is permissible only as long as the military value of the target exceeds the harm done by attacking it. The criteria of *jus in bello* are fiercely debated. The boundaries between combatants and non-combatants are not always clear, and it is extremely difficult to determine what is proportionate damage, especially when the factors being compared (the value of a military target and some harm to innocents) often differ considerably.

Not everybody agrees with the precepts of just war theory. Pacifists reject entirely the idea that war can be just. Others, including some proponents of **Realism**, suggest that labelling wars as 'just' leads to undesirable consequences by making war appear to be morally righteous. It is better, according to this perspective, to view war as an occasionally necessary lesser evil. Just war theory is an ethical theory, not a legal construct, but the laws of war are informed by and draw on it for inspiration. During the **Cold War**, just war theory attracted little attention. In the past decade debates over issues such as **humanitarian intervention**, **preventive war**, and the treatment of prisoners in the **Global War on Terrorism** have given the subject a new salience.

Further reading
Alex J. Bellamy, *Just Wars: From Cicero to Iraq* (Cambridge: Polity, 2006)
James Turner Johnson, *Morality and Contemporary Warfare* (New Haven: Yale University Press, 1999)
Michael Walzer, *Just and Unjust Wars*, 3rd edition (New York: Basic Books, 2000)

KONGRA-GEL, see PARTIYA KARKEREN KURDISTAN (PKK)

LAND POWER

Land power refers to the capacity of states to capture and control land as well as to force others to do their will through the application of military power on land. Although **sea power** and **air power** are very often considered as entirely separate subjects, they are in fact essential supporting elements to land power, events at sea and in the air having a significant impact on events on the ground. Land power does what sea power and air power cannot, namely seize land and hold it. It derives from a combination of military firepower and manoeuvre. It is a product of the size and quality of armed forces, factors which in turn depend on numbers, training, and technology, and thus on the extent of a state's industrial, technological and human resources.

All other things being equal, victory in battle is more likely to go to the side with the larger numbers of personnel and equipment. As Napoleon Bonaparte noted, 'God is on the side of the big battalions'. All other things are rarely, however, equal, and it is not uncommon for a better equipped or better trained army to defeat one much larger than itself. Size also carries certain disadvantages. In particular, large armies require greater logistical support and tend to be slower moving. A small, fast moving force may be superior to a large, slow one. The current process of military **transformation** thus aims to make Western armed forces more powerful by reducing their size while enhancing their technological capabilities through **network-centric warfare** and **C4ISR**. Nevertheless, when it comes to occupying and holding ground, the essential tasks of land power, recent experience suggests that when judging land power, numbers still matter.

Further reading
GlobalSecurity.org, *Land Power*, www.globalsecurity.org/military/ops/land. htm
Stephen Biddle, 'Land Warfare: Theory and Practice' in John Baylis, James Wirtz, Eliot Cohen, and Colin S. Gray (eds), *Strategy in the Contemporary World: An Introduction to Strategic Studies* (Oxford: Oxford University Press, 2002), pp. 91–112

LATIN AMERICAN NUCLEAR-FREE ZONE TREATY – see TREATY FOR THE PROHIBITION OF NUCLEAR WEAPONS IN LATIN AMERICA

LAW OF THE SEA, see UNITED NATIONS CONVENTION ON THE LAW OF THE SEA (UNCLOS)

LIBERATION TIGERS OF TAMIL EELAM (LTTE)
The Liberation Tigers of Tamil Eelam (LTTE), commonly referred to as the Tamil Tigers, are a separatist Tamil organization in Sri Lanka.

The LTTE's original goal was the creation of an independent Tamil state, but this aim has been scaled down to that of an autonomous Tamil homeland within Sri Lanka. The LTTE has carried out a prolonged campaign of **guerrilla warfare** against the Sri Lankan government and security forces since being founded in 1976 by Velupillai Prabhakaran. It has combined conventional military tactics with guerrilla operations and **terrorism**, and is noted for its assassinations of important political figures and its use of **suicide terrorism**. LTTE suicide bombers assassinated former Indian Prime Minister Rajiv Gandhi in May 1991 and Sri Lankan President Ranasinghe Premadasa in May 1993, and injured Sri Lankan President Chandrika Kumaratunga in December 1999. The LTTE controls much of the north and east of Sri Lanka, and has established fundraising networks among the Tamil diaspora in North America, Europe, and Asia. In February 2002, with the help of Norwegian mediators, the LTTE and the Sri Lankan government signed a ceasefire agreement and subsequently entered into negotations. These failed to produce a final settlement. In 2006 the ceasefire collapsed and the LTTE renewed its campaign of terror.

Further reading
Edward V. Linden (ed.), *Foreign Terrorist Organizations: History, Tactics, and Connections* (New York: Nova Science, 2004)
Chris Smith, 'The Eelam Endgame', *International Affairs*, vol. 83, no. 1, January 2007, pp. 69–86

LIMITED TEST BAN TREATY – see PARTIAL TEST BAN TREATY

LIMITED WAR

The concept of limited war refers to both the ends being pursued during a **war** and the means adopted to achieve those ends. A limited war is one fought for goals which fall short of the complete destruction of the enemy, and one fought without using all the resources available to the state. The concept may also refer to a war in which the combatants exercise restraint in terms of restricting those people and things which are considered legitimate targets, and also to a war which is limited geographically. In these ways, limited war can be contrasted to **total** or **absolute war**. It must be borne in mind that what may be limited war from the perspective of one combatant may not be from the point of the other. In addition, it can be argued that all wars are limited to some extent. Even in the Second World War, which came as close to absolute war as any other conflict, the belligerents did not use all the means at their disposal. They refrained from the use of chemical weapons, for instance. There is no clear dividing line between limited and total and absolute war. The destruction wreaked by the two world wars in the twentieth century, followed by fears of the apocalypse which could result from nuclear war, encouraged strategists during the **Cold War** to find ways of limiting war so as to avoid **escalation** into total war. The concept of limited war gained considerable traction in this period. Opponents of the idea complained that self-handicapping during war merely led to defeat. The restraints placed on US forces in Vietnam is one example. On the other hand, it is entirely sensible to limit force to avoid an escalation of conflict that leads to losses which are disproportionate to the intended goal, and also to avoid levels of violence which create an undesirable political backlash in domestic and international public opinion. This logic means that limited war has been the norm for the wars fought by Western states since the end of the Second World War.

Further reading
Robert E. Osgood, *Limited War Revisited* (Boulder: Westview, 1979)
John Garnett, 'Limited War', in John Baylis, Ken Booth, John Garnett, and Phil Williams, *Contemporary Strategy: Theories and Policies* (New York: Holmes and Meier, 1975), pp. 114–31

LORD'S RESISTANCE ARMY

The Lord's Resistance Army (LRA) is a guerrilla organization operating primarily in the lands of the Acholi people in northern Uganda, out of bases in southern Sudan. Founded in 1987, and led by Joseph Kony, the LRA wishes to overthrow the Ugandan government and install a new regime based on the biblical Ten Commandments. The LRA has been accused of numerous atrocities, most particularly of abducting children in order to turn them into soldiers. The LRA and the Ugandan government agreed on a truce in August 2006, but attempts to negotiate a final **peace** settlement have in part been hampered by the decision of the **International Criminal Court** to indict Kony and other LRA leaders for **war** crimes, with the result that they now fear arrest should they agree to surrender.

Further reading
Tim Allen, *Trial Justice: The International Criminal Court and the Lord's Resistance Army* (London: Zed Books, 2006)
Anna Sabasteanski (ed.), *Patterns of Global Terrorism 1985–2005: US State Department Reports with Supplementary Documents and Statistics* (Great Barrington: Berkshire Publishing Group, 2005)

MERCENARIES

Mercenaries have participated in **war** for thousands of years, but from the 17th century onwards, with the advent of nation states and those states' efforts to monopolize the use of force, they became increasingly unpopular and illegitimate. Intervention by mercenaries in the internal affairs of African states in the 1960s and 1970s led to measures to outlaw their use. In 1977, article 47 of Additional Protocol I of the **Geneva Conventions** defined mercenaries and stated that they were not entitled to be treated as prisoners of war if captured. The use of mercenaries is also regulated by the 1989 International Convention against the Recruitment, Use, Finance, and Training of Mercenaries.

According to article 47 of Additional Protocol I of the Geneva Conventions, a mercenary is anyone who is specially recruited to fight and does fight in an armed conflict, is motivated essentially by the desire for private gain, is neither a national or a resident of a party to the conflict, is not a member of the armed forces of a party to the conflict, and has not been sent by a state which is not party to the conflict on official duty as a member of its armed forces. This definition leaves many loopholes through which individuals can claim not to be mercenaries. For instance, military advisors and support staff would appear to be excluded because they do not actually fight. Members of 'foreign legions' such as the French Foreign Legion and the British Gurkha battalions are also excluded because they are formally enrolled in a country's armed forces. As a result of such exclusions, the legal definition is considered inadequate by some critics.

The post-**Cold War** era has seen a revival in the use of mercenaries worldwide. It is estimated, for instance, that 20,000 Russian mercenaries have participated in wars in the Former Soviet Union, and another 2,000 in the former Yugoslavia. The tremendous growth in **Private Military Companies (PMCs)** is further evidence of this trend, although those who work for PMCs deny that they are mercenaries and claim that they operate within the bounds of both national and **international law**.

Further reading
Thomas K. Adams, 'The New Mercenaries and the Privatization of Conflict', *Parameters*, vol. 39, no. 2, Summer 1999, pp. 103–16
Steven Brayton, 'Outsourcing War: Mercenaries and the Privatization of Peacekeeping', *Journal of International Affairs*, vol. 55, no. 2, Spring 2002, pp. 303–29

MI5, see SECURITY SERVICE

MI6, see SECRET INTELLIGENCE SERVICE

MIGRATION

Migration is the movement of people across national borders. While migration brings many benefits both to the migrants and to the countries to which they move, it can also pose problems for both international and **national security**. Mass immigration of people who do not share the culture of the recipient society may undermine its cultural identity and so threaten **societal security**. It may also lead to racism and even violent clashes between the immigrants and members of the host society, especially if the latter feel that the former are lowering wages and taking jobs. This in turn may radicalize the immigrants, creating the environment in which **terrorism** can flourish. Diaspora groups may maintain contacts with their original homelands, providing funds to terrorists overseas as well as shelter to terrorists coming from abroad. They may also maintain networks facilitating transnational **organized crime**, such as drug and human trafficking. On occasion, forced migrations of large numbers of people who have subsequently been sheltered in refugee camps have seriously destabilized the receiving country. The examples of Palestinian refugees in Lebanon in the late 1970s and early 1980s, and of Rwandan refugees in the Congo in the mid-1990s, are cases in point. In both instances the refugees helped to cause **civil war** and then intervention by outside powers.

Despite these problems, some analysts claim that the **securitization** of migration may have negative consequences. Viewing migrants as a **threat** to **security** encourages a 'them' and 'us' attitude which inhibits their integration into their new homes, thereby making the problem worse. Some also claim that the alleged link between migration and phenomena such as rises in organized crime is exaggerated, and that any problems caused by migration are outweighed by its benefits.

Further reading
Thomas Faist, ' "Extension de la domaine de la lutte". International Migra-tion and Security before and after September 11, 2001', *International Migration Review*, vol. 36, no. 1, Spring 2002, pp. 7–14
Elspeth Guild and Joanne van Selm (eds), *International Migration and Security: Opportunities and Challenges* (Abingdon: Routledge, 2005)
John Tirman, *The Maze of Fear: Migration and Security after September 11th* (New York: The New Press, 2004)

MILITARIZATION AND WEAPONIZATION OF SPACE
Militarization of space includes any use of space for military pur-poses. Weaponization of space is a subset of militarization of space which refers to the deployment of weapons in space. The weaponiza-tion of space is not entirely prohibited, but is restricted by the **Outer Space Treaty**, which prohibits the placing of **weapons of mass destruction** in outer space as well as the use of the moon and other celestial bodies for military purposes. At present, the militarization of space is well advanced, but the weaponization of space has not yet begun.

Examples of the militarization of space include the use of satellites for the collection of meteorological data, for military communica-tions, for navigational assistance (through use of global positioning systems), for early warning of attack, and for **intelligence** gathering and target acquisition.

One of the main arguments against the weaponization of space is the 'sanctuary' theory. This emphasizes that space systems play a vital role in the **verification** of **arms control** treaties and in providing early warning of surprise attack. In this way they strengthen **deterrence** and enhance international stability. For this reason, developments which threaten space systems should be avoided and space should remain a weapon-free sanctuary.

By contrast, the theory of 'space control' views space as a military environment just like the land, air and sea. Those who can control space and deny its use to others will have a decisive advantage in future conflict. Accordingly, proponents of the weaponization of space, principally in the United States, argue that weaponization is inevitable. They advise that the USA should take the lead in this field and secure space domination for the foreseeable future. Opponents of the weaponization of space argue that this could lead to a new **arms race** in outer space which would prove prohibitively expensive, and also point out that the US is so dependent on its space systems that it might be unwise to encourage others to develop weapons to threaten these. They also challenge the assumption that weaponization is inevitable, noting its financial costs as well as the clear advantages to states from keeping space weapons-free.

Had it ever reached fruition, the Strategic Defence Initiative (SDI, popularly known as 'Star Wars') unveiled by US President Ronald Reagan would have been a major step towards the weaponization of space, as it envisaged the placing of **ballistic missile** defence components in space. The less ambitious **National Missile Defence** system which has supplanted SDI is land-based and does not involve placing weapons in space. Internationally, there is a broad consensus against the weaponization of space. In 2002 the United Nations General Assembly voted 156-0 in favour of a resolution on the Prevention of an Arms Race in Outer Space (with Israel and the USA abstaining), but this statement of intention has yet to translate into a binding international treaty.

Further reading
Michael Krepon with Christopher Clary, *Space Assurance or Space Dominance? The Case against Weaponizing Space* (Washington DC: Henry L. Stimson Center, 2003)
Matthew Mowthorpe, *The Militarization and Weaponization of Space* (Lanham: Lexington Books, 2003)
United Nations Institute for Disarmament Research, *Outer Space and Global Security*, UNIDIR/2003/26 (Geneva: UNIDIR, 2003)

MILITARY–INDUSTRIAL COMPLEX (MIC)

The phrase 'Military–Industrial Complex (MIC)' was coined by US President Dwight Eisenhower in his farewell address of 1961, and subsequently became popular in the United States during the Vietnam War. Eisenhower warned of the conjunction of 'an immense military establishment and a large arms industry' which had acquired undue and potentially dangerous influence over domestic and foreign politics. In addition to the armed forces and defence industries, potential members of the MIC include politicians, think-tanks, and academic security experts. Critics say that these combine to produce exaggerated analyses of potential **threats** to **national security**, which in turn justify increased defence expenditure, perpetuating what some analysts call a 'permanent war economy' or the 'warfare state'. As the MIC expands, the number of persons with an interest in maintaining it grows similarly, making it difficult to reverse the expansion: military officers fear that they will lose equipment and promotions; academics fear the loss of research grants; defence industries fear the loss of profits; workers fear they will lose their jobs; and politicians, in the face of lobbying, fear that they will not be re-elected if those jobs are lost. The result is a distortion of state budget priorities, with negative economic consequences. At the same time, the perpetual state of fear induced by the MIC risks pushing the state into foreign military adventures, and can threaten civil liberties as the state seeks to reassure citizens that it is taking action to ensure their **security**. Some critics therefore regard the MIC as a threat to democratic society. Others, though, point out that the MIC, in so far as it exists, is far from being a homogenous, unified conspiracy, and that it contains many competing interests.

The term 'military–industrial complex' is primarily used with reference to the United States, although during the Cold War it was also applied to the Soviet Union, and the origins of the MIC are generally seen as lying in the massive expansion of defence spending in the USA during the Second World War. The phrase is nevertheless applicable to any state in which military, industrial, and other interests have combined to produce an inflated and overly powerful defence sector.

Further reading
Carroll W. Pursell Jr (ed.), *The Military–Industrial Complex* (New York: Harper and Row, 1972)
Alex Roland, *The Military–Industrial Complex* (Washington, DC: Society for the History of Technology, 2001)
Sam Sarkesian (ed.), *The Military–Industrial Complex: a Reassessment* (Beverly Hill: Sage, 1972)

MINISTRY OF STATE SECURITY (CHINA), see GUOJIA ANQUAN BU

MISSILE TECHNOLOGY CONTROL REGIME
The Missile Technology Control Regime (MTCR) is an informal association of states which have undertaken to voluntarily control the

export of technologies which could be used to construct delivery systems for **weapons of mass destruction** (WMD), namely **ballistic missiles**, **cruise missiles**, and unmanned aerial vehicles. The MTCR was created in 1987 by the countries of the G-7 organization (Canada, France, West Germany, Italy, Japan, the UK and USA), and has by now expanded to include 34 members. The most notable addition to the regime was Russia, which joined in 1995. China, although not a member, has pledged that it will abide by the regime's guidelines. The MTCR holds plenary meetings every year, but has no permanent secretariat.

The MTCR establishes a common set of export guidelines and a list of controlled items. Members are to establish national export control policies restricting the circumstances in which the listed items may be exported. They are supposed to assure themselves that the recipient of the technology will not use it for the creation of delivery systems of WMD, and if unable to do so, should not permit the export. The regime is purely voluntary, so it is up to each member to make these judgements for itself, and there are no designated punishments for transferring controlled items. In an effort to ensure compliance, the United States Congress passed in 1990 the Missile Technology Control Act. By this, the US government gives itself the power to impose **economic sanctions** on countries or companies who violate the MTCR, regardless of whether they are members of the regime.

The MTCR has been credited with limiting the **proliferation** of ballistic missiles. For instance, Argentina abandoned its Condor missile project in the 1990s, in part, though not entirely, because the costs of missile development had been raised by the MTCR. However, some key missile proliferators, notably North Korea, Pakistan, and Iran, remain outside the MTCR. For this and other reasons, the MTCR has been supplemented in recent years by other initiatives, such as the **Proliferation Security Initiative**.

Further reading

Dinshaw Mistry, *Containing Missile Proliferation: Strategic Technology, Security Regimes, and International Cooperation in Arms Control* (Seattle: University of Washington Press, 2003)

Istvan Gyarmati, Edmundo S. Fujita, Kapil Kak, Aaron Karp, and Wang Qun, *Missile Development and its Impact on Global Security* (New York: United Nations Department for Disarmament Affairs, 1999)

Missile Technology Control Regime website, www.mtcr.info/English/index.html

MOSCOW TREATY, see STRATEGIC OFFENSIVE REDUCTIONS TREATY

MOSSAD

Founded in 1949, Mossad is Israel's foreign **intelligence** agency. With an estimated 1,200 staff, its activities involve intelligence gathering and **covert action** beyond Israel's borders; analysis and dissemination of strategic, political, and operational intelligence; liaison with foreign intelligence services; counter-**proliferation**; preventing terrorist acts against Israeli targets abroad; and bringing Jews to Israel from countries where official agencies are not allowed to operate. Prominent Mossad operations include: the kidnappings of Nazi war criminal Adolf Eichmann in 1960 and of Israeli nuclear technician Mordecai Vanunu, who had revealed the existence of Israel's **nuclear weapons** to the British press, in 1986; the assassination of members of the Black September terrorist organization responsible for murdering Israeli athletes at the 1972 Olympic Games; and assistance provided to the operation to bring Ethiopian Jews to Israel in 1984. Mossad's operations have on occasion embarrassed the Israeli government and strained relations with allies, as in the case of two Mossad agents caught carrying forged Canadian passports during a failed attempt to assassinate **Hamas** official Khaled Meshaal in Jordan in 1997, and in the case of two more agents imprisoned in New Zealand in 2004 for attempting to acquire passports under false pretences. Despite such incidents Mossad continues to possess a reputation for efficiency.

Further reading
Thomas Gordon, *Gideon's Spies: The Secret History of the Mossad* (London: Macmillan, 1999)
Claire Hoy and Victor J. Ostrovsky, *By Way of Deception: a Devastating Insider's Portrait of the Mossad* (Toronto: Stoddart, 1990)
Mossad website: www.mohr.gov.il/Mohr/MohrTopNav/MohrEnglish/MohrAboutUs/

MULTILATERALISM

Multilateralism is the practice of three or more states coordinating national policies in accordance with mutually-agreed principles. This may be done in an ad-hoc fashion or through formal institutions with set rules. It can be contrasted with unilateralism, which is the principle and practice of states acting on their own in international affairs, with a minimum of consultation and agreement with others, and perhaps even in opposition to the will of others. In the past century, multilateralism has become increasingly important in the arena of international **security** and the number of multilateral institutions has grown significantly. Notable institutions include the **United Nations**, the **North Atlantic Treaty Organization**, and the **Organization for Security and Cooperation in Europe**.

Multilateralism has many advantages over unilateralism, and consequently many people assign it a moral quality, considering multilateralism not only a principle and practice which is beneficial but also one which states *ought* to follow. Multilateralism reflects the limits of **national power**. Even a state enjoying notional **hegemony**, such as the United States at the present time, cannot do everything it wishes without some assistance from others. Coordinating its policies with others enhances its power. Furthermore, many of the **threats** to contemporary security cannot be dealt with adequately on a purely national basis. International cooperation, and thus multilateral arrangements, are required. The threats posed by international **terrorism**, **organized crime**, and climate change are examples. Finally, multilateralism further enhances power by providing legitimacy to international action.

These benefits come at the cost of agreeing to abide by certain rules and practices, which serve to protect weaker members of multilateral arrangements from the power of the stronger. More powerful states may sometimes resent the restrictions that multilateralism thereby imposes on them. In addition, because multilateralism requires the creation of consensus among many states, it may result in inaction or action which reflects the lowest common denominator, and thus prove ineffective. These drawbacks mean that states occasionally opt to act unilaterally instead. Most notably, in recent years many critics have accused the United States of abandoning multilateralism in favour of unilateralism, especially under the presidency of George W. Bush. The US refusal to ratify the Kyoto Protocol and other treaties such as the **Ottawa Convention**, the **Comprehensive Test Ban Treaty**, and the treaty establishing the **International Criminal Court**, are all evidence of this unilateral tendency. Nevertheless, unless a state isolates itself in the manner of North Korea, complete unilateralism is impossible in the modern world, and the unilateralist tendencies of the USA are counterbalanced by its continued participation in, and often leadership of, numerous multilateral institutions.

Further reading
Robert O. Keohane, 'Multilateralism: an Agenda for Research', *International Journal*, vol. 45, no. 4, Autumn 1990, pp. 731–64
John Gerard Ruggie, 'Multilateralism: the Anatomy of an Institution', *International Organization*, vol. 46, no. 3, Summer 1992, pp. 561–98

MULTIPOLARITY, see UNIPOLARITY

MUTUALLY-ASSURED DESTRUCTION (MAD)

Mutually-Assured Destruction (MAD) is an essential element of the **strategy** of nuclear **deterrence**. The term first came into use in the mid-1960s, but the key concepts behind it developed in the United States in the 1950s, as American strategists sought to determine how to respond to the Soviet development of **nuclear weapons**. A condition of mutually-assured destruction exists when two potential opponents both possess sufficient numbers of nuclear weapons that neither will be able to destroy all of the other's weapons in a nuclear first strike. This will guarantee that if attacked, either party will be able to inflict an unacceptable degree of damage on the attacker in response (a level defined in the 1960s by the US Secretary of Defence Robert McNamara as the destruction of 20–33 per cent of the Soviet population and 50–75 per cent of its industrial capacity). In other words, the result of any attack will be mutual destruction. The desire to avoid this means that the **threat** of mutually-assured destruction, according to its supporters, can prevent the outbreak of nuclear **war**.

The theory of MAD relies on a degree of rationality among those who are to be deterred, and assumes that they will consider the **risk** of nuclear retaliation too large to carry out a first strike. Opponents of MAD argue that these assumptions are not necessarily correct. Creating a massive arsenal of nuclear weapons in order to ensure MAD could in fact increase the likelihood of nuclear war by raising mutual suspicions and fears, as well as increase the possibility of accidental launches and theft of nuclear materials by terrorists or others. Nevertheless, the concept of MAD remained the cornerstone of nuclear strategy for most of the **Cold War** and continues to influence discussions about nuclear deterrence in the twenty-first century.

Further reading
Lawrence Freedman, *The Evolution of Nuclear Strategy*, 2nd edn (Basingstoke: Macmillan, 1989)
Alan J. Parrington, 'Mutually Assured Destruction Revisited: Strategic Doctrine in Question', *Airpower Journal*, vol. 11, no. 4, Winter 1997, pp. 4–19

NATIONAL INTEREST

The defence of the national interest against internal and external **threats** is often considered to be the essential task of **national security** policy. The national interest consists of those things which are valued by a society and its leaders. These are, among others, physical survival, territorial integrity, the pursuit of ideology, national honour and prestige, economic well being and trade, and the maintenance of international stability. Different persons and different groups within a society will attach different values to each of these, and the pursuit of some of these interests will benefit some people and groups and not others. It is possible, therefore, to deny that there is such a thing as the national interest, there merely being individual and group interests. Despite this, most observers would agree that there are some things that are of sufficient importance to a sufficiently large majority of people within a nation to constitute a national interest, and without the concept to guide them state leaders would find it difficult to determine the purpose of their policies.

National interests are traditionally divided into two types: vital and secondary. Vital interests are considered to be those which affect the very life and existence of the nation. These are so important that a nation should go to **war** to defend them. Defence of secondary interests should in theory call for methods short of war. In practice, there are no firm criteria for determining what is a vital and what is a secondary interest, and it is not clear that statesmen distinguish between them. In addition, national interests are not always complementary, indeed may conflict with one another. A leader may consider that spreading human rights and democracy is a national interest, but then find that attempting to do this antagonizes foreign countries who are potential trade partners, so harming a separate interest. Just as there are no clear guidelines for distinguishing between vital and secondary interests, there are none for determining priorities among interests. Thus, although many speak of the national interest as though it were an objective fact, interpretations of it are inevitably very subjective.

Further reading
Joseph Frankel, *National Interest* (London: Macmillan, 1970)
Michael G. Roskin, 'National Interest: From Abstraction to Strategy', *Parameters*, vol. 24, no. 4, Winter 1994/1995, pp. 4–18
Fred A. Sonderman, 'The Concept of National Interest', *Orbis*, vol. 21, no. 1, Spring 1977, pp. 121–138

NATIONAL MISSILE DEFENCE (NMD)

National Missile Defence (NMD) is the name of a programme being developed by the United States to protect the entire territory of the USA against attack by **ballistic missiles**. The origins of NMD lie in the Strategic Defence Initiative (SDI) launched by President Ronald Reagan in the 1980s. Unlike SDI, NMD does not aim to protect the United States against a full-scale missile attack by the Russian Federation. Rather, it aims more modestly at being able to shoot down a handful of missiles launched by a **rogue state** such as North Korea. The NMD program was mandated by the US Congress in the National Missile Defence Act of 1999, which requires the President to deploy NMD as soon as technologically feasible. NMD will use a system currently known as Ground-Based Midcourse Defence, based in Alaska. Satellites and ground-based radars will detect incoming ballistic missiles, which will then in theory be destroyed by 'ground-based interceptors'. These will, if they work as desired, strike their targets while the latter are still in space.

National Missile Defence is highly controversial. Many doubt that there exists a serious enough ballistic missile **threat** to justify the system, and say that an enemy wishing to use **nuclear weapons** against the United States would be unlikely to use a ballistic missile as its delivery system. Second, NMD is hugely expensive, costing tens of billions of dollars at a time when US defence budgets are being stretched by operations in Iraq, Afghanistan, and elsewhere. Third, there is no guarantee that the system will ever work as planned, and tests carried out so far have had mixed results. Fourth, there is a danger that if an effective NMD system is ever developed, it will merely encourage other states to increase their ballistic missile capability in order to overwhelm it, thus inciting a new **arms race**. Fifth, NMD is vulnerable to counter-measures, such as decoys. And sixth, in order to put NMD into action, the USA has had to withdraw from the **Anti-Ballistic Missile Treaty** with Russia, arguably undermining the whole **arms control** structure of the past 30 years. Supporters of

NMD, on the other hand, argue that the **proliferation** of ballistic missile technology makes some form of national ballistic missile defence system ever more important, and that the creation of an effective NMD will strengthen America's position vis-à-vis rogue states.

Further reading
Richard L. Garwin, 'Holes in the Missile Shield', *Scientific American*, vol. 291, no. 5, November 2004, pp. 70–79
George Lewis, Lisbeth Gronlund, and David Wright, 'National Missile Defense: an Indefensible System', *Foreign Policy*, no. 117, Winter 1999–2000, pp. 120–131
Missile Defense Agency website, www.mda.mil
Keith B. Payne, 'The Case for National Missile Defense', *Orbis*, vol. 44, no. 2, Spring 2000, pp. 187–196

NATIONAL POWER

National power is a measure of a state's ability to get others to do what it wishes them to do. This is dependent on the possession of certain capabilities and the willingness to use them, and also on others' perceptions of those capabilities and will. The sources of the objective capabilities of national power include human resources (such as the size of the nation's population and its skills), natural resources (such as land area and raw materials), and economic resources (both industrial and financial). Subjective power is dependent on matters of reputation or prestige. However much objective power one possesses it is of little use if others do not believe that one possesses it or has the will to use it. Another way of examining national power is to divide it into hard power and **soft power**. The former reflects a state's ability to coerce or bribe others; the latter reflects its ability to persuade them to positively want what it wants.

States exercise national power through a number of instruments: military, economic and diplomatic. All of these instruments and sources of power are highly situational. Hard, military power, for instance, may be extremely useful in one situation and entirely useless, even counterproductive, in another. On occasions, the different forms of power may complement each other; on others they may work against each other. For proponents of **Realism**, the pursuit of the **national interest** and **national security** is synonymous with the expansion of national power. This theory is contested by others, who note that states often behave in ways which cannot easily be explained purely by the pursuit of power.

Further reading
David Jablonsky, 'National Power', *Parameters*, vol. 37, no. 1, Spring 1997, pp. 34–54
Hans Morgenthau, *Politics among Nations: The Struggle for Power and Peace*, 7th edition (Guildford, CT: McGraw-Hill, 2005)

NATIONAL SECURITY

National **security** refers to the protection of nation states from external and internal **threats** to their **national interests**. Different observers emphasize different interests and different threats, and also define those interests in different manners and disagree over the nature and scale of the threats. They also disagree over the appropriate responses. As a result, the core objectives of national security policy are often hotly contested.

The state's primary national security concern is survival. Strong states, whose internal stability is assured, have historically tended to frame their national security in terms of protection from military threats from outside their borders. Weaker states, by contrast, have tended to do so in terms of protection from internal dangers, such as **revolution**, **coup d'état**, and **insurgency**. The former we may refer to as 'military security', and the latter as 'political security'. Political security can also encompass efforts to defend or spread one's political ideology. These are not the only potential aspects of national security. Military and political power are dependent on economic power. This makes **economic security** and **energy security** essential elements of national security. This is true not only because they are vital for maintenance of state power, but also because one of the tasks of national security policy is the protection of the quality of life of citizens, a task which is itself dependent on economic success. This task also demands that the state protect its citizens from the dangers posed by **organized crime**. While this is normally framed as a law enforcement issue, if organized crime acquires excessive dimensions it may threaten social order and the existence of the state, and thus become a national security problem. Citizens may also be concerned about threats to their culture and identity, such as that posed by mass

migration, and demand that the state protect them against these. Such concerns come under the rubric of **societal security**. Finally, some analysts broaden the concept of national security to include **environmental security**, on the grounds that environmental degradation can severely degrade the quality of life of individuals, damage the economy, and spark **resource conflicts**.

Realism posits that states seek to enhance national security by seeking to maximize **national power**, especially military power. This does not always achieve the desired effect. The workings of the **security dilemma** mean that efforts to strengthen military power, for instance, can provoke an **arms race**, which leaves the state facing greater external dangers than it did before. There is no necessary correlation between power and security. Small or poor states are often more secure, or at least feel more secure, than large and powerful ones who have more enemies.

Some critics argue that the language of national security can have negative effects. The invocation of national security may be used to silence opposition within states and to enhance the power of the state and its leaders at the expense of their citizens and their human rights. Opponents of the practice of **securitization** argue that it may be best to restrict the national security label to traditional issues such as military security, and to avoid describing dangers such as environmental degradation as national security problems. Others posit that a better approach would be to abandon the discourse of 'national' security and think instead in terms of 'international' security. The former encourages states to adopt policies which put them in opposition to each other, whereas the latter encourages them to consider finding common solutions to the problems which threaten them all. **Cooperative security** of this sort can protect states and their interests better in the long term than policies based on a narrow understanding of national security. While arguments of this sort have had some influence on state policy since the end of the **Cold War**, in general leaders continue to view policy in fairly traditional terms, a tendency strengthened by the onset of the **Global War on Terrorism**.

Further reading
Barry Buzan, *People, States and Fear: an Agenda for International Security in the Post-Cold War Era*, 2nd edn (London: Harvester Wheatsheaf, 1991)
Melvyn P. Leffler, 'National Security', *The Journal of American History*, vol. 77, no. 1, June 1990, pp. 143–152

Robert Mandel, *The Changing Face of National Security: a Conceptual Analysis* (Westport: Greenwood, 1994)

NATIONAL SECURITY AGENCY (NSA)

The National Security Agency (NSA) is the signals **intelligence** and **information security** agency of the United States of America. Created in 1952, the NSA is based in Fort Meade, Maryland, and intercepts electronic signals using platforms on land, sea, air, and space. It also has stations outside the USA, such as that at Menwith Hill in the United Kingdom. The largest and most secretive of the many US intelligence organizations, it is part of the Department of Defence. It possesses close ties to, and shares information with, many foreign signals intelligence agencies, such as the British **Government Communications Headquarters (GCHQ)**. The NSA is responsible for the collection, analysis, and dissemination of signals intelligence to the US government, as well as for protecting government information systems from hostile attack. Over the 50 years of its existence, the NSA has played an important role in the development of computer technology due its need for tools to aid in cryptanalysis and in collation of the millions of messages intercepted by its listening stations each day.

The ability of the NSA to intercept communications has caused much fear that its power might be abused for domestic political purposes in breach of personal privacy. The NSA's mandate authorizes it to collect information concerning foreign intelligence or counter-intelligence, but not to spy on American citizens within the USA. In the late 1970s, it was revealed that despite this the NSA had spied on anti-Vietnam war protesters, as a result of which the Foreign Intelligence Surveillance Act (FISA) was passed. This permits the NSA to intercept communications within the USA, but only after receiving a warrant from the FISA court. In 2005, however, the NSA was shown to have been carrying out warrantless wiretaps within the USA as part of the **Global War on Terrorism**. In January 2007, President George W. Bush announced that this practice would cease. Nevertheless, the revelations about it have renewed debate about the appropriate limits of the NSA's powers.

Further reading
James Bamford, *Body of Secrets: Anatomy of the Ultra-Secret National Security Agency* (London: Arrow, 2002)
National Security Agency website: www.nsa.gov

NATIONAL SECURITY COUNCIL (NSC)

The National Security Council (NSC) is the primary agency within the government of the United States of America for formulating high-level foreign and **security** policy and for integrating the work of the various departments involved in the making of such policy. It provides a forum in which the President can discuss foreign and security matters with his most senior advisors, and by bringing those advisors into one committee facilitates coordination of their activities. Founded by the National Security Act of 1947, the NSC originally consisted of just four members – the President, Vice-President, Secretary of State, and Secretary of Defence. Under President Clinton, the membership was expanded to include the Secretary of the Treasury. The National Security Advisor also attends meetings, as do the Director of National Intelligence and the Chairman of the Joint Chiefs of Staff as statutory advisors. The Chief of Staff to the President and the Assistant to the President for Economic Policy can also be invited, as occasionally are other officials.

The NSC contains two primary committees: the NSC Principals Committee (NSC/PC), consisting of the Secretary of State, the Secretary of the Treasury, the Secretary of Defence, the Chief of Staff to the President, and the National Security Advisor who chairs the meetings; and the NSC Deputies Committee (NSC/DC), composed of the deputies of the government agencies with an interest in security issues. The prime role of the NSC/DC is to act as an interagency forum to consider policy issues affecting American **national security**.

The NSC is supported by a staff of 200, led by the Assistant to the President for National Security Affairs, more commonly known as the National Security Advisor. Critics of the NSC complain that what was designed as a simple structure allowing the president and his senior security advisors to consult and make decisions has become a large and unwieldy bureaucracy which focuses too much on short-term policy detail and pays insufficient attention to its function of integrating the work of other security agencies. On occasions, the staff of the NSC have acted almost as independent policy actors, as for instance in the notorious Iran-Contra affair in the 1980s, when NSC staff arranged secret sales of arms to Iran and provided support to the Nicaraguan Contra guerrillas. On other occasions, however, Presidents have chosen to bypass the NSC when making important policy decisions. The power of the NSC has thus varied over time, an important determinant being the personalities and relationships of the main players, most particularly the President and the National Security Advisor.

Further reading
Karl F. Inderfurth and Loch K. Johnson (eds), *Fateful Decisions: Inside the National Security Council* (New York and Oxford: Oxford University Press, 2004)
David Rothkopf, *Running the World: The Inside Story of the National Security Council and the Architects of American Power* (New York: Public Affairs, 2005)

NEOCONSERVATISM
Neoconservatism is an intellectual movement believed to have had an important influence on the **security** policy of the United States under the presidency of George W. Bush. In particular, neoconservatives such as former Deputy Secretary of Defence Paul Wolfowitz are supposed to have played a significant role in pushing the United States into adopting the policies of **regime change** and **preventive war**.

In terms of security policy, neoconservatism argues that the internal regimes of foreign states play an important role in determining their international policies. Non-democratic regimes are believed to be inherently likely to adopt positions hostile to American interests, and thus US security is ultimately dependent on the spread of democracy and human rights. Furthermore, the neoconservatives firmly believe that American norms and values are inherently superior to others, and are universally applicable. They argue that the United States should exploit its moment of **hegemony** to actively promote democracy overseas and overthrow non-democratic regimes. In this way, through the use of its power, and in particular its military power, they hold that the USA can act as a force for good in the world. While neoconservatism does not entirely reject **multilateralism** in the pursuit of this policy, it maintains that the USA should not allow any concessions to multilateralism to give other states a veto over US policy. When necessary, the United States should act unilaterally in pursuit of its interests and the greater moral good.

Critics of neoconservatism, particularly those associated with **Realism**, accuse it of excessive idealism and of underestimating the difficulties of exporting democracy and human rights by force. They also accuse the neoconservatives of overemphasizing the military instrument of **national power** to the detriment of other instruments, and of being uncritically pro-Israeli in their foreign policy prescriptions for the whole Middle East region. Many portray the difficulties being experienced by the United States due to the **insurgency** in Iraq as a consequence of these errors of neoconservative policy. It would be wrong, however, to pin these difficulties entirely on the chests of neoconservatism, since the leading figures in the Bush administration at the time of the invasion of Iraq, such as Donald Rumsfeld, Condoleezza Rice, and Colin Powell, were not neoconservatives. The problems in Iraq have put neoconservatism on the defensive, but many of its adherents continue to occupy influential positions in government, academia, and think tanks, and it cannot yet be written off as a political force.

Further reading

Max Boot, 'Neocons', *Foreign Policy*, no. 140, January/February 2004, pp. 20–28

Gary Dorrien, 'Consolidating the Empire: Neoconservatism and the Politics of American Dominion', *Political Theology*, vol. 6, no. 5, 2005, pp. 409–428

Francis Fukuyama, *America at the Crossroads: Democracy, Power, and the Neoconservative Legacy* (New Haven: Yale University Press, 2006)

Adam Wolfson, 'Conservatives and Neoconservatives', *The Public Interest*, no. 154, Winter 2004, pp. 32–48

NETWAR

Netwar is a term developed by American theorists John Arquilla and David Ronfeldt. They use it to refer to military and political conflicts in which one side operates using networked organizations and strategies. A network, for these purposes, is considered to be a web consisting of a large number of dispersed but interconnected nodes, with a common ideology but little by way of hierarchy or central command. This distinguishes networks from the hierarchical cell structures previously favoured by terrorist organizations. The existence of networks is facilitated by developments in information technology, in particular the internet and email. These enable the nodes of the network to communicate with one another and the outside world.

Thus, despite being dispersed, the nodes are able to share ideas and experience, and when desirable to practise **swarming**.

Netwar is particularly attractive to non-state actors, such as terrorists, transnational criminal organizations, and radical political pressure groups. It is difficult to defeat as there is no single target whose destruction would threaten the entire network. **Al Qaeda**, particularly after its leadership was dispersed by American forces in Afghanistan in late 2001, can be seen as an example of a networked group. Anti-globalization protestors also practise netwar and swarming. Members of such networks can use the internet not only to communicate with each other, but also to propagandize their cause, and to mobilize non-governmental organizations on their behalf. They can also bypass traditional media, which may be under government control, to broadcast their message. Netwar can pose a serious challenge to state structures which remain wedded to slower moving and more hierarchical systems.

Further reading
John Arquilla and David Ronfeldt, *The Advent of Netwar* (Santa Monica: RAND, 1996)
John Arquilla, David Ronfeldt, Graham Fuller, and Melissa Fuller, *The Zapatista Social Netwar in Mexico* (Santa Monica: RAND, 1998)

NETWORK-CENTRIC WARFARE (NCW)

Network-centric warfare (NCW), sometimes referred to also as 'network-enabled operations', is an important element of the **Revolution in Military Affairs (RMA)** and defence **transformation**. It relies heavily on the use of modern information technologies and communications systems. NCW aims to empower armed forces to act with greater rapidity and efficiency, by linking, or networking, all relevant command, control and information systems with weapons and decision-makers. It is similar to **C4ISR**. In theory, those commanding the weapons should be able to have almost immediate access through a computer network to a fused picture of all significant **intelligence**, allowing them to strike targets very rapidly and accurately. NCW thus enhances combat power and provides military forces with a decisive information superiority over those who lack it. The relevance of NCW, as also of the RMA, to **asymmetric warfare** and **Fourth Generation War** is open to debate.

Further reading
Office of Force Transformation, *The Implementation of Network-Centric Warfare* (Washington, DC: US Government Printing Office, 2005)
Thomas P. N. Barnett, 'The Seven Deadly Sins of Network Centric Warfare', *US Naval Institute Proceedings*, vol. 125, no. 1, January 1999, pp. 36–39
John Ferris, 'Netcentric Warfare, C4ISR and Information Operations: Towards a Revolution in Military Intelligence?', in L. V. Scott and Peter Jackson (eds), *Understanding Intelligence in the Twenty-First Century* (London: Routledge, 2004), pp. 54–77

NON-PROLIFERATION TREATY (NPT)

The 'Treaty on the Non-Proliferation of Nuclear Weapons', more commonly known as the Non-Proliferation Treaty (NPT), was signed on 1 July 1968 and entered into force on 5 March 1970. The treaty was to last twenty-five years from entering into force, after which time a conference was to be held to decide whether it should be extended indefinitely or for another fixed period. In 1995 the appropriate conference decided to extend the treaty indefinitely. Subsequent review conferences have taken place in 2000 and 2005. States have the right to withdraw from the treaty if they feel that 'extraordinary events' have jeopardized their 'supreme interests'. One country, North Korea, has taken advantage of this clause, withdrawing from the treaty in 2003.

The NPT places different obligations on 'nuclear weapons states' and 'non-nuclear weapons states'. Five countries are designated as the former – China, France, Russia (as successor to the USSR), the United Kingdom, and the United States. All other states are considered the latter. Under the terms of the treaty, the nuclear weapons states undertake not to transfer **nuclear weapons** to any recipient, and not to assist or encourage any non-nuclear weapons state to acquire nuclear explosive devices. They also undertake to pursue negotiations in good faith to achieve complete nuclear **disarmament**, although no specific date is given for this goal. All states are prohibited from providing others with special fissionable materials suitable for making nuclear weapons and with equipment designed to process, use or produce such materials. Non-nuclear weapons states undertake not to receive from anybody else nuclear weapons or other nuclear explosive devices, and not to manufacture or otherwise acquire these. They are obliged to conclude agreements with the **International Atomic**

Energy Authority (IAEA) to implement safeguards to ensure their compliance. In return, the NPT grants all parties an 'inalienable right to develop research, production and use of nuclear energy for peaceful purposes without discrimination', and obliges all parties to facilitate the 'fullest possible exchange of equipment, materials, and scientific and technological information for the peaceful uses of nuclear energy'. In effect, the NPT represented a bargain by which the nuclear weapons states persuaded others to forego nuclear weapons in return for a guarantee of assistance in the development of peaceful uses of nuclear power.

The NPT has been relatively successful in its stated aim of reducing the **proliferation** of nuclear weapons. No state has yet tested a nuclear device while remaining a party to the treaty. However, the NPT has not been able to prevent the spread of nuclear weapons entirely. Three states have not signed the NPT and have developed a nuclear weapons capability, namely India, Israel, and Pakistan. In addition, North Korea has left the treaty and exploded a nuclear device in October 2006. Furthermore, the nuclear weapons states have not lived up to their obligation in the treaty to work towards complete nuclear disarmament, nor do they show any inclination of doing so, as witnessed by the UK's recent decision to renew its independent nuclear deterrent.

One perceived weakness in the NPT is that it allows states to develop all the industrial apparatus required for the construction of a nuclear device, as long as the use of that apparatus remains entirely peaceful. Once a state has acquired all it needs, there is nothing stopping it from leaving the treaty and converting its legally obtained nuclear capacity into a tool for making weapons, precisely as North Korea did (a phenomenon known as 'breakout'). The example of Iraq, which came close to building a nuclear weapon prior to 1991, also suggests that the safeguards system managed by the IAEA can be circumvented. Many commentators in the nuclear weapons states therefore now favour amending the NPT to make it harder for non-nuclear weapons states to acquire nuclear materials even for peaceful purposes. Unsurprisingly, this idea is resisted by the non-nuclear weapons states, who see it as a negation of the original bargain which led to the NPT. Efforts to strengthen the NPT at the 2005 review conference ended in failure after disagreements over a variety of issues, such as the desire to tighten controls on fissile materials, the need to ratify the **Comprehensive Test Ban Treaty**, and the failure of the weapons states to disarm.

Further reading
Jayantha Dhanapala, *Multilateral Diplomacy and the NPT* (Geneva: United Nations Institute for Disarmament Research, 2005)
Thomas Graham Jr and Damien J. LaVera, *Cornerstones of Security: Arms Control Treaties in the Nuclear Era* (Seattle: University of Washington Press, 2003)
United Nations, *Weapons of Mass Destruction: Treaty on the Non-Proliferation of Nuclear Weapons*, disarmament2.un.org/wmd/npt/index.html

NORTH AMERICAN AEROSPACE DEFENCE COMMAND (NORAD)

The North American Aerospace Defence Command (NORAD) is a joint Canadian and US organization, with responsibility for aerospace warning and control for North America. The organization was established in 1958 to provide a means of protecting North American airspace against possible incursions by Soviet aircraft. Radar systems across northern Canada detect incoming aircraft which can then be intercepted by Canadian and US forces. In addition to this basic air defence role, NORAD has over time acquired additional tasks, such as the tracking of objects in space and early warning of **ballistic missile** attack. It also monitors aircraft suspected of illegal drug smuggling, and since 11 September 2001 has provided support to the civil authorities in Canada and the United States to prevent further instances of aerial **terrorism**. The headquarters of NORAD is in Colorado Springs, USA. The commander of the organization is always a senior American officer, and the deputy commander a Canadian. The treaty creating NORAD has been renewed on several occasions since 1958, most recently in 2006.

Further reading
David L. Bashow, 'The Case for Norad', in David L. Bashow, *Canada and the Future of Collective Defence* (Kingston: Centre for International Relations, 1998), pp. 11–22
Ann Denholm Crosby, 'A Middle-Power Military in Alliance: Canada and NORAD', *Journal of Peace Research*, vol. 34, no. 1, pp. 37–52
NORAD website: www.norad.mil/

NORTH ATLANTIC TREATY ORGANIZATION (NATO)

The North Atlantic Treaty Organization (NATO) is a military and political alliance which currently has 26 member countries in Europe and North America. The alliance was created in 1949 in order to provide for the **collective defence** of Europe against the **threat** posed by the Soviet Union. In this regard, the critical article of NATO's founding charter, the North Atlantic Treaty, is Article Five, which stipulates that an attack on any member of NATO shall be considered an attack on all. This article was invoked for the first time following the terrorist attacks on the United States on 11 September 2001.

Since 1966, the headquarters of NATO has been located in Brussels, Belgium. Supreme political authority within the alliance rests in the North Atlantic Council, which consists of the ambassadors to NATO of each of the member states. Meetings of the Council are chaired by the Secretary General of NATO, who with his staff is also responsible for the administration of the organization. Direction of military affairs is the responsibility of the Military Committee, which consists of the 26 senior officers accredited as Military Representatives by the member states. Until 2003, the conduct of military operations and planning was delegated to three commands, European, Atlantic, and Channel, under three 'supreme commanders', Supreme Allied Commander Europe (SACEUR), Supreme Allied Commander Atlantic (SACLANT), and Allied Commander-in-Chief Channel (CINCHAN). In 2003, a reorganization abolished these commands, and replaced them with two new ones: Allied Command Transformation (ACT), responsible for the **transformation** of NATO forces to better suit the changed international **security** situation after the Cold War, and Allied Command Operations (ACO), responsible for the planning and conduct of NATO operations worldwide. The commander of ACO retains the title of SACEUR and is based in the Supreme Headquarters Allied Powers Europe (SHAPE) in Mons, Belgium.

Throughout the Cold War, NATO concentrated on the defence of Western Europe. The collapse of communism left it without an obvious role. Since 1990, NATO has sought to convert itself from a collective defence to a **collective security** organization, and also to spread its influence within and beyond the boundaries of Europe. The **Partnership for Peace** programme, established by NATO in 1994, aims to encourage democratization and promote stability in Eastern Europe and the Former Soviet Union through a series of bilateral agreements on security cooperation between NATO and partner countries. NATO has also substantially enlarged its membership, expanding to take in ten former communist states in Eastern Europe. In 1995, NATO launched air strikes against Serbian forces in Bosnia in an effort to end the **civil war** in that country, and in 1999 it undertook a three-month air campaign against Yugoslavia in response to Belgrade's actions in the Serbian province of Kosovo. Subsequent to these operations, NATO forces occupied both Bosnia and Kosovo. The military campaigns indicated NATO's move away from concepts of defence to embrace **humanitarian intervention, peace enforcement**, and **peacebuilding** outside of NATO's borders. Since 2001, NATO troops have also been fighting the **Taliban** in Afghanistan.

Although notionally an alliance of equals, NATO has always been dominated by the United States. In recent years, there have been growing efforts to balance this through the creation of a **Common European Security and Defence Policy (CESDP)**, which will give greater strength to the European arm of NATO. Some opponents of CESDP fear that it could in the long term make NATO redundant and lead to the organization's demise. In the short term, however, there is little indication that NATO's members wish to replace the alliance with anything radically different, and it seems likely that NATO will remain an important player on the international scene for some time to come.

Further reading

Peter Duignan, *NATO: Its Past, Present, and Future* (Stanford: Hoover Institution Press, 2000)

Carl Cavanagh Hodge, *Atlanticism for a New Century: the Rise, Triumph and Decline of NATO* (Upper Saddle River: Pearson/Prentice Hall, 2005)

Lawrence S. Kaplan, *The Long Entanglement: NATO's First Fifty Years* (London: Westport, 1999)

NUCLEAR NON-PROLIFERATION TREATY,
see NON-PROLIFERATION TREATY

NUCLEAR, BIOLOGICAL, AND CHEMICAL WEAPONS (NBC),
see WEAPONS OF MASS DESTRUCTION (WMD)

NUCLEAR SUPPLIERS GROUP (NSG)

The Nuclear Suppliers Group is a nuclear export control regime established in 1975 after the **nuclear weapons** test conducted by India in 1974 revealed significant weaknesses in existing systems to prevent the **proliferation** of nuclear weapons. The group consists of 45 nuclear supplier countries who have agreed to coordinate their controls on the export of nuclear and nuclear-related equipment to non-nuclear weapons states. To this end, the NSG has produced two sets of guidelines listing nuclear materials which are subject to export controls. NSG members should not export such materials to other states without receiving assurances that they will not be used for weapons purposes. The final destination of the materials must also be subject to **International Atomic Energy Authority** safeguards. Members' agreement to restrict their exports according to NSG guidelines is entirely voluntary, and there is no enforcement mechanism. The NSG meets annually to amend the guidelines and discuss their operation.

Further reading
Richard T. Cupitt and Igor Khripunov, 'New Strategies for the Nuclear Suppliers Group', *Comparative Strategy*, vol. 16, no. 3, July–September 1997, pp. 305–15
Seema Gahlaut and Victor Zaborsky, 'Do Export Control Regimes Have Members They Really Need?', *Comparative Strategy*, vol. 23, no. 1, January–March 2004, pp. 73–91
Nuclear Suppliers Group website, http://www.nuclearsuppliersgroup.org/default.htm

NUCLEAR TRIAD, see DETERRENCE

NUCLEAR WEAPONS
Nuclear weapons are weapons which use a nuclear reaction to cause an explosion. This reaction may be of two types. The first is a fission reaction, in which a heavy molecule (either Uranium-235 or Plutonium-239) is split when bombarded with neutrons. This in turns causes more neutrons to be dispersed, splitting more molecules, and setting off a chain reaction which releases enormous energy in a brief moment. The second is a fusion reaction, in which two lighter molecules are combined to produce a heavier one, again producing energy in the process. To produce the heat required to start a fusion reaction, a fission reaction is first necessary. Nuclear weapons which make use of fission reactions alone are known as atomic bombs; those which use a combined fission–fusion reaction are known as

thermonuclear or hydrogen bombs. Together with **biological weapons** and **chemical weapons**, both types of nuclear weapons are considered **weapons of mass destruction**.

Nuclear weapons produce a powerful blast wave which in the case of larger thermonuclear weapons can destroy and kill everything within a radius of several kilometres. They also cause damage by producing extreme heat and radiation. The latter can contaminate the blast area long after the initial explosion. Nuclear weapons vary considerably in power; the smallest have the strength of only a few thousand tons of explosives (kilotons); the largest the strength of several million tons (megatons). Devices designed to strike enemy military forces on the battlefield are generally on the lower end of the scale and are referred to as 'tactical' nuclear weapons. These can be delivered by air or by artillery. Devices designed to strike enemy targets behind the front lines are referred to as 'strategic' nuclear weapons. These can be delivered by air or by **cruise** and **ballistic missiles**.

Because of their immense destructive power, nuclear weapons are of limited use for fighting wars. An exchange of nuclear weapons would cause damage out of all proportion to any possible **war** aim. Their primary purpose is, therefore, not to be used as weapons but to act as a **deterrent** against attack. Some countries also see the possession of nuclear weapons as a question of national prestige. At present, nine countries are known or believed to possess them – the United States, United Kingdom, France, China, Russia, Israel, India, Pakistan, and North Korea. South Africa at one point owned nuclear weapons, but dismantled them at the end of the apartheid era. Preventing the further **proliferation** of nuclear weapons is a priority of the **national security** policy of many states. The development, deployment, and use of nuclear weapons, as well as of the materials required to produce them, is restricted by a large number of **arms control** treaties, most notably the **Non-Proliferation Treaty**. Other important nuclear-related treaties include the **Outer Space Treaty**, the **Partial Test Ban Treaty**, the **Seabed Treaty**, the **Strategic Arms Limitation** and **Strategic Arms Reduction Treaties**, and the **Treaty for the Prohibition of Nuclear Weapons in Latin America**.

Further reading

Richard W. Mansbach, 'The Special Case of Nuclear Weapons', in Richard W. Mansbach, *The Global Puzzle: Issues and Actors in World Politics*, 3rd edn (Boston: Houghton Mifflin, 2000), pp. 331–67

L. W. McNaught, *Nuclear Weapons and their Effects* (London: Brassey's, 1984)

Steve Tulliu and Thomas Schmalberger, 'Nuclear Weapons', in *Coming to Terms with Security: A Lexicon for Arms Control, Disarmament and Confidence-Building*, UNIDIR/2003/22 (Geneva: UNIDIR, 2003)

OPEN SKIES, see **TREATY ON OPEN SKIES**

OPERATIONAL LEVEL OF WAR, see **STRATEGY**

ORGANIZATION OF AMERICAN STATES (OAS)

The Organization of American States is an international organization consisting of all 35 independent states in North and South America, although only 34 members participate actively as the membership of Cuba has been suspended. A General Assembly of the foreign ministers of all members meets once a year to establish policy. The organization's goals include social and economic development, promoting democracy, protecting human rights, combating corruption and the drugs trade, and strengthening **peace** and **security**. The OAS security agenda, adopted in October 2003, took a broad interpretation of security, including issues such as poverty, environmental degradation, and HIV/AIDS, but the organization has also taken some interest in more traditional security issues. In 1999, for instance, the OAS established an Inter-American Committee Against Terrorism to better coordinate members' efforts to counter **terrorism**. To date, however, the OAS has not played a major role in **conflict prevention**, **conflict resolution**, or **peacekeeping** in the Americas. While the desire to strengthen cooperation exists, as yet the OAS remains a relatively minor player in questions of international security.

Further reading

Michael W. Collier, 'The Hemispheric Security Agenda', *Hemisphere: a Magazine of the Americas*, vol. 16, Spring 2006, pp. 14–17

Kent den Heyer and Jeremy King, 'Security and Peacekeeping: the Experience of the OAS', *Peacekeeping and International Relations*, vol. 25, no. 3, May/June 1996, pp. 15–16

Organization of American States website: http://www.oas.org/

ORGANIZATION FOR SECURITY AND COOPERATION IN EUROPE (OSCE)

The Organization for Security and Cooperation in Europe (OSCE) is an international organization with fifty-six members in Europe, North America, and Central Asia. The origins of the OSCE lie in the Conference on Security and Cooperation in Europe (CSCE), established in 1973. In 1975 CSCE members agreed the Helsinki Final Act, in which the states of the two main **Cold War** blocs undertook to respect each others' **sovereignty** and territorial borders, to renounce force, and to respect human rights. Thereafter the CSCE met regularly over the next two decades to review these commitments and monitor their implementation, but the conference lacked a permanent institutional basis. This changed in 1994, when the CSCE became the OSCE and acquired permanent institutions, including a secretariat based in Vienna.

The OSCE deals with three dimensions of **security**, namely politico-military security, **economic** and **environmental security**, and **human security**. These include **arms control**, **confidence and security building measures**, promotion of human rights, democratization and election monitoring, **counter-terrorism**, and economic and environmental activities. OSCE missions have been deployed to numerous former communist countries in Eastern Europe and Central Asia, the largest missions being in Bosnia, Kosovo, and Georgia. In the last example, the OSCE acts as a mediator in the conflict between Georgia and its autonomous regions of South Ossetia and Abkhazia, and provides forces to monitor the border zones. Despite these activities, the OSCE remains overshadowed in the security field by the **North Atlantic Treaty Organization** and the European Union's developing **Common European Security and Defence Policy**.

Further reading
Organization for Security and Cooperation in Europe website: http://www.osce.org/
V. Shustov, 'OSCE's Place in Europe's Architecture', *International Affairs: a Russian Journal of World Politics, Diplomacy and International Relations*, vol. 48, no. 1, 2002, pp. 38–48
Gérard Stoudmann, 'The OSCE: Still Relevant to the New Global Security Environment?', *Helsinki Monitor*, no. 3, 2005, pp. 198–203

ORGANIZED CRIME

There is no agreed definition of what constitutes organized crime. The term suggests criminal activity involving two or more people, but usually many more, within some organized social system. In this, there should be some hierarchy, division of labour, group rules, and common purpose. Studies of organized crime suggest that hierarchies are often loose and informal. Groups may consist of networks rather than formal structures. As a result, some experts even argue that the phrase 'organized crime' is inaccurate, as what people consider to be criminal organizations are often not 'organized' at all, in the sense of having some form of rigid central control. Nevertheless, it is clear that, however structured, large groups of criminals do sometimes work together for common cause, and that the concept of organized crime, even if poorly defined, describes a real phenomenon.

Organized crime is increasingly seen as a threat to both national and international **security**. This is especially true of transnational criminal organizations, whose members operate in more than one country. Typical activities of transnational criminal organizations include drug and human trafficking, kidnapping, extortion, fraud, money laundering, gambling, prostitution, and weapons smuggling. These are often accompanied by violence, and even murder. At a low level, these are purely law enforcement issues. At some point, however, they may become matters of either national or international security in a number of ways. First, some criminal organizations have acquired enormous wealth. With this, they can subvert state authority through massive bribery of state officials, to the extent that corruption undermines the ability of government organizations, including the security services, to carry out their functions efficiently. Second, criminal organizations may lend support to **terrorism**, and terrorists may fund their activities through the practice of organized crime, so that the two activities become indistinguishable. Third, transnational criminal organizations may smuggle weapons, including **weapons of mass destruction**, across borders to terrorists, insurgents, and other groups seeking to undermine **national security**. Fourth, **rogue states** may engage in organized crime in order to finance their regimes or gain access to weapons. Allegations that North Korea has carried out large scale counterfeiting of US dollars is a case in point.

For all these reasons, there are legitimate reasons for considering organized crime to be a security issue. There are also some drawbacks in doing so. **Securitization** of organized crime may lead to inappropriate military responses, such as in the so-called 'war on drugs'. Such responses have had little or no success, as witnessed by failed efforts by military forces to eradicate coca production in South America and poppy production in Afghanistan. Arguably, states need to find new methods which step outside the traditional national security framework if they are to successfully combat the threat of transnational criminal organizations.

Further reading

Mats Berdal and Monica Serrano (eds), *Transnational Organized Crime and International Security: Business as Usual?* (Boulder: Lynne Rienner, 2002)
James D. Torr (ed.), *Organized Crime* (San Diego: Greenhaven, 1999)
Emilio C. Viano, *Global Organized Crime and International Security* (Aldershot: Ashgate, 1999)
Alan Wright, *Organized Crime* (Cullompton: Willian, 2006)

OTTAWA CONVENTION

The 'Convention on the Prohibition of the Use, Stockpiling, Production and Transfer of Anti-Personnel Mines and on Their Destruction' was signed in Ottawa in December 1997 and is more commonly known as the Ottawa Convention. It entered into force in March 1999. At present, 154 states have signed, and 151 have ratified, the treaty. Significant states which have not signed the treaty include China, Russia, and the United States. These remain bound instead by the less restrictive Protocol II of the **Certain Conventional Weapons Convention**.

The preamble to the convention states that its aim is to 'put an end to the suffering and casualties caused by anti-personnel landmines that kill or maim hundreds of persons every week, mainly innocent and defenceless civilians'. To this end, the convention prohibits signatories from using anti-personnel landmines, and from developing, producing, or otherwise acquiring, stockpiling, retaining or transferring them to anyone. It also prohibits them from assisting, encouraging or inducing anyone to engage in such activities. The parties to the treaty also undertook to destroy all anti-personnel mines in their possession within four years. The convention does not contain any intrusive **verification** measures, but if a state requests clarification of an issue from another state and this is not forthcoming, a special meeting of the state parties to the convention may authorize a fact-finding mission to the state in question to investigate.

The Ottawa Convention is unusual in that the impetus behind it came not from states but from an international alliance of non-governmental organizations. It is possibly the most tangible product of the **human security** agenda of the 1990s.

Further reading
Foreign Affairs and International Affairs Canada, *Canada's Guide to the Global Ban on Landmines*, http://www.mines.gc.ca/menu-en.asp
Thomas Graham Jr and Damien J. LaVera, *Cornerstones of Security: Arms Control Treaties in the Nuclear Era* (Seattle: University of Washington Press, 2003)
International Campaign to Ban Landmines, www.icbl.org/
Richard A. Matthew, Bryan McDonald, and Kenneth R. Rutherford, *Landmines and Human Security: International Politics and War's Hidden Legacy* (Albany: State University of New York Press, 2004)

OUTER SPACE TREATY

Formally known as the 'Treaty on Principles Governing the Activities of States in the Exploration and Use of Outer Space, Including the Moon and Other Celestial Bodies', the Outer Space Treaty was originally signed by the UK, USA, and USSR in January 1967 and came into force on 10 October 1967. There are currently 125 signatories to the treaty, which states that outer space, including the moon and other celestial bodies, are not subject to national appropriation by claim of **sovereignty**, occupation, or any other means. The treaty also prohibits the placing of **weapons of mass destruction** in orbit around the earth, on celestial bodies, or in outer space in any other manner. It states that the moon and other celestial bodies shall be used for exclusively peaceful purposes and forbids the establishment of military bases, the testing of weapons, or the carrying out of military manoeuvres on them. All signatories of the treaty are to allow each others' representatives access into any installations that they may build on the moon and other celestial bodies. It is important to note that while the treaty prohibits the placing of weapons of mass destruction in outer space, it does not prohibit their transit, thus permitting the use of **ballistic missiles** with nuclear warheads which pass outside the earth's atmosphere but then return to earth. The treaty thus partially prohibits the **weaponization of space**, but does not prohibit the **militarization of space** through the placing of military-related equipment, such as military communications and imagery satellites, in space.

Further reading

Arms Control and Disarmament Agreements (New Brunswick: Transaction, 1984)

Coit D. Blacker and Gloria Duffy (eds), *International Arms Control: Issues and Agreements* (Stanford: Stanford University Press, 1984)

Thomas Graham Jr and Damien J. LaVera, *Cornerstones of Security: Arms Control Treaties in the Nuclear Era* (Seattle: University of Washington Press, 2003)

PALESTINE LIBERATION ORGANIZATION (PLO)

The Palestine Liberation Organization (PLO) is an umbrella organization containing a variety of groups, such as **Fatah** and the **Popular Front for the Liberation of Palestine (PFLP)**. The PLO was formed in 1964, and set as its goal the destruction of the state of Israel and the creation of an independent Palestinian state. In 1969, Fatah leader Yasser Arafat became chairman of the PLO, since when Fatah has remained the dominant group within the organization. The PLO has won widespread international recognition as the official representative of the Palestinian nation, and in 1974 was granted observer status at the **United Nations**.

After the defeat of an Arab coalition by Israel in the Six-Day War of 1967, the prospect of Arab states being able to liberate Palestine from Israeli occupation appeared to vanish, and the Palestinian populations of the West Bank and Gaza Strip also fell under Israeli control. The PLO therefore abandoned its previous reliance on the Arab states as liberators and began a campaign of **terrorism** against Israel which has continued to this day. In 1970, the Jordanian government expelled the PLO's fighters in what was known as 'Black September', and thereafter the PLO waged its battle against Israel from southern Lebanon, as well as worldwide through terrorist actions such as airplane hijackings and the murder of Israeli athletes at the 1972 Olympic Games. The Israeli invasion of Lebanon in 1982 then forced Arafat and thousands of PLO fighters to flee the country. From exile in Tunisia, Arafat began secret negotiations with the Israeli government, which led in 1993 to the Oslo agreement, setting up an autonomous Palestinian Authority under PLO control, and supposedly laid out a path towards the creation of an independent Palestinian state. At this point Arafat renounced those clauses in the PLO charter which called for the destruction of Israel, and a Declaration of Principles of September 1993 committed the PLO to a two-state solution to the Israeli-Palestinian dispute.

Nevertheless, especially since 2000, some groups within the PLO have continued to use violence against Israeli targets, including Arafat's own Fatah movement via the **Al Aqsa Martyrs Brigade**. The perceived corruption and incompetence of PLO officials running the Palestinian Authority, as well as their inability to negotiate a final **peace** settlement with Israel, have undermined popular support for the organization. As a result, in 2006 **Hamas** defeated Fatah in elections to the Palestinian parliament. Following Arafat's death in 2004, the chairmanship of the PLO passed into the hands of Mahmoud Abbas, who in January 2005 also became President of the Palestinian Authority.

Further reading
Anat N. Kurz, *Fatah and the Politics of Violence: The Institutionalisation of a Popular Struggle* (Brighton: Sussex Academic Press, 2005)
Jamal R. Nassar, *The Palestine Liberation Organization: From Armed Struggle to the Declaration of Independence* (New York: Praeger, 1991)

PALESTINIAN ISLAMIC JIHAD
Palestinian Islamic Jihad (PIJ) is the name of a Palestinian terrorist organization, founded by Palestinian students in Egypt in 1979. Its objectives are the destruction of the state of Israel and the creation of an Islamic state in Palestine. Its aims are very similar to those of **Hamas**, but despite some evidence of collaboration the two organizations are often seen as rivals. PIJ is much smaller and lacks Hamas's social and political networks. It has carried out numerous terrorist attacks, including acts of **suicide terrorism**, in Israel, the West Bank, and the Gaza Strip. Its most notable operation was the suicide bombing of the Maxim restaurant in Haifa on 4 October 2003, which killed 21 people. PIJ is believed to maintain close contacts with **Hizballah**, and to receive support from Iran and from Syria, where PIJ's headquarters is currently located.

Further reading
Edward V. Linden (ed.), *Foreign Terrorist Organizations: History, Tactics, and Connections* (New York: Nova Science, 2004)
Intelligence and Terrorism Information Center, *Profile of Palestinian Islamic Jihad*, http://www.intelligence.org.il/eng/sib/3_05/pji.htm

PANDEMIC

A pandemic is a disease which spreads over a wide geographic area and infects a large proportion of the population. Notable examples are the influenza pandemic which killed millions of people worldwide in 1918 and 1919, and the HIV/AIDS virus which has so far killed some 25 million people. The numbers killed by pandemics are dependent on a number of factors: the speed with which they spread (slowly in the case of HIV/AIDS, very rapidly in the case of influenza); the deadliness of the disease – it must kill, but not too quickly if it is to be passed onto others; and the effectiveness of the medical response. Societies are not helpless in the face of pandemics. They can prepare in advance by stockpiling medicines and vaccines, and can restrict the spread of disease through the use of quarantine and by tightening border controls to prevent infected persons from carrying diseases over national boundaries. Fears that Severe Acute Respiratory Syndrome (SARS) would become a worldwide pandemic in 2003 proved to be ill-founded. After a slow start, governments eventually reacted effectively to contain the disease. Many commentators are suggesting that the H5N1 strain of avian influenza (commonly referred to as 'bird flu'), may become the next pandemic. At present humans can catch H5N1 from birds, but the disease cannot pass from human to human. If that were to change, the disease might spread worldwide with great rapidity, killing very large numbers of people.

Analysts disagree as to whether pandemics should be considered a **security** issue. Opponents of **securitization** argue that attaching the security label to diseases contributes little if anything to preventing and curing them. Indeed, the culture of secrecy which surrounds security issues may inhibit the search for solutions, as may the habit of viewing security in national, rather than international, terms. By contrast, proponents of securitization point out that disease can have a debilitating effect on **national security** institutions. For instance, the incidence of HIV/AIDS among soldiers in some African countries is extremely high, with negative consequences in terms of military effectiveness. In broader terms, pandemics can cause mass death and severe societal and economic disruption. The consequences of an H5N1 pandemic, for instance, might be to almost completely shut down international trade, as states closed their borders to halt the spread of the disease. In many countries, especially in Africa, diseases such as HIV/AIDS, tuberculosis, and malaria cause far more harm than **war** or other **threats** to security. It makes some sense, therefore, to consider pandemics a security issue. Following this logic, in 2000 the **United Nations Security Council** officially declared HIV/AIDS to be a threat to **peace** and security in Africa.

Further reading
Stefan Elbe, 'Should HIV/AIDS be Securitized? The Ethical Dilemmas of Linking HIV/AIDS and Security', *International Studies Quarterly*, vol. 50, no. 1, March 2006, pp. 119–144
Christian Enemark, 'Pandemic Influenza and National Security', *Australian Defence Force Journal*, no 171, 2007, pp. 18–32
Henry Feldbaum, Kelley Lee and Preeti Patel, 'The National Security Implications of HIV/AIDS', *PLoS Medicine*, vol. 3, no. 6, June 2006, pp. 774–78

PARTIAL TEST BAN TREATY
The Partial Test Ban Treaty (PTBT) is the usual appellation of the 'Treaty Banning Nuclear Weapons Tests in the Atmosphere, in Outer Space and Under Water', also sometimes known as the Limited Test Ban Treaty. Originally signed by the United States, United Kingdom and Soviet Union in August 1963, this treaty was subsequently signed by over 120 other parties. The treaty prohibits any **nuclear weapon** test explosions in the atmosphere, in outer space, and under water, as well as in any other environment if such an explosion causes radioactive debris to be present outside the territorial limits of the state conducting it. In this way the treaty aims to reduce contamination of the environment by radioactive substances. Among the nuclear powers, France and China did not sign the PTBT. France carried out 41 atmospheric nuclear explosions until 1975 when it moved its tests underground. In addition, although the UK, USA and USSR did cease atmospheric tests after signing the PTBT, they did not cease tests altogether, merely shifting their focus to underground explosions. The impact of the PTBT was, therefore, limited. The preamble to the treaty stated an eventual ambition to discontinue all nuclear tests. It may in that way have helped pave the way for the later **Comprehensive Nuclear Test Ban Treaty**.

Further reading
Arms Control and Disarmament Agreements (New Brunswick: Transaction, 1984)

Coit D. Blacker and Gloria Duffy (eds), *International Arms Control: Issues and Agreements* (Stanford: Stanford University Press, 1984)

Thomas Graham Jr and Damien J. LaVera, *Cornerstones of Security: Arms Control Treaties in the Nuclear Era* (Seattle: University of Washington Press, 2003)

PARTIYA KARKEREN KURDISTAN (PKK)

The Kurdistan Workers' Party (Partiya Karkeren Kurdistan – PKK) is a secular, socialist political party and terrorist/guerrilla organization dedicated to creating an independent Kurdish state. Founded by Abdullah Ocalan in 1974, since 1984 it has carried out a prolonged campaign of **insurgency** and **terrorism** in Turkey in which over 30,000 people have died. The PKK has established networks throughout the Kurdish diaspora in Europe and North America, and uses these to fund its operations. In 1999, Ocalan was captured in Kenya and taken back to Turkey. Under threat of a death sentence, he called upon the PKK to cease its armed struggle. The PKK responded to this call, and the scale of Kurdish terrorism in Turkey temporarily diminished, but in 2004 the organization announced a resumption of military activities. In 2002, the PKK renamed itself Kadek, and in 2003 it changed its name again to Kongra-Gel. In 2005 it reverted to PKK.

Further reading

'The Case of the PKK: History, Ideology, Methodology, and Structure (1978–99)', *Ankara Papers*, vol. 9, no. 1, 2004, pp. 21–59

Michael Radu, 'The Rise and Fall of the PKK', *Orbis*, vol. 45, no. 1, Winter 2001, pp. 47–63

PARTNERSHIP FOR PEACE (PfP)

The Partnership for Peace (PfP) was established by the **North Atlantic Treaty Organization (NATO)** in 1994. It is a programme to enhance international stability, to promote democratic reform, and to strengthen the **security** relationship between NATO and countries in Europe and the Former Soviet Union who are not members of the organization. Currently there are 23 such Partners. PfP works through bilateral agreements reached between NATO and each Partner. The latter agree to make a number of far-reaching political commitments to preserve democracy, to maintain the principles of **international**

law, and to settle disputes peacefully. They also make specific commitments to promote transparency in national defence planning and budgeting and to develop the capacity for joint action with NATO in **peacekeeping** and humanitarian operations. In return, NATO provides the Partners with assistance in meeting these commitments. For instance, NATO has aided PfP members to reform defence institutions, has provided them with training in **counter-terrorism** and in the disposal of surplus weapons, and has engaged in joint military exercizes with them. In 1997, the Euro-Atlantic Partnership Council (EAPC) was created. This brings together the 26 members of NATO and the 23 PfP Partners in a forum for consultation and cooperation. Since 2005, an EAPC Security Forum has also been meeting to discuss important security issues and look at how NATO and Partner countries can best address them together.

Further reading
John Borawski, 'Partnership for Peace "Plus": Joint Responsibility for Euro-
    Atlantic Security', *Defense Analysis*, vol. 15, no. 3, 1999, pp. 323–32
Partnership for Peace website, http://www.nato.int/issues/pfp/index.html

PASDARAN

The Pasdaran, known in English as the Islamic Revolutionary Guards Corps, is an Iranian paramilitary organization created after the Islamic Revolution of 1979 as a counterweight to the Iranian military, which the new regime regarded as ideologically suspect. Whereas the armed forces are officially responsible for protecting Iran's borders from external attack, the Pasdaran is responsible for protecting the **revolution** itself. To this end, it acts as a **security intelligence** agency within Iran, collecting information about enemies of the regime. It has also developed a military structure parallel to that of the armed forces, with its own army, navy, and airforce, and controls Iran's **ballistic missiles**. Pasdaran's Al Quds (Jerusalem) Brigade is responsible for activities beyond Iran's borders, including **intelligence** and **covert action**. In the 1980s, the organization was believed to have provided training for **Hizballah** in Lebanon, and more recently it has been accused of providing weapons to insurgents in Iraq. Pasdaran is a significant political force within Iran, with several members of the government, such as President Mahmoud Ahmadinejad, having either served in it or being closely associated with it.

Further reading
Ed Blanche, 'Pasdaran Power', *The Middle East*, no. 360, October 2005,
  pp. 22–24
Anthony H. Cordesman, *Iran's Developing Military Capabilities* (Washington,
  DC: CSIS, 2005)
Kenneth Katzman, *The Warriors of Islam: Iran's Revolutionary Guards*
  (Boulder: Westview, 1993)

PEACE

In its simplest form, peace implies an absence of **war**, though it may
also refer to an absence of tension and of quarrels, in the sense of
neighbours living in peace with one another. This is often known as
'negative peace', as opposed to 'positive peace', defined below. The
idea of peace as a prolonged and stable period during which war is
entirely absent is relatively new. Before the nineteenth century, war
was often the norm. Thus the ancient Greek concept of *eirene* considered peace to be merely an interlude of rest in the normal state of
war. Negative peace can also be interpreted in terms of forcible paci-
fication, such as the *Pax Romana*, or in terms of the more utopian
'perpetual peace' or **democratic peace theory**, which derives from the
writings of German philosopher Immanuel Kant and which suggests
that the spread of democratic forms of government will eventually
eliminate war between states.

Many commentators consider the concept of negative peace to be
too narrow. They argue that a situation without **war** in which people
suffer injustice and poverty and are divided into mutually hostile
groups, be it ethnic groups, social classes, or any others, cannot truly
be described as peace. A negative peace such as the *Pax Romana*
which is built and maintained by conquest and repression similarly
does not deserve the title 'peace'. Some therefore contrast negative
peace with 'positive peace', a situation in which exploitation and
oppression are minimized, and in which the structural divisions
which lead to conflict are absent. Positive peace should in theory be
more stable and long lasting than negative peace, since it is a situation in which the causes of conflict have been eliminated.

Positive peace represents an ideal which has yet to be achieved. It
can also be viewed in many ways. St. Augustine presented an early
vision of it as 'the tranquillity of order', in other words 'the arrange-
ment of things equal and unequal in a pattern which assigns to each
its proper position'. Modern thinkers generally reject such a hierar-

chical view of peace, and instead speak in terms of social justice, economic development, and political democracy.

The idea of positive peace allows one to concentrate not on the symptoms but on the causes of conflict, whereas a concentration on negative peace may fail to address those causes, thereby making conflict more likely. However, there clearly is a distinction between situations where war is present and those where it is absent, and there needs to be some word to describe the latter. Furthermore, the majority of discussions concerning positive peace are still concerned with the absence of war, viewing positive peace as the means by which negative peace is achieved. Contrasting negative peace with a truer positive peace may even make war more likely as it suggests that war may be preferable to a 'false' peace that currently exists. Thus, while the concept of positive peace has some advantages, it is not without its dangers.

Further reading
David P. Barash and Charles P. Webel, *Peace and Conflict Studies* (Thousand Oaks: Sage, 2002)
Johan Galtung, *Peace: Research, Education, Action: Essays in Peace Research*, vol. 1 (Copenhagen: Christian Ejlers, 1975)

PEACEBUILDING
Peacebuilding consists of actions taken by outside parties once an internal conflict, such as a **civil war** or **insurgency**, has ended, in order to prevent it from resuming and to establish the conditions for long-term **peace**. Peacebuilding seeks to address the root causes of conflict by eliminating human rights abuses, creating legitimate institutions of government, and supporting economic development, thereby reshaping societies so that they become more peaceful. In this regard it is considerably more ambitious than **peacekeeping**, but despite the problems associated with such ambition it has to a large degree replaced peacekeeping in the post-**Cold War** world. As practised in recent years, peacebuilding rests on a model which suggests that the establishment of liberal democratic institutions and free market economies will reduce the tensions within societies which cause **war** and create a true 'positive' peace which can endure.

Typical peacebuilding activities can be divided into three types: **security** tasks, such as the **disarmament** and demobilization of the warring factions, and the training of police and soldiers; political tasks, which include writing constitutions, organizing and holding democratic elections, and establishing independent and honest judicial institutions; and socio-economic tasks, which include post-conflict reconstruction and reforming economic systems in accordance with free market theories. In order to carry out these tasks, peacebuilding may even involve taking over the government of the country involved. Whereas peacekeeping operations were almost exclusively a preserve of the **United Nations**, peacebuilding involves many other national and international institutions, including the **North Atlantic Treaty Organization (NATO)**, the European Union, the International Monetary Fund, and the World Bank, as well as non-governmental organizations. Examples of peacebuilding operations include the United Nations Transition Assistance Group (UNTAG) in Namibia in 1989, the United Nations Transitional Authority in Cambodia (UNTAC) in 1991, and the NATO missions in Bosnia and Kosovo from 1995 and 1999 respectively.

Peacebuilding missions have had mixed results to date. Success depends on a variety of factors. First, it depends to some degree on whether the parties involved in civil conflict are sufficiently exhausted and lacking in confidence in the benefits which resumed war might bring. Second, it rests on the external **balance of power**. During the Cold War, the tendency of the superpowers to intervene in internal conflicts to support their proxies hampered successful peacebuilding. Since the late 1980s, Western **hegemony** has made it easier for Western states to enforce peace settlements. Third, much depends on the actual terms of each settlement and the manner in which it is carried out. While it may be true that strong liberal democratic institutions in the long term tend to reduce the incidence of violent conflict, it is also true that in the short term the opportunity to voice dissent can exacerbate tensions within societies. The suitability of the specific model of political and economic transformation preferred by peacebuilders in the post-Cold War world is debatable, and it is possible that it may on occasion have made matters worse rather than better.

Further reading

Charles-Philippe David, 'Does Peacebuilding Build Peace?', *Security Dialogue*, vol. 30, no. 1, March 1999, pp. 25–41

Fen Osler Hampson, *Nurturing Peace: Why Peace Settlements Succeed or Fail* (Washington, DC: United States Institute of Peace Press, 1996)

Roland Paris, *At War's End: Building Peace after Civil Conflict* (Cambridge: Cambridge University Press, 2004)

PEACE ENFORCEMENT

Peace enforcement involves the use or **threat** of force to impose, maintain or restore a **peace** settlement and may be seen as a means of imposing **collective security** on those who threaten international peace and **security**. In some instances, such as in Kosovo in 1999, it may involve an outside party drawing up a peace settlement and ordering the warring factions to abide by its terms on pain of military attack. In other instances, it may involve similar threats and use of force to punish those who are in breach of an existing settlement.

Peace enforcement came to the fore in the 1990s with international operations in Somalia and the former Yugoslavia. The new emphasis on peace enforcement reflected a frustration with the failings of the traditional model of **peacekeeping**, which relied on the consent of all parties involved. Peace enforcement differs from peacekeeping in that those enforcing the peace will do so without the consent of all parties, and do not limit the use of force to self-defence. It may be a more effective way of keeping the peace because through the threat and use of force a third-party intervenor can deter, prevent and punish violations of a ceasefire in a manner which is not possible during a peacekeeping operation. On the other hand, critics argue that peace enforcement has little to do with peace and is merely **war** by another name. In addition, there are dangers in crossing the line of consent established for peacekeeping operations. Doing so destroys any pretence of impartiality and may simply heighten resistance to the intervenor. Once the line of consent has been breached, it may be impossible ever to restore it. Thus, while on occasion peace enforcement operations have managed to impose a ceasefire on combatants, as in Kosovo in 1999, on other occasions they have merely exacerbated existing problems, as was the case in the failed **United Nations** intervention in Somalia in 1993. The record of peace enforcement is mixed.

Further reading

Jane Boulden, *Peace Enforcement: the United Nations Experience in Congo, Somalia, and Bosnia* (New York: Praeger, 2001)

Peter Viggo Jakobsen, 'National Interest, Humanitarianism or CNN: What Triggers UN Peace Enforcement after the Cold War?', *Journal of Peace Research*, vol. 33, no. 2, May 1996, pp. 205–15

Ramesh Thakur, 'From Peacekeeping to Peace Enforcement: The UN Operation in Somalia', *The Journal of Modern African Studies*, vol. 32, no. 3, September 1994, pp. 387–410

PEACEKEEPING

Peacekeeping takes place when those fighting a **war** have agreed to a ceasefire, but tension between them remains. It consists of the deployment of a third party intervention force in order to prevent the resumption of hostilities. The peacekeepers aim to preserve the ceasefire, prevent the conflict from spreading, and create the conditions in which the opposing sides can formulate a long-term settlement. Peacekeeping includes three different types of operations: monitoring and observation missions, which have no mandate to influence the actors involved but merely monitor a ceasefire and report any violations; supervisory missions, which have a mandate to request, but not to order, actors to change their behaviour; and security force missions, which are tasked with keeping the parties physically apart by interposing themselves and creating a buffer zone. Successful peacekeeping has often been seen as being dependent on a number of factors, the most important of which are: the existence of an established ceasefire; the consent of all parties involved; the impartiality of the peacekeepers; and the non-use of force in circumstances other than self-defence.

Peacekeeping may be carried out by the armed forces of any state or international organization. Generally, though, the practice is associated with the **United Nations**, which has the benefit of being considered impartial. The first United Nations peacekeeping operation was the UN Treaty Supervision Organization (UNTSO), which was set up at the end of the first Arab-Israeli war, tasked with observing the ceasefire and reporting any violations. This was followed in 1949 by the UN Military Observer Group in India and Pakistan (UNMOGIP). Both of these were very limited observation missions. Larger-scale peacekeeping operations began with the United Nations Expeditionary Force (UNEF), which was sent to Egypt in 1956 as part of the resolution of the Suez crisis. This was the first peacekeeping operation tasked with separating the combatants and establishing a demilitarized zone between them, taking peacekeeping one step further and setting the pattern for future operations. Overall, the UN has now dispatched over 50 peacekeeping operations, the great majority of which have taken place since the end of the **Cold War**, this being because of the reduced likelihood of a great power veto in the United Nations Security Council.

Opinion is divided as to whether peacekeeping has been successful. Critics point out that many peacekeeping operations, such as UNTSO, have notably failed to keep the **peace**. It may also be the case that they simply freeze conflicts along ceasefire lines, while failing to resolve the fundamental problems which led to the eruption of war. Peacekeeping also does nothing to prevent crises from developing into war in the first place. On the other hand, the deployment of a peacekeeping force may provide a face-saving device for warring nations to agree to a ceasefire. One example would be the expansion of the UN peacekeeping force in southern Lebanon and the cessation of fighting between Israel and **Hizballah** in the summer of 2006. Peacekeeping may also prevent minor ceasefire violations from escalating into a full-scale resumption of fighting, and create a calmer environment in which politicians can address problems without the emotional stress caused by combat. Nonetheless, dissatisfaction with the peacekeeping model has meant that in recent years it has been increasingly replaced by more ambitious attempts at **peacebuilding**.

Further reading
Alex Bellamy, Stuart Griffin and Paul Williams, *Understanding Peacekeeping* (Oxford: Policy, 2003)
Boutros Boutros-Ghali, *An Agenda for Peace* (New York: United Nations, 1995)
Steven R. Ratner, *The New UN Peacekeeping* (Basingstoke: Macmillan, 1995)
Adam Roberts, *The Crisis in Peacekeeping* (Oslo: Institut for forsvarsstudier, 1994)

PEACEMAKING
Peacemaking is action undertaken during a violent conflict to bring the hostile parties to end the violence. The peacemaking action is undertaken not by the hostile parties themselves but by a third party, such as another state or an international organization. The normal focus of peacemaking efforts is on negotiation, mediation, and diplomacy, although it can also involve offers of external financial and administrative assistance, as well as more coercive measures, including **economic sanctions** and the **threat** and use of force. In this way peacemaking may on occasion slip into **peace enforcement**. Although peacemaking is not the exclusive prerogative of the **United Nations**, and is often undertaken by other organizations, the UN has very often played a leading role, due to its ability to act as an impartial outside mediator and to mobilize resources from the international community to provide positive incentives to make **peace**. Peacemaking refers

only to actions undertaken to create peace until such time as **war termination** is achieved. After that point, **peacekeeping** and **peacebuilding** efforts take over. Peacemaking is, therefore, only one step on the road towards a permanent settlement of a conflict. The success of peacemaking depends on a variety of factors, including the willingness of the warring parties to resolve their differences peacefully and the amount of leverage possessed by the third party. The latter is in turn largely dependent on the level of commitment by the international community to the peacemaking process.

Further reading
Boutros Boutros-Ghali, *An Agenda for Peace* (New York: United Nations, 1995)
J. Michael Greig and Paul F. Diehl, 'The Peacekeeping-Peacemaking Dilemma', *International Studies Quarterly*, vol. 49, no. 4, December 2005, pp. 621–46
Tom Woodhouse and Robert Bruce (eds), *Peacekeeping and Peacemaking: Towards Effective Intervention in Post-Cold War Conflicts* (Basingstoke: Macmillan, 1998)

PEACE OPERATIONS
Peace operations, often referred to as peace support operations, is an umbrella term covering all operations designed to create, enforce, and preserve **peace**. It includes **peacebuilding**, **peace enforcement**, **peacekeeping**, **peacemaking**, preventive deployments of military forces in a crisis prevention role, and the delivery of humanitarian aid in a **war** zone. Any state or international organization may engage in peace operations, but they are most often associated with the **United Nations**, whose endorsement can provide them with the legitimacy they require to be successful. Since the end of the **Cold War**, the number of United Nations peace operations has increased dramatically. In addition, whereas during the Cold War the focus of peace operations was on peacekeeping, since 1990 it has shifted towards other types of operations, especially peacebuilding. The ending of Cold War rivalries has reduced the possibility of a veto in the United Nations Security Council, and so made it easier to reach international agreement to commence a peace operation. In addition, public pressure on democratic politicians to intervene in war zones for humanitarian reasons has increased, and there is a growing perception that globalization makes **national security** dependent on the

establishment of a system of **collective security** and the maintenance of peace not only at home but also worldwide.

Further reading
Christopher Bellamy, *Knights in White Armour: the New Art of War and Peace* (London: Pimlico, 1996)
Boutros Boutros-Ghali, *An Agenda for Peace* (New York: United Nations, 1995)
Peter Viggo Jakobsen, 'The Transformation of United Nations Peace Operations in the 1990s', *Cooperation and Conflict*, vol. 37, no. 3, 2002, pp. 267–82

PEACE SUPPORT OPERATIONS, see PEACE OPERATIONS

PETERSBERG TASKS, see COMMON EUROPEAN SECURITY AND DEFENCE POLICY (CESDP)

POPULAR FRONT FOR THE LIBERATION OF PALESTINE

The Popular Front for the Liberation of Palestine (PFLP) is a secular, socialist terrorist organization fighting for the formation of a Palestinian state. Founded in 1967 by a Palestinian Christian, George Habash, the PFLP soon split into three factions: the PFLP, the Popular Front for the Liberation of Palestine – General Command (PFLP-GC), and the Democratic Front for the Liberation of Palestine (DFLP). The PFLP gained particular notoriety for carrying out a number of plane hijackings. Since the start of the second Palestinian *intifada* in 2000, the PFLP has undertaken numerous attacks against Israeli targets both in Israel and the occupied territories, most notably assassinating the Israeli minister of tourism, Rehavam Zeevi, in October 2001. From 2002 it has also engaged in acts of **suicide terrorism**. The PFLP has rejected the Oslo peace accords signed with Israel by the leader of the **Palestinian Liberation Organization (PLO)**, Yasser Arafat, and continues to oppose a two-state solution for the Israeli-Palestinian conflict. The second largest group within the PLO after **Fatah**, the PFLP is nevertheless a relatively small player on the Palestinian political scene, having lost ground in recent years to Islamic organizations such as **Hamas**.

Further reading

Yonah Alexander, *Palestinian Secular Terrorism* (Ardsley: Transnational Publishers, 2003)

Edward V. Linden (ed.), *Foreign Terrorist Organizations: History, Tactics, and Connections* (New York: Nova Science, 2004)

PRE-EMPTIVE WAR, see PREVENTIVE WAR

PREVENTIVE WAR

A preventive **war** is one fought by a state to eliminate a distant **threat**. Those who begin the war believe that if they wait the threat will become more severe and their ability to deal with it will decline. They calculate that it is better to strike early while the odds are relatively in their favour. The term is often conflated with 'pre-emptive war', but many commentators distinguish between the two. With a pre-emptive war, the threat is imminent. With a preventive war, it is not. Pre-emptive war is considered less controversial in terms of **international law** and **just war theory**. While the Charter of the **United Nations** and other instruments of international law prohibit war except for self-defence, a pre-emptive attack on an enemy who is poised to attack you can be considered a form of anticipatory self-defence, and thus legitimate. The key determinant is the question of imminence. The traditional viewpoint is that expressed by US Secretary of State Daniel Webster in response to the *Caroline* incident of 1837, when British forces sank a vessel supporting Canadian rebels in US waters. According to Webster, pre-emptive war was permissible if the danger was 'instant, overwhelming, leaving no choice of means, and no moment of deliberation'. This formulation makes preventive war illegitimate, as the danger being pre-empted is neither instant nor overwhelming.

An example of a pre-emptive war is that begun by Israel in 1967 to counter what was believed (probably mistakenly) to be an imminent attack by Arab states. An example of a preventive war is the Anglo-American invasion of Iraq in 2003. In that case, there was no evidence of a threat which was either instant or overwhelming, and the logic used by the invaders was that they were acting to eliminate a danger which might emerge at some point in the distant future. The doctrine of preventive war has regained popularity in some circles, particularly within the United States, in the aftermath of the terrorist attacks of 11 September 2001. In its 2002 National Security Strategy, the US government claimed a right to take preventive action against states it believed might pose a future threat to US **security** on the grounds that the dangers posed by **terrorism** and **weapons of mass destruction** are so great that once the threat of attack becomes imminent, it will be too late to take action.

From the practical point of view, preventive war relies on accurate **intelligence** about distant dangers, something which is all too often lacking. In the absence of such intelligence, it is all too likely that states will wage war against non-existent, mistaken threats. From the moral point of view, preventive war is also incompatible with the 'last resort' criterion of just war theory – because the threat is not imminent, one has sufficient time to consider alternative solutions other than war. Furthermore, the doctrine is open to abuse: any state may claim that any other will pose some future danger to it, and then use this as an excuse to wage aggressive war. Consequently, while the current governments of the United States and United Kingdom have adopted the idea of preventive war and put it into action in Iraq, it remains extremely controversial.

Further reading
John L. Hammond, 'The Bush Doctrine, Preventive War, and International Law', *The Philosophical Forum*, vol. 36, no. 1, Spring 2005, pp. 97–111
Harry S. Laver, 'Preemption and the Evolution of America's Strategic Defense', *Parameters*, vol. 35, no. 2, Summer 2005, pp. 107–120
Franklin Eric Webster, 'Preemption and Just War: Considering the Case of Iraq', *Parameters*, vol. 34, no. 4, Winter 2004–05, pp. 20–39

PRIVATE MILITARY COMPANIES (PMCs)

Private Military Companies (PMCs), sometimes referred to as 'private contractors', are corporate entities which provide services linked to warfare. Historical antecedents of modern PMCs include organizations such as the Free Companies in the Hundred Years War, the *condottieri* in fourteenth and fifteenth-century Italy, and the military entrepreneurs of the 30 Years War. In the aftermath of the last of these, nation states gradually took over control of military affairs, and private military organizations declined in importance. In a reversal of this trend, PMCs have experienced a massive growth since the end of the **Cold War**. Tens of thousands of employees of PMCs have served alongside British and American armed forces in Iraq, and the private military industry is now worth billions of dollars annually. A number of factors may explain this growth: the downsizing of Western militaries in the 1990s put a large number of trained soldiers and weapons on the market; there were a series of state failures with which domestic military forces were unable to cope without external assistance; and PMCs capitalized on the trend in the Western world towards the privatization of services, built on the belief that private corporations can provide those services more efficiently and at less cost than the state itself.

Commentators disagree as to whether those working for PMCs should be considered **mercenaries**. PMCs differ from previous mercenary bodies in that they are legally incorporated and their goal is corporate not individual profit, although those who work for them often do profit substantially. They provide a variety of services. At the harder end of the spectrum, they engage in combat on behalf of the state which employs them, an example being the company Executive Outcomes which fought in Angola and Sierra Leone. Companies involved in such activities are hard to distinguish from mercenaries. This is less true for PMCs involved in providing other services. These include: training military and police personnel; management and servicing of military equipment; **intelligence** gathering and analysis; logistical services, including delivery of supplies and equipment and construction of military facilities; mine clearing and post-conflict reconstruction; protection of personnel and property, both government and commercial; and kidnap response, including negotiations and advice on hostage situations. Companies providing the more peaceful of these services, and those providing services to private clients, are sometimes referred to as 'private security companies' (PSCs), rather than PMCs, to distinguish them from their more military-orientated competitors. The largest providers of PMCs and PSCs are the United States, United Kingdom, and South Africa. Notable examples are ArmorGroup, Blackwater Security Consulting, Control Risks Group, DynCorp, Group 4 Falck, Kellogg, Brown and Root, and MPRI.

PMCs claim that they operate according to high moral and legal standards, and that their standards are indeed often higher than those of many local actors in conflict zones. Critics note, however, that PMCs will always be concerned with financial profit rather than morals, the laws of war, professional military standards, or the **national interest** of their country of origin. They also operate in a legal grey area. As their employees are not members of armed forces, they are not subject to military discipline, but they are also often outside the control of civilian authorities. This means that they fall between the cracks of military and domestic law, making it hard, if not impossible, to hold them to account for their actions. As a result, many consider the recent growth in PMCs to be a matter of serious concern.

Further reading
Christopher Kinney, *Corporate Soldiers and International Security: the Rise of Private Military Companies* (London and New York: Routledge, 2006)
David Shearer, *Private Armies and Military Intervention*, Adelphi Paper 316 (Oxford: Oxford University Press, 1998)
Peter W. Singer, *Corporate Warriors: the Rise of the Privatized Military Industry* (Ithaca and London: Cornell University Press, 2003)
Peter W. Singer, 'Outsourcing War: Understanding the Private Military Industry', *Foreign Affairs*, vol. 84, no. 2, March/April 2005, pp. 119–132

PROLIFERATION

Proliferation refers to the spread of weapons and the technologies associated with them. The term is most commonly used with reference to the spread of **weapons of mass destruction (WMD)** and **ballistic missiles**, although there is increasing concern in some circles about the spread of other weapons, especially small arms. 'Vertical proliferation' relates to increases in the quality and quantity of weapons among those who already possess them; 'horizontal proliferation' describes the spread of weapons to those who previously did not have them.

Since the end of the **Cold War** the horizontal proliferation of WMD has become one of the primary **security** concerns of Western states, with great efforts being put into counter-proliferation to prevent WMD from falling into the hands of **rogue states** and terrorists. Among Western policy makers and security analysts the language of proliferation and counter-proliferation has largely replaced that of **arms control** and **disarmament**. This has led to objections that Western states are seeking to restrict the spread of weapons technology to others while not accepting any reciprocal obligation to reduce their own arsenals. These competing discourses of proliferation, arms control and **disarmament** are most obviously visible in current disputes between the existing **nuclear weapons** powers and others over revision of the **Non-Proliferation Treaty (NPT)**.

A number of international treaties have been signed to limit proliferation of WMD, including the NPT, the **Biological and Toxin Weapons Convention**, and the **Chemical Weapons Convention**. Various international groups and export-control regimes have also been established to try to restrict the export of WMD-related materials. These include the **Australia Group**, the **Nuclear Suppliers Group**, and the **Missile Technology Control Regime**. The groups create lists of restricted items and require their members not to export these if there is reasonable suspicion that they will be used to create prohibited weapons.

Further reading

David Mutimer, *The Weapons State: Proliferation and the Framing of Security* (Boulder: Lynne Rienner, 2000)

Office of the Secretary of Defense, *Proliferation: Threat and Response* (Washington DC: Department of Defense, 2001)

PROLIFERATION SECURITY INITIATIVE

Unveiled by President George W. Bush in May 2003, the Proliferation Security Initiative (PSI) is an American-led multilateral effort to control the **proliferation** of **weapons of mass destruction (WMD)** and the means of delivering them. Its focus is primarily on the interdiction of shipments of WMD being transported by sea. Initially, ten nations, Australia, Canada, France, Germany, Italy, Japan, Netherlands, Poland, Portugal, and Spain, agreed in Madrid in June 2003 to join the United States in launching the initiative. The United States now claims that there are over 20 states involved in PSI, and another 40 who 'support' it, but since the names of the states and the level of their involvement have not all been made public, this cannot be verified.

The PSI does not create any formal obligations for its members, and has not resulted in the establishment of any formal organization. Joining the initiative implies abiding by the terms of the Statement of Interdiction Principles agreed by the original eleven participants in September 2003. These call upon states to undertake measures to interdict the transfer or transport of WMD, their delivery systems, and related materials; to adopt streamlined procedures for the sharing of information concerning suspected proliferation activity; to review and strengthen their laws to accomplish these objectives, and to work with others to modify **international law** accordingly; at their own initiative, or at the request of another state, to board and search any vessel flying their own flag that is reasonably suspected of transporting WMD, and to seize any such cargoes as are identified; and finally to stop and search in their internal waters or territorial seas any vessels that are reasonably suspected of carrying such cargoes. PSI participants have conducted several joint interdiction exercises.

The PSI has no legal authority, and as such does not grant its participants the right to stop and search ships flying another country's flag outside their own internal or territorial waters, beyond what is already granted by international law (one may stop a ship which is not properly registered, or is suspected of piracy, but not because it is suspected of transporting WMD). Being a purely voluntary initiative, it imposes no binding obligations on any states. In order to bypass the existing prohibition on intercepting vessels on the high seas, the United States has signed bi-lateral shipboarding pacts with several states, giving it the right to intercept and board ships registered in those countries. How extensive and effective the PSI will be in the long term remains to be seen.

Further reading

Mark J. Valencia, *The Proliferation Security Initiative: Making Waves in Asia*, Adelphi Paper 376 (London: IISS, 2005)

Sharon Squassoni, *Proliferation Security Initiative (PSI)*, CRS Report for Congress, 7 June 2005, available online at: http://fpc.state.gov/documents/organization/48624.pdf

US Department of State, *Proliferation Security Initiative*, http://www.state.gov/t/np/c10390.htm

PROPAGANDA

Propaganda consists of communications designed to influence the attitudes and behaviour of a target audience in a manner that supports the objectives of the communicator. It does this by shaping the audience's perceptions of the world and suggesting appropriate reactions to those perceptions. In a military context it is related to, and is in some ways synonymous with, **information warfare** and **psychological operations**. Propaganda may be directed at both hostile and friendly audiences. In the former case, possible aims may be to undermine morale, to reduce the legitimacy of a foreign government, to sow dissent within enemy organizations, or to encourage surrender. In the latter case, the aims include boosting support for a **war** effort, inciting hatred of the enemy, or promoting confidence in the legitimacy and eventual triumph of the cause.

Propaganda is divided into three types: white, grey, and black. White propaganda accurately identifies the source of the information being conveyed: those at the receiving end know who sent the message. Grey propaganda does not identify the source. Black propaganda actively pretends to be from a source other than the real one. The term 'propaganda' usually has negative connotations, reflecting a popular perception that it involves at best manipulation of the facts and at worst outright falsehood. This need not be the case. Generally, it is felt that propaganda is most likely to be successful if it is based on truth, since this maintains the credibility of the source. Nonetheless, the propagandist does attempt to shape perceptions of which facts are important and what they mean. In the struggle against many contemporary **threats** to **security**, such as **insurgency** and **terrorism**, the fight for hearts and minds is often as important as, if not more important than, physical combat and destruction of the enemy. Some commentators believe that Western states are ill-equipped in this regard, and that while they are able to defeat groups such as **Al Qaeda** on the battlefield, they risk losing the propaganda battle against them. Successful propaganda requires a good knowledge of the target audience, its culture, ideology, and modes of thought, and also needs to be directed at those audiences which will be most receptive. Good propaganda is, therefore, in part dependent on good **intelligence**.

Further reading
Robert Jackall (ed.), *Propaganda* (New York: New York University Press, 1995)
Nicholas Jackson O'Shaughnessy, *Politics and Propaganda: Weapons of Mass Seduction* (Manchester: Manchester University Press, 2004)
Garth S. Jowett and Victoria O'Donnell, *Propaganda and Persuasion*, 3rd edn (Thousand Oaks: Sage, 1999)

PROVISIONAL IRISH REPUBLICAN ARMY, see IRISH REPUBLICAN ARMY (IRA)

PSYCHOLOGICAL OPERATIONS (PSYOPS)

Psychological operations (PSYOPS) are activities undertaken in order to influence the emotions, reasoning, and most importantly the behaviour of a target audience, be it a foreign government, an organization, a group, or an individual, in a direction favourable to the party carrying out the operations. PSYOPS can take place during both **peace** and **war**, although they are most commonly associated with military operations in wartime. They include **propaganda** and other activities designed to influence attitudes and behaviour. For instance, a physical attack on an enemy target could be considered a psychological operation as long as the primary purpose of the attack was psychological rather than physical. PSYOPS can be used to undermine the credibility of enemy leaders, to reduce others' confidence in the success or the legitimacy of their cause, to undermine morale, or to encourage desertion or surrender. In a military context, television and radio broadcasts, leaflet drops, and loudspeakers are common PSYOPS dissemination methods. Those responsible for PSYOPS must have a good knowledge of the target and its mode of thought. Successful PSYOPS are thus dependent on good **intelligence**. If well applied, PSYOPS can save life by reducing others' will to fight and inducing them to surrender without fighting.

Further reading
Randall G. Bowdish, 'Information-Age Psychological Operations', *Military Review*, vol. 76, no. 6, December 1998–February 1999, pp. 29–35
Carnes Lord and Frank R. Barnett (eds), *Political Warfare and Psychological Operations: Rethinking the US Approach* (Washington, DC: National Defense University Press, 1989)
Ron D. McLaurin (ed.), *Military Propaganda: Psychological Warfare and Operations* (New York: Praeger, 1982)

RADIOLOGICAL WEAPONS
A radiological weapon is a device that disperses radioactive material without a nuclear explosion. As yet, radiological weapons remain hypothetical, as none have ever been used, but some terrorists associated with **Al Qaeda** are known to have expressed an interest in them. The simplest form of radiological weapon is the one commonly referred to as a 'dirty bomb'. Here, the radioactive material is attached to conventional explosives which when detonated disperse the radioactive substance. More sophisticated devices could use other methods of dispersal, such as turning the material into a vapour. This would have the advantage of spreading the contamination over a wider area.

The harm done by a radiological weapon would be largely dependent on the type of radioactive material and the method chosen to disperse it. A crude dirty bomb using a lightly radioactive substance would be unlikely to kill many people, and would also be unlikely to spread material far beyond the initial blast area, although some could be transmitted further by the wind or by contaminated individuals. A more effective device might contaminate an area of several square kilometres with sufficient radioactive material to kill tens or even hundreds of people and to cause sickness in hundreds more. Making such a device would be far more difficult than making a simple dirty bomb, and if sufficiently highly radioactive material was used, those making the weapon might be killed in the process of constructing it. Experts disagree as to whether it would actually be possible for terrorists to build a radiological weapon capable of contaminating a large area and killing large numbers of people. In fact, it is most unlikely that such a weapon would be capable of causing a sufficient number of deaths to be classified correctly as a **weapon of mass destruction (WMD)**. Its primary effects would be psychological and economic. Even a small dirty bomb would be likely to cause immense panic as well as serious financial damage. This fact means that even if they could not cause mass destruction, radiological weapons could be attractive tools for some terrorist organizations.

Further reading
Andrew J. Grotto, *Defusing the Threat of Radiological Weapons: Integrating Prevention with Detection and Response* (Washington DC: Center for American Progress, 2005)
Peter D. Zimmerman with Cheryl Loeb, 'Dirty Bombs: The Threat Revisited', *Defense Horizons*, no. 38, January 2004, pp. 1–11

REAL IRISH REPUBLICAN ARMY, see IRISH REPUBLICAN ARMY (IRA)

REALISM

For many years the dominant theory in studies of **security** and international relations, Realism seeks to explain how the international system operates and why inter-state conflict happens. Realism's intellectual origins lie in the works of writers such as E. H. Carr and Hans Morgenthau, who saw states as the most important actors on the international stage. It contains various different strands which differ on important issues but share a core of vital assumptions which mark them off from other theories.

According to the Realist model, states pursue their own **national interest**, which is measured in terms of maximizing **national power**, which in turn is generally measured in terms of military power. International relations are characterized by a continuous struggle for power between states in which states will tend, consciously or unconsciously, to pursue policies which lead to a **balance of power**. For Realists such as Morgenthau this was an inevitable product of human nature, which is seen as essentially selfish and aggressive. This particular point of view is now known as 'classical realism'. 'Neo-realists' or 'structural realists', such as Kenneth Waltz, disagree. For them, the crucial determinant in state behaviour is not human nature, since political leaders are assumed to be rational actors, but the structure of the international system, and in particular the absence of world government. This means that states live in a system of **anarchy**. Anarchy obliges states to assume the worst about the **threats** posed by others, and to take measures to protect themselves as they cannot rely on others to do it for them. However, these preparations in turn threaten other states, leading to the **security dilemma**, and so make it difficult for states to cooperate for their mutual benefit. Anarchy thus makes conflict an inevitable and tragic part of international politics.

This view of the world can be defined as 'offensive realism', since it assumes an essentially offensive relationship among states. 'Defensive realism', by contrast, maintains that states do not live in a condition of perpetual external threat and that the security dilemma occurs comparatively rarely. Thus, violent competition between states need not be an endemic feature of international politics.

The name 'Realism' implies a view of the world based not on naïve idealism but a self-described hard-headed 'realistic' conception of how international politics actually works. Critics of Realism complain that the theory's concentration on states and **national security** does not describe the world accurately. Some also maintain that it has negative consequences in terms of security. In the first place, the idea that states are engaged in a perpetual struggle for power is contestable. Human nature may not be inherently selfish and aggressive, and the international system is not entirely anarchic – elements of an international society exist along with growing **security communities**. Second, the rise of non-state actors in the modern world challenges the idea that states are the most important players on the international stage. Third, the security interests of states do not necessarily coincide with those of their citizens – indeed concentrating on states' security needs can lead to neglect of the **human security** requirements of individuals. To proponents of the school of **critical security studies**, Realism is responsible for perpetuating policies which emphasize military solutions to security problems and ignore the individual needs of the powerless in favour of the wishes of those with power. Against this, it must be noted that many Realists, far from being militarists, have been deeply concerned with learning to understand what causes inter-state **war** in order to find mechanisms for reducing its incidence.

Further reading

John H. Herz, *Political Realism and Political Idealism: A Study in Theories and Realities* (Chicago: University of Chicago Press, 1951)

Robert O. Keohane (ed.), *Neorealism and its Critics* (New York: Columbia University Press, 1986)

Hans Morgenthau, *Politics among Nations: The Struggle for Power and Peace*, 7th edn (Guildford, CT: McGraw-Hill, 2005)

REGIME CHANGE

Regime change is the forcible overthrow by one country of the government of another. The term has acquired public prominence since the United States declared a right to engage in regime change in its National Security Strategy document of 2002. Nevertheless, regime change is nothing new, and there have been numerous examples over the centuries. Recent cases include the American invasions of Grenada in 1983, Panama in 1989, Haiti in 1994, Afghanistan in 2001, and Iraq in 2003. Further back, examples include the Vietnamese invasion of Cambodia in 1978/79 to overthrow the Khmer Rouge, and the Tanzanian invasion of Uganda in 1979 to overthrow the regime of Idi Amin.

The current US predeliction for regime change is influenced by the ideas of **neoconservatism, democratic peace theory**, and **preventive war**. According to the policy's proponents, some regimes are by their nature inherently bad and the only sure path to **peace** and international **security** is their replacement by more democratic governments. Supporters of regime change claim that the practice may be justified to remove governments which commit significant human rights abuses, and which violate **international law** and threaten international security, for instance through the **proliferation** of **weapons of mass destruction** or by providing safe havens for **terrorism**. Opponents of the policy argue that the principle of state **sovereignty** makes regime change illegal under international law. In addition, while it may often be easy to overthrow a regime, it is often extremely difficult to create a replacement one which is stable and effective. The result of regime change may simply be to replace a **rogue state** with a **failed state**, thus harming international security rather than benefitting it.

Further reading
Dieter Janssen, 'Preventive Defense and Forcible Regime Change: a Normative Assessment', *Journal of Military Ethics*, vol. 3, no. 2, 2004, pp. 105–128
Stephen Kinzer, *Overthrow: America's Century of Regime Change from Hawaii to Iraq* (New York: Times Books, 2006)
W. Michael Reisman, 'Why Regime Change is (Almost Always) a Bad Idea', *The American Journal of International Law*, vol. 98, no. 3, July 2004, pp. 516–525

RENDITION
Rendition is a practice developed by the **Central Intelligence Agency (CIA)** of the United States in which terrorist suspects are arrested or abducted and sent to other countries, where they are imprisoned and interrogated. The CIA has felt that it would be unwise or impossible to try such suspects in US courts, either because the evidence is inadmissible in court or because revealing it would threaten its source. Removing the individuals to other countries with less stringent legal procedures provides an alternative way of putting them out of action.

At first, rendition was used only in cases where the suspect had already been charged by the criminal system in another country. After the terrorist attacks on America on 11 September 2001, the program was expanded to include persons merely suspected of having connections with **terrorism**. Rendition of this sort is known as 'extraordinary rendition', as it takes place outside of normal legal procedures. In cases of extraordinary rendition, the suspects are not formally arrested or deported, merely abducted from countries outside of the USA, sometimes without the knowledge of the country in question. It is estimated that at least 150 persons have suffered rendition or extraordinary rendition at the hands of the United States since 2001, their most common final destinations being Egypt, Syria, and Jordan. Prominent examples are the cases of Maher Arar, a Canadian citizen who was flown from the United States in September 2002 to Syria; of Khaled El-Masri, a German car salesman, who was seized in Macedonia in January 2004, and then flown by the CIA to Afghanistan; and of Hassan Mustafa Osama Nasr, who was kidnapped by the CIA in Italy in February 2003, and flown to Egypt.

Those rendered have often been tortured. Critics of rendition have alleged that this is one of the reasons that it has proved so popular since 2001. They argue that US **intelligence** agencies, being banned by law from practising torture, have in effect outsourced it by sending suspects to places whose agencies are less scrupulous in their interrogation practices, hoping thereby to obtain information that they are unable to extract themselves. US officials deny this allegation, and claim that suspects are never rendered to locations where it is definitely known that they will be tortured. However, the term 'known' allows a large degree of flexibility (for instance to send people to places where it is merely very likely that they will be tortured), besides which the US definition of what constitutes torture is sufficiently narrow that even this denial may not be especially meaningful.

Moral and legal aspects aside, there is considerable disagreement as to the practical benefits of the rendition programme. US officials have argued that it has saved lives by removing dangerous terrorists from circulation. Others have countered that many of those rendered, such as Maher Arar and Khaled El Masri, have been innocent, and that information extracted from the suspected terrorists once rendered is of limited use and often deeply unreliable. For instance, false evidence provided by **Al Qaeda** member Ibn al-Sheikh al-Libi after his rendition to Egypt is believed to have played an important role in convincing US leaders of a non-existent link between Al Qaeda and the Iraqi government of Saddam Hussein. Despite such criticism, the US government continues to affirm its right to carry out both ordinary and extraordinary renditions in the future.

Further reading
Stephen Grey, *Ghost Plane: the True Story of the CIA Torture Program* (New York: St Martin's Press, 2006)

Aziz Z. Huq, 'Extraordinary Rendition and the Wages of Hypocrisy', *World Policy Journal*, Spring 2006, pp. 25–35

Jane Mayer, 'Outsourcing Torture: the Secret History of America's "extraordinary rendition" program', *The New Yorker*, vol. 81, no. 1, 14 February 2005, pp. 106–123

RESOURCE CONFLICT

A resource conflict is a **war** fought to gain or maintain control of scarce natural resources, such as oil, water, or diamonds. Such conflicts may be either internal or external in nature. American military intervention in the Persian Gulf, for instance, is often interpreted in terms of the United States' desire to maintain access to Gulf oil. Similarly, some recent internal conflicts in Africa have centred around struggles to control the trade in diamonds and other valuable commodities.

Some commentators believe that as the world's population grows and resources become increasingly scarce, the incidence of resource conflict will increase. They say that 'water wars' in particular will become more common. Others argue that the link between resource scarcity and conflict is unproven. On the one hand, it is true that **civil war** is especially common in countries which are heavily reliant on the export of natural resources. On the other hand, these countries tend to be poorer and have weaker state structures than those which are more heavily industrialized, and this may be the real cause of their internal violence.

The pursuit of natural resources undoubtedly plays a role in sparking some conflicts, such as in the Middle East, but it is never the sole factor, and so the extent to which these are truly 'resource conflicts' is disputable. In addition, it may often be the case that the presence of valuable natural resources is not so much the cause of a conflict as an enabling factor: it is not that the warring parties are fighting for control of the resources, but that the existence of the resources provides them with the funds to finance a conflict they otherwise could not maintain. Finally, scenarios predicting rising resource conflict due to increasing scarcity rely on a Malthusian model of demand outstripping supply which may not be reliable. Even when environmental scarcity does exist, this can sometimes push groups into finding new ways of cooperating to collectively manage resources rather than push them into war. While some analysts consider that the desire to control natural resources is the primary cause of both international and internal war, many others disagree.

Further reading

Macartan Humphreys, 'Natural Resources, Conflict, and Conflict Resolution', *Journal of Conflict Resolution*, vol. 49, no. 4, August 2005, pp. 508–537

Michael T. Klare, *Resource Wars: the New Landscape of Global Conflict* (New York: Owl, 2001)

Jan Selby, 'Oil and Water: the Contrasting Anatomies of Resource Conflicts', *Government and Opposition*, vol. 40, no. 2, Spring 2005, pp. 200–224

RESPONSIBILITY TO PROTECT

The concept of a 'responsibility to protect' was established by the International Commission on Intervention and State Sovereignty (ICISS), created by the Canadian government in 2001. Building on the idea of **human security**, the ICISS report, entitled *The Responsibility to Protect*, challenged the Westphalian model of **sovereignty** and argued that sovereignty does not grant states the right to treat their citizens in any way they choose. Rather it carries a responsibility to respect their human rights. In the event that states are unable or unwilling to fulfill that responsibility it falls upon other members of the international community to do so. This provides a justification for **humanitarian intervention** in the case of extreme human rights abuses. Indeed, by changing the language of the debate from a discussion about whether states had a 'right' to intervene to one which describes intervention as a duty, the ICISS significantly strengthened the interventionist position.

The concept of the responsibility to protect was endorsed by a **United Nations (UN)** High Level Panel on Threats, Challenges, and Change which reported to the UN Secretary General in December 2004. This stated that the responsibility should be exercised by the UN Security Council, and that humanitarian intervention in response to human rights abuses would be permissible under certain conditions drawn from the tenets of **just war theory**: the **threat** to human security should be sufficiently great to justify force; the primary aim of the mission should be to eliminate the threat; the use of force should be a last resort; the force used should be the minimum required and proportionate to the threat; and there should be a reasonable chance of the intervention succeeding.

The establishment of the principle of a responsibility to protect is part of a broader recent attempt to create new international norms regarding state sovereignty and human rights. In theory, its adoption should deter potential human rights abusers as well as provide a mechanism by which those who are not deterred can be stopped. However, there exists a danger that by weakening previous restrictions against the use of armed force, the principle may instead open the door to abuse, as strong powers assert the responsibility to protect as justification for what are in fact acts of aggression. Furthermore, in the wake of the **wars** in Afghanistan and Iraq, the appetite of the international community for military intervention may well be sated for some time. International inaction in the face of humanitarian crises in places such as Darfur suggests that much needs to be done before the responsibility to protect can be said to have been widely accepted in practice rather than in theory.

Further reading
David Chandler, 'The Responsibility to Protect? Imposing the Liberal Peace', *International Peacekeeping*, vol. 11, no. 1, Spring 2004, pp. 59–81
High Level Panel on Threats, Challenges, and Change, *A More Secure World: Our Shared Responsibility* (United Nations, 2004)
International Commission on Intervention and State Sovereignty, *The Responsibility to Protect* (Ottawa: ICISS, 2001)
S. Neil Macfarlane, Carolin J. Thielking, and Thomas G. Weiss, 'The Responsibility to Protect: Is Anyone Interested in Humanitarian Intervention?', *Third World Quarterly*, vol. 25, no. 5, 2004, pp. 977–992

REVOLUTION
In the context of politics, a revolution is an effort to overthrow a political regime by unconstitutional methods. Revolutions differ from **coups d'état** in that they involve mass participation and aim to produce radical social, economic or political change. Scholars have carried out substantial research into the subject of revolutions, but have as yet to reach definite conclusions as to what causes them, and why they occur in some states and not in others.

A necessary condition for a revolution is widespread discontent with the existing order, both among the mass of the population and among a crucial element of the elite. This is often associated with poverty and/or dictatorial or corrupt government. But while these may be necessary conditions, they are not sufficient; there are many states with impoverished populations and dictatorial governments which have not experienced revolution. Indeed, some revolutions take place not when people get poorer, but when rapid economic progress disrupts existing social relations, or when government reform opens up space for political opposition. Other factors need to be taken into consideration, such as the role of leadership and of ideology. In the former case, the presence of a charismatic leader may make a crucial difference, but even the strongest personality is not able to make a revolution in the absence of the appropriate preconditions. The introduction of new ideas may also shake the foundations on which the regime bases its legitimacy, but on their own ideas are also insufficient; those which take root in one society may not in another. One theory posits that revolutions occur when a conjunction of many of these factors comes about. In addition, chance may make an important contribution. Some catastrophic event, such as defeat in **war**, may be required to tip a society over the edge, but even this does not guarantee revolution. Revolutions occur in the absence of such catastrophes, and often do not occur even when they are present.

Just as there is no single explanation of revolutions, there is no single type. Revolutions may be class-based, or may involve nearly the whole of society united against the ruling regime. They may be peaceful or may be violent. They may draw most of their support from the cities or from the countryside. They may lead to social collapse and even to **civil war**, or they may witness a rapid restoration of order. Their effects may be confined within the borders of the country in question, or may spread beyond them. In short, revolutions are extremely complex and heterogeneous, and it seems unlikely that it will ever be possible to explain them all within the confines of a single theory.

Further reading
John Foran, 'Theories of Revolution Revisited: Toward a Fourth Generation?', *Sociological Theory*, vol. 11, no. 1, March 1993, pp. 1–20
Jack A. Goldstone, 'The Comparative and Historical Study of Revolutions', *Annual Review of Sociology*, vol. 8, 1982, pp. 187–207
Jack A. Goldstone, 'Toward a Fourth Generation of Revolutionary Theory', *Annual Review of Political Science*, vol. 4, no. 1, 2001, pp. 139–187

REVOLUTION IN MILITARY AFFAIRS (RMA)

The term 'Revolution in Military Affairs' (RMA) was developed by American military thinkers in the early 1990s. It evolved from an earlier concept developed by Soviet strategists, who predicted that advances in computer technology and precision weaponry would create what they called a 'military-technological revolution', which would fundamentally alter the character of **war**. This prediction then seemed to be confirmed by the ease of the US victory over Iraq in the Gulf War of 1991.

There has been considerable debate as to what defines a revolution in military affairs, and whether recent developments do in fact constitute one. The phrase is associated with precision weapons, high-technology **intelligence** and surveillance systems, and their integration into command and control systems through the use of modern computer technology. The RMA offers the prospect of armed forces being able to acquire near perfect knowledge of the state of the battlefield and being able to target enemy units with great rapidity and accuracy. The RMA is therefore closely linked to popular contemporary military phraseology such as **C4ISR**, **Network-centric Warfare**, and **Information Warfare**. Proponents of the RMA argue that developments in these areas are changing the nature of war in a revolutionary fashion, dramatically quickening the pace of operations, reducing the requirement for mass in favour of smaller, lighter and more rapidly responding formations using precision weapons, and making 'information dominance' the key to military success. The logic of the RMA is therefore fundamental to the current US policy of military **transformation**.

Theorists postulate that there have been several RMAs over the centuries. Significant changes in military technology do not by themselves constitute an RMA. It is possible to have an RMA without any new recent technology, and for new technologies to arrive without there being an RMA. An RMA is deemed to have taken place when new technologies combine with changes in military doctrine and organization to produce a fundamental change in the way that military operations are conducted. Thus, the invention of the tank did not by itself constitute an RMA – that took place only when the Germans invented the concept of blitzkrieg, established new forms of military organization (such as tank divisions), and trained soldiers to operate in a new fashion, giving greater freedom for lower-level commanders to use their initiative to exploit the speed of their armoured formations.

It remains to be seen whether modern developments in information technology have truly resulted in an RMA of this sort. Critics cast doubt on the idea that it is ever possible to fundamentally alter the nature of war, arguing that technology will never enable one to fully overcome the 'fog of war'. Another criticism is that that while the technology associated with the RMA is useful when an army fights another army, it is of limited use when combating **terrorism, insurgency, guerrilla warfare**, and other manifestations of what some refer to as **Fourth Generation Warfare** or **asymmetric warfare**. In these situations, more traditional tools and formations may be more useful than the small, rapid, high-technology armies favoured by the spokespersons of the RMA.

Further reading
John Arquilla and David Ronfeld, *In Athena's Camp: Preparing for Conflict in the Information Age* (Santa Monica: RAND, 1997)
Eliot A. Cohen, 'A Revolution in Warfare', *Foreign Affairs*, vol. 75, no. 2, March/April 1996, pp. 37–54
Williamson Murray, 'Thinking about Revolutions in Military Affairs', *Joint Force Quarterly*, Summer 1997, pp. 69–76

REVOLUTIONARY WAR, see INSURGENCY AND GUERRILLA WARFARE

RISK
The term 'risk' refers to the probability that harm may result from a given **threat**, combined with an assessment of the extent of the likely harm should the threat materialize. Risks are present in almost all forms of human activity. The dangers which are most likely to become a reality tend to be the least harmful; those which are more harmful tend to occur more rarely. Looked at in terms of **national security**, the risk of **terrorism** occurring is high, but the likely damage an act of terrorism would cause is low; the risk of nuclear war occurring is low, but the harm which would result would be enormous. Risk management involves weighing up these two factors and then determining which dangers should receive priority and which ones can be ignored, as well as deciding what precautionary measures should be taken. As a general rule, humans tend to perform poorly at this task. For a number of psychological reasons they underestimate the risks of some potential hazards and exaggerate the risks of others. A citizen of a Western society is, for instance, many thousand times more likely to be killed in a car accident than by an act of terrorism, but terrorism generates far more public concern. In this case, this is

because one becomes habituated to dangers which occur regularly, and because events which happen repeatedly but cause only limited harm each time they occur are less emotionally compelling than others which happen rarely but cause substantial damage when they do.

Some commentators believe that the risk assessment skills of people in modern Western societies are particularly poor, and that we live in a 'culture of fear' in which we worry unduly about very unlikely dangers, ranging from bird flu, mad cow disease and deep-vein thrombosis through to **rogue states** providing terrorists with **weapons of mass destruction (WMD)**. This may be a reflection of the development of what German sociologist Ulrich Beck has called the 'risk society'. In extreme cases this may lead the leaders of Western states to engage in 'risk-transfer **war**'. Here, in order to avoid even the merest possibility of others harming them, leaders launch **preventive wars**, in effect transferring the possibility of harm onto the citizens of the country which they attack. The current predeliction in some circles for preventive war is is indicative of what appears to be an especially low risk tolerance in Western societies in the aftermath of the terrorist attacks on America in September 2001.

Further reading
Ulrich Beck, *Risk Society: Towards a New Modernity* (London: Sage, 1992)
Frank Furedi, *The Culture of Fear: Risk-taking and the Morality of Low Expectation*, revised edition (London: Continuum, 2005)
Peter L. Bernstein, *Against the Gods: The Remarkable Story of Risk* (New York: John Wiley and Sons, 1996)

ROGUE STATES
The term 'rogue states' is used to refer to states that are considered anti-democratic and oppressive towards their citizens, possess **weapons of mass destruction**, are guilty of external aggression, and have links with international **terrorism**. The leaders of rogue states are often depicted as irrational. As such they do not respond to the normal rules of **deterrence** and must be confronted rather than merely contained or deterred. The term became popular in public and official discourse in the early 1990s, especially after the Gulf War of 1991. During the later years of the Clinton administration in the

United States, the phrase 'countries of concern' officially replaced 'rogue states', but the latter regained popularity during the presidency of George W. Bush. The United States has in the past designated seven states as 'rogue states' or 'countries of concern': Cuba, Iran, Syria, Libya, North Korea, Pakistan, and Iraq before the fall of Saddam Hussein. In the absence of a major conventional **threat** to Western powers, as previously posed by the Soviet Union, many commentators see rogue states as providing the greatest dangers to Western **security**. In particular, many fear that rogue states may pass weapons of mass destruction to terrorists in order to use them against Western targets.

The list of rogue states appears to be somewhat arbitrary. Many states who are non-democratic do not appear on it, while some who are on the list do not appear to meet all the criteria which supposedly qualify one for membership of the rogues' gallery. Cuba, for instance, has no proven links with international terrorism, and appears to be on the list for domestic political reasons in the United States. Pakistan, which does have nuclear weapons and links to terrorism, has been removed from the list, as its aid is required in fighting the **Taliban** in Afghanistan. Critics suggest that the label of 'rogue state' tells one only that the leadership of the state in question is hostile to US foreign policy. It is also argued that labelling a state in this way becomes a self-fulfilling prophecy. By demonizing states and seeking to isolate and even overthrow their ruling regimes, those who favour calling states 'rogues' further antagonize them and drive them more certainly into hostile behaviour. Commentators have also noted that the term conveniently came into favour at a time when the threat which justified military budgets, namely the Soviet Union, had vanished, and describe it as a rhetorical tool for justifying continued high defence expenditure. Regardless of its roots, the term has acquired a dominant role in the discourse of security affairs, and it seems unlikely to disappear from public rhetoric in the near future.

Further reading

Michael Klare, *Rogue States and Nuclear Outlaws* (New York: Hill and Wang, 1995)

Miroslav Nincic, *Renegade Regimes: Confronting Deviant Behavior in World Politics* (New York: Columbia University Press, 2005)

Raymond Tanter, *Rogue Regimes: Terrorism and Proliferation* (New York: St Martin's Griffin, 1999)

SEABED TREATY

Formally known as the 'Treaty on the Prohibition of the Emplacement of Nuclear Weapons and Other Weapons of Mass Destruction on the Seabed and the Ocean Floor and in the Subsoil Thereof', the Seabed Treaty was signed on 11 February 1971 and came into force on 18 May 1972. Parties to the treaty undertake not to place on the seabed, the ocean floor, or the subsoil of the ocean floor, beyond a 12 mile coastal limit, any **weapons of mass destruction (WMD)**, or any structures and installations designed for storing, testing or using such weapons. Signatories have the right to observe the activities of parties to the treaty on the seabed and ocean floor, and if doubts persist as to the nature of these activities, to refer the matter to the **United Nations** Security Council. Conferences to review the operation of the treaty were held in 1977, 1983, and 1992.

Further reading
Arms Control and Disarmament Agreements (New Brunswick: Transaction, 1984)
Coit D. Blacker and Gloria Duffy (eds), *International Arms Control: Issues and Agreements* (Stanford: Stanford University Press, 1984)
Thomas Graham Jr and Damien J. LaVera, *Cornerstones of Security: Arms Control Treaties in the Nuclear Era* (Seattle: University of Washington Press, 2003)

SEA POWER

Sea power is a measure of a state's strength in maritime trade and commerce, of its control of ocean resources, and of its capacity to project military force into and from the sea. It is therefore more than a purely military matter. The great American naval strategist Alfred Thayer Mahan identified six conditions of sea power: geographic position, natural resources and climate, extent of territory, population, character of the people, and character of the government. Possession of civilian shipping, fisheries, ports and undersea resources such as oil may all also be considered elements of sea power. Military sea power entails the ability to protect the other forms of sea power and deny their use to enemies.

Historically, sea power has been vital to prosperity in **peace** as well as to success in **war**. Sea power allows one to protect one's own trade and communications as well to to strike enemies from the sea. To this end it is desirable to obtain 'command of the sea' or 'sea control', the ability to use the sea for one's own purposes while denying that ability to the enemy. Mahan suggested that the best method to achieve such control was by means of a decisive naval battle to destroy the enemy's navy. Later naval strategists, such as Sir Julian Corbett, placed less stress on the decisive battle and more on preserving sea lines of communication. Corbett stressed that sea power must be used in conjunction with **land power** to be of maximum benefit.

Uses of sea power in war include protection of lines of communication, sea denial (i.e. denying use of the sea to the enemy), blockades of enemy territory, and amphibious operations (i.e. using the sea to place land forces on the enemy's coast). Since the end of the **Cold War**, Western, and especially American, naval dominance has become so great that command of the sea is assured for the foreseeable future. The focus of naval operations has shifted from protection of lines of communication to what is known as littoral warfare, in which naval forces are placed close to an enemy's coast from where they can launch attacks on enemy territory (using for instance cruise missiles and aircraft and helicopters based on aircraft carriers). In peacetime naval forces may also be used for naval diplomacy and nuclear **deterrence**.

Further reading
Julian S. Corbett, *Some Principles of Maritime Strategy* (London: Longman, Green and Co., 1911)
Colin S. Gray, *The Navy in the Post-Cold War World: the Uses and Value of Strategic Sea Power* (University Park: Pennsylvania State University Press, 1994)
Alfred Thayer Mahan, *The Influence of Sea Power upon History, 1660–1783* (New York: Hill and Wang, 1962)
Sam J. Tangredi, 'Sea Power: Theory and Practice', in John Baylis, James Wirtz, Eliot Cohen, and Colin S. Gray (eds), *Strategy in the Contemporary World: An Introduction to Strategic Studies* (Oxford: Oxford University Press, 2002), pp. 113–136

SECRET INTELLIGENCE SERVICE (SIS)

The Secret Intelligence Service (SIS) is the foreign **intelligence** service of the United Kingdom, popularly known by its former title, MI6. SIS is responsible to the Foreign Secretary, and is governed by the terms of the 1994 Intelligence Services Act. The head of SIS is known as

'C' after the organization's first director, Captain Sir George Mans-field-Cumming, who used to sign letters 'C' in green ink. The Intelligence Services Act directs SIS to obtain information relating to the acts and intentions of persons overseas in order to protect the **national security** and economic well-being of the United Kingdom. This it does primarily through the use of human intelligence, though also through liaison with foreign intelligence services. The organization works closely with other British intelligence agencies such as the **Security Service** and **Government Communications Headquarters (GCHQ)**, and contributes intelligence to the **Joint Intelligence Committee**. The Intelligence Services Act also directs SIS to carry out 'other tasks', thereby mandating it to engage in **covert action** overseas.

Further reading
National Intelligence Machinery (London: The Stationery Office, 2006)
Philip H. J. Davies, *MI6 and the Machinery of Spying* (London: Frank Cass, 2004)
Stephen Dorrill, *MI6: Fifty Years of Special Operations* (London: Fourth Estate, 2001)

SECURITIZATION
Securitization refers to the labelling of an issue as a '**security**' issue, thereby implying that it is a matter of special significance in terms of national or human survival. Securitization theory argues that security is a 'speech act'. The fact that something is considered a matter of security does not mean anything other than that somebody has successfully labelled it as such. This act suggests that something of importance is threatened, and that emergency measures need to be taken to protect it. In this way, securitization moves issues out of the realm of normal politics and into that of emergency politics, justifying action which otherwise would not be considered justifiable. In theory, anybody may securitize any issue, but in practice not all attempts at securitization will be accepted by others. Much depends on the power of the person making the attempt, and on the credibility of the claim itself.

Proponents of the practice of securitization argue that the application of the security label gives issues additional urgency and helps to mobilize popular and government resources towards solving it. They therefore recommend the application of the language of security to matters such as the protection of the natural environment and the **emancipation** of individuals from poverty and oppression. In contrast, critics of securitization argue that there is no clear data supporting the assertion that it helps to solve problems. There is, for instance, no evidence that the use of the term '**environmental security**' has helped to mobilize resources towards solving environmental problems. In addition, there are some dangers in securitization. The language of security often implies an 'us versus them' relationship, which may not be conducive to solving the issues in question. It can also be used to justify otherwise unwarranted extensions of government power and restrictions on human rights and civil liberties. Some commentators therefore argue in favour of de-securitization rather than securitization.

Further reading
Rita Taureck, 'Securitization Theory and Securitization Studies', *Journal of International Relations and Development*, vol. 9, no. 1, March 2006, pp. 53–61
Ole Waever, 'Securitization and Desecuritization', in Ronnie D. Lipschutz (ed.), *On Security* (New York: Columbia University Press, 1995), pp. 46–86

SECURITY

Security implies freedom from **threat**. Some analysts see this as an absolute condition: either one is secure, or one is not. More commonly they regard it as a relative one: there are varying degrees of security. It is also possible to view it as both an objective and a subjective matter. The former refers to the reality of one's situation, whether one truly is threatened and adequately protected; the latter refers to one's perception of the situation and one's desire not merely to be free from threat but to feel free. Of course, one may argue that those who feel threatened when they are not are merely misinformed. Nevertheless, misperception is common and drives much of human behaviour in the realm of security.

The concept of security as freedom from threat is clear, but it raises a number of questions. Whom and what is one protecting? And from which threats? In principle, security can apply to anyone or anything. One may speak of global security, international security, **national security**, regional security, and the security of organizations, groups, and individuals. Similarly, the concept may apply to any threats. At its most basic, security is about survival. States wish to protect themselves against overthrow or external invasion; individuals wish to protect themselves against those who might threaten their lives and the lives of those that they love. Less fundamentally, they wish to be free from threats to their property (or in the case of states to their territory or **sovereignty**), their core values, and their general well-being. Building on the last of these concerns, some commentators define security less in negative terms of freedom from threat and more in positive terms of the promotion of general well-being and quality of life.

Interpreted in this way, the concept of security runs the risk of losing focus. Within the arena of international security, political leaders and academics have sought to avoid this by restricting discussions of security to a narrower set of objects. Reflecting the dominance of the philosophy of **Realism**, they have tended to define security in terms of the security of nation states and the protection of **national interests** against military threats. Over the past twenty-five years, many in the academic community have increasingly contested this practice. They have sought to both widen and deepen the meaning of security, widening it to include subjects other than military security, such as **economic security** and **environmental security** (a process known as **securitization**), and deepening it to change the referent object of security studies from the state to individuals and to recognize that for most individuals in the world the primary threats to their security come not from **war** but from problems such as **disease** and poverty. They hold that an approach to international security based on promoting individual **human security** may provide longer term solutions to the problems which cause conflict, and thus a better guarantee of lasting **peace** and true security, than the traditional approach centred on national security and military concerns.

While there is much in favour of these arguments, they are not without difficulties. Nation states remain extremely important actors and do have significant security concerns, many of which are military in character. War, **terrorism**, **insurgency**, the **proliferation** of **weapons of mass destruction**, and so on, continue to threaten the lives and well-being both of states and of their populations. Conflating these issues with others such as economic development and disease by bringing them all together under the rubric of security ignores the fact that they may require very different responses. Indeed, the securitization of problems such as environmental degradation may result in the development of inappropriate policies. In practice, traditional definitions of security continue to determine the direction of most national and international security policies, but the influence of broader and deeper understandings of the concepts has grown since the end of the **Cold War**. The outcome of the intellectual debate about the meaning of security is of more than theoretical impact and has the capacity to shape the making of security policy in the future.

Further reading
David A. Baldwin, 'The Concept of Security', in Paul F. Diehl (ed.), *War*, vol. 1 (London: Sage, 2005), pp. 1–24

Barry Buzan, *People, States and Fear: an Agenda for International Security in the Post-Cold War Era*, 2nd edn (London: Harvester Wheatsheaf, 1991)

Michael Sheehan, *International Security: an Analytical Survey* (Boulder: Lynne Rienner, 2005)

Richard H. Ullman, 'Redefining Security', *International Security*, vol. 8, no. 1, Summer 1983, pp. 129–153

SECURITY COMMUNITY

A security community is a group of states that have become so integrated in terms of institutions, practices, and a sense of communal identity, as to have created an expectation among them that problems and disagreements will be solved by peaceful means. The concept was first developed by Karl Deutsch in 1957. Deutsch identified two types of security community: 'amalgamated' communities, in which states have merged to form new, larger states; and 'pluralistic' communities in which the states retain their independence but have a sufficient sense of community for there to be a real expectation that disputes will not be settled by force. Deutsch believed that three preconditions were essential for the establishment of a pluralistic community: compatibility of major values; a capacity of political units to respond to each others' needs and messages; and mutually predictable behaviour. If these conditions are present, pluralistic communities may then be built through transactions such as trade and travel, which over time create the desired sense of mutual trust and common identity. The creation of security communities allows states to overcome the **security dilemma** and thus offers a model which could contribute to the construction of more peaceful international relations.

Further reading
Emanuel Adler and Michael Barnett (eds), *Security Communities* (Cambridge: Cambridge University Press, 1998)
Karl W. Deutsch, *Political Community at the International Level* (Garden City, NY: Archon, 1970)
Karl W. Deutsch et al., *Political Community and the North Atlantic Area: International Organization in the Light of Historical Experience* (Princeton: Princeton University Press, 1957)

SECURITY DILEMMA

The 'security dilemma' describes a situation in which one state's efforts to enhance its **security** threaten the security of others. These then take measures to protect themselves, which then further threaten the original state. Efforts to heighten security thus end up reducing it. The **Cold War arms race** may be seen as a typical expression of the security dilemma – fearing each other's weapons, the Soviets and Americans each increased their own military expenditure, thus making each other feel even more insecure and inspiring further expenditure, in a potentially endless spiral. According to the theory of **Realism**, the security dilemma is a product of **anarchy** in the international system. Some Realists believe it to be inevitable; others argue that it is relatively rare and can be avoided. Misperceptions of others' motives play an important role in the process of the security dilemma. Given uncertainty as to others' motives, states tend to assume the worst, interpreting defensive measures as potentially offensive, and responding accordingly. Opportunities for mutually beneficial cooperation are therefore lost. However, if the costs of conflict and the benefits of cooperation are both high, rationally acting states may be able to overcome the security dilemma, especially if communications can be improved to avoid misperception. **Confidence and security building measures** may sometimes play an important role in this regard. The existence of **arms control** agreements and of **security communities** suggests that overcoming the security dilemma is possible.

Further reading
Charles L. Glaser, 'The Security Dilemma Revisited', *World Politics*, vol. 50, no. 1, 1990, pp. 171–201
Robert Jervis, 'Cooperation under the Security Dilemma', *World Politics*, vol. 30, no. 2, January 1978, pp. 167–214

SECURITY INTELLIGENCE

Security intelligence refers to **intelligence** regarding **threats** to **security**. The term is most often used with regard to internal security threats rather than dangers overseas. It is a subset of intelligence, and its subjects include **terrorism**, subversion, espionage, and **organized crime**. It excludes most political, economic and tactical military intelligence. Security intelligence is distinct from **information security**, which refers to activities to protect information, although the two overlap in the area of counter-intelligence. Examples of security intelligence agencies are the **Security Service (MI5)** in the United Kingdom, the **Federal Bureau of Investigation (FBI)** in the United States, and the **Federal'naia Sluzhba Bezopastnosti (FSB)** in the Russian Federation.

Further reading

Peter Chalk and William Rosenau, *Confronting the Enemy 'Within': Security Intelligence, the Police, and Counterterrorism in Four Democracies* (Santa Monica: RAND, 2004)

Michael Herman, *Intelligence Power in Peace and War* (Cambridge: Cambridge University Press, 1996)

SECURITY SERVICE (MI5)

The Security Service is the formal title of the United Kingdom's internal **security intelligence** agency, popularly known by its old name, MI5. The organization was established in 1909 and is now governed according to the terms of the Security Services Act of 1989. It is responsible to the Home Secretary and provides **intelligence** on **security** issues to the **Joint Intelligence Committee**. The Security Services Act gives the Security Service the functions of: protecting **national security** against the threats of espionage, **terrorism**, and sabotage, the agents of foreign powers, and efforts to overthrow parliamentary democracy; safeguarding the economic well-being of the United Kingdom; and assisting the police in combating **organized crime**. During the **Cold War**, the primary focus of the service's activities was countering Soviet espionage and subversion. Since the end of the Cold War, it no longer carries out work in the area of counter-subversion, and although it is still involved in counter-espionage, this now accounts for only a small percentage of its activities. Until the mid-1990s, responsibility for **counter-terrorism** in the United Kingdom belonged to the Metropolitan Police Special Branch. In 1995, however, the Security Service took over this role, and since the terrorist attacks on America of 11 September 2001 it has focused ever more on the **threat** from terrorism. According to official figures, counter-terrorism now absorbs some 87 per cent of the Security Service's finances. Following the creation of the Serious Organized Crime Agency in 2006, the Security Service no longer undertakes work on organized crime, in order to allow it to concentrate on its counter-terrorist role.

Further reading
Mark Hollingsworth and Nick Fielding, *Defending the Realm: Inside MI5 and the War on Terrorism* (London: André Deutsch, 2003)
National Intelligence Machinery (London: The Stationery Office, 2006)
Security Service website: http://www.mi5.gov.uk/

SHABAK
Shabak, often referred to by its original title, Shin Bet, is Israel's **security intelligence** agency. Together with the military **intelligence** branch, Aman, it is responsible for combating **terrorism** within Israel and the occupied territories, through both intelligence gathering and **covert action**. As part of the latter, Shabak cooperates with the Israel Defence Forces (IDF) to carry out 'targetted killings' of suspected terrorists; Shabak provides the IDF with details of a terrorist's location, after which the armed forces kill him by means of a precision air strike. The organization is also responsible for combatting extremist groups within Israel, for counter-intelligence operations, and for the protection of critical infrastructure. Shabak has had considerable successes in all these activities, but a number of scandals have tarnished its reputation. These include the murder in 1984 by Shabak agents of two terrorists originally taken alive by the IDF; the failure to prevent the assassination of Prime Minister Yitzhak Rabin in 1995; and allegations that Shabak tortured prisoners. Responding to complaints about the last of these, in 2000 the Israeli Supreme Court ruled that the organization's coercive interrogation techniques contravened the law and prohibited their further use.

Further reading
Federation of American Scientists, *Shabak*, http://www.fas.org/irp/world/israel/shin_bet/
Samuel M. Katz, *Guards without Frontiers: Israel's War against Terrorism* (London: Arms and Armour, 1990)

SHANGHAI COOPERATION ORGANIZATION (SCO)

Founded in June 2001, the Shanghai Cooperation Organization (SCO) is an international organization with six full members, namely China, Russia, Kazakhstan, Kyrgyzstan, Tajikistan, and Uzbekistan, and four observer members, India, Iran, Mongolia, and Pakistan. The organization grew out of the 'Shanghai Five' mechanism, created in the 1990s as a means for China, Russia, Kazakhstan, Kyrgyzstan, and Tajikistan to deepen mutual trust and reduce military forces in border regions. With the addition of Uzbekistan in 2001, the Shanghai Five became the SCO. The organization's primary areas of concern are economic and **security** cooperation. In particular, in 2004, the SCO created a Regional Antiterrorism Structure (RATS), a permanent body based in Tashkent with responsibility for fighting **terrorism**, separatism, and extremism. SCO members have also held joint military exercises. Some commentators in Western countries view the development of the SCO with alarm, considering it to be a potential future rival to the **North Atlantic Treaty Organization** and a means by which China and Russia are seeking to undermine American **hegemony** and restore the global **balance of power**. At present, however, that possibility remains somewhat remote.

Further reading
Shanghai Cooperation Organization website, http://www.sectsco.org
Gregory Logvinov, 'The Shanghai Cooperation Organization: a New Qualitative Step Forward', *Far Eastern Review*, vol. 30, no. 3, 2002, pp. 18–28
Sun Zhuangzhi, 'New and Old Regionalism: the Shanghai Cooperation Organization and Sino-Central Asian Relations', *The Review of International Affairs*, vol. 3, no. 4, Summer 2004, pp. 600–612

SHIN BET, see SHABAK

SLUZHBA VNESHNEI RAZVEDKI (SVR)

The Sluzhba Vneshnei Razvedki (SVR) is Russia's foreign **intelligence** service. Until 1991, it was the First Chief Directorate of the Soviet **security** and intelligence service, the KGB. In that year the KGB was split up into several parts, and the SVR became an independent service. The SVR is subordinated to the President of the Russian Federation, and its workings are guided by the Law on Foreign Intelligence Organs, passed by the Russian State Duma in

1996. Among other things, this tasks the SVR with acquiring, processing, and analysing information vital to the Russian Federation's interests, and with conducting activities to benefit the scientific and technological development of Russia. To this end, the SVR seeks information about the political intentions of foreign states, engages in industrial espionage against them, and seeks to infiltrate foreign intelligence services. It has also broadened its activities to include work countering the **proliferation** of **weapons of mass destruction** and combating international **terrorism** and **organized crime**. This has necessitated efforts to cooperate with the intelligence services of other states, but these have been complicated by the SVR's continued operations against those states. The expulsion of a suspected SVR agent from Canada in 2006 would appear to indicate that the organization remains active in the West.

Further reading
Gordon Bennett, *The SVR: Russia's Intelligence Service* (Camberley: The Conflict Studies Research Centre, 2000)
Amy Knight, *Spies without Cloaks: the KGB's Successors* (Princeton: Princeton University Press, 1996)

SOCIETAL SECURITY
Societal security relates to the maintenance and protection, within the limits of natural evolution, of collective identity, as embodied in culture, religion, language, political and social values, and so forth. Societal security is a particular concern for small communities who fear integration and assimilation by larger ones. The march of globalization and the spread of the English language arguably threaten the existence of many cultures and languages worldwide, and thus for some people societal security may be a matter of primary significance. Meanwhile, even members of well-established Western nations fear that their culture may be overwhelmed and extinguished by mass **migration** or be subsumed into some larger supranational body, such as the European Union. Such fears are not entirely without foundation, as large-scale immigration, for instance, can lead to certain peoples becoming a minority or almost a minority in their own land, as happened with Jewish immigration into Palestine in the 1930s and 1940s and with Russian immigration into Latvia and Estonia during the period of Soviet rule. Current debates about the assimilation of

Muslim immigrants into European states, such as the UK and the Netherlands, further illustrate the fears which many have that their collective identity may be extinguished. The language used in such debates may, however, cause additional problems. For instance, encouraging groups to view immigrants as **threats** may inadvertently encourage racism and thus inhibit integration and worsen problems such as **terrorism**. Given the importance of identity in peoples' lives, there are clear grounds for concern about anything which threatens collective identity, but it is not altogether obvious whether framing these issues in terms of **security** helps societies to find solutions to them, and thus whether the concept of societal security is a useful one.

Further reading

Barry Buzan, *People, States and Fear: an Agenda for International Security Studies in the Post-Cold War Era*, 2nd edn (London: Harvester Wheatsheaf, 1991)

Michael Sheehan, *International Security: an Analytical Survey* (Boulder: Lynne Rienner, 2005)

SOFT POWER

Power is a measurement of one's ability to get others to do what one wants. First coined by Joseph S. Nye Jr. in 1990, the term 'soft power' refers to the ability to get others to do this not because they have been forced or bribed to do so, but because they actually want to. It therefore reflects a capacity to make others want what one wants. This differentiates it from 'hard power', which is a measurement of the ability to get others to do what one wants by means of coercion or inducements. Sources of soft power include cultural attraction, ideology, and international institutions. The example of a state's domestic and foreign policies, as well as its people's way of life, may incite admiration in others and encourage them to emulate its behaviour as well to ally themselves with its cause.

Soft power attracts. This fact gives it many advantages over hard power. For example, many analysts believe that the spread of democracy will enhance international **security**, but democracy is more likely to develop deep roots and prosper if those who are democratizing do so by choice rather than because they have been made to do so by force. It must be noted, however, that soft power may not be suitable in all circumstances. In addition, it is hard to apply soft power to a specific goal. The attraction of soft power tends to be of a more general kind. Hard and soft power may both enhance and interfere with one another. For instance, it may be difficult to employ soft power in **war** zones. Some use of force may be required to provide the minimum level of security in which reconstruction, state building, democratization, and so forth can take place. Hard power in this way can support soft power. A state which possesses large reserves of soft power will also find it easier to use its hard power as others are more likely to give it the benefit of the doubt and to consider its actions legitimate. On the other hand, excessive use of hard power may undermine soft power. A state which insists on using hard power in situations which others consider inappropriate will eventually squander the goodwill it has previously built up. Others will no longer admire its values and consequently will no longer want what it wants.

Hard power may well be becoming less important in international affairs. For a variety of reasons, there is much less tolerance in most parts of the world for the use of military force. Furthermore, hard power does not provide a suitable solution for many of the **security** problems faced by contemporary society, such as environmental degradation, the spread of disease, and **terrorism**. In these circumstances, soft power is likely to become ever more vital.

Further reading
Joseph S. Nye Jr, *Bound to Lead: The Changing Nature of American Power* (New York: Basic Books, 1990)
Joseph S. Nye Jr., *Soft Power: The Means to Success in World Politics* (New York: Public Affairs, 2004)

SOVEREIGNTY
Sovereignty implies possessing sole authority over one's own domain. In terms of international **security**, the term is most commonly used with reference to state sovereignty and the concept that nation states have sole authority within their own territorial borders. This concept is traditionally seen as having arisen in Europe in the sixteenth and seventeenth centuries, and to have been enshrined in **international law** by the Treaty of Westphalia in 1648. The treaty established the principle that the internal politics of each state were its own affair

and that disagreements about another state's internal arrangements did not constitute legitimate grounds for intervention. This principle was then cemented further into international law by the Charter of the **United Nations**, which prohibited the waging of **war** on grounds other than self-defence.

While the idea that sovereignty implies a single authority within a given area is clear, commentators disagree about its basis: does it imply the possession of sole *legal* authority, or is it rather a measure of power? If a state lacks the means to enforce its authority, is it truly sovereign? And is a state which controls its own territory, but lacks international recognition, sovereign? Further disagreements surround the issue of where sovereignty lies: does it, or ought it to, lie in the state, its institutions and leaders, or in the people whom the state in theory serves? The answers to these questions have important consequences. If, for instance, sovereignty lies in the state, then an armed intervention by an outside power to remove a despotic regime is clearly a breach of sovereignty; if, however, it lies in the people, then intervention could be seen as a restoration of their sovereignty, and thus justifiable under international law.

According to its traditional definition, sovereignty is indivisible. This idea, like much else on the subject, has come under increasing challenge in recent years. The constitutional arrangements of the European Union, in particular, seem to have created a unique system in which it is not clear where sovereignty lies. Some commentators argue that trends associated with globalization, such as the spreading power of transnational corporations, mean that nation states can no longer truly claim to possess sole authority within their borders. Meanwhile, proponents of the **human security** agenda have established new international norms of **humanitarian intervention** and the **responsibility to protect**, which suggest that states do have the right to intervene in each other's internal affairs in order to prevent extreme human rights abuses. In this way, the Westphalian model of sovereignty is apparently being undermined. On the other hand, interventions remain very rare, and many states continue to fiercely assert their sovereignty. Like much else in the arena of international affairs, the demise of sovereignty remains a matter of considerable dispute.

Further reading
Ersun N. Kurtulus, 'Theories of Sovereignty: an Interdisciplinary Approach', *Global Society*, vol. 18, no. 4, October 2004, pp. 347–371

Hans Morgenthau, 'Sovereignty', in Hans Morgenthau, *Politics among Nations: The Struggle for Power and Peace*, 7th edn (Guildford, CT: McGraw-Hill, 2005)
Christopher Rudolph, 'Sovereignty and Territorial Borders in a Global Age', *International Studies Review*, vol. 7, 2005, pp. 1–20

SPACE, see MILITARIZATION AND WEAPONIZATION OF SPACE, AND OUTER SPACE TREATY

SPECIAL RELATIONSHIP

The 'special relationship' is a phrase normally used to describe the particularly close ties which supposedly exist between the United States and the United Kingdom, above all in the realms of defence and **intelligence**. The closeness of the relationship dates back to the alliance formed during the Second World War, which then continued throughout the **Cold War**. It is made possible by a common language, similar cultures, and a shared belief in democracy and free market capitalism. For the past sixty years, the United Kingdom has received privileged access to US military technology, including nuclear technology, and, along with Canada and Australia, has participated in an unparalleled system of intelligence sharing. In return, the USA has found the UK to be an especially reliable ally. Despite this, critics of the concept of the special relationship argue that it is a one-sided affair: the USA gains far more from it than the UK. Indeed some claim that the concept is an almost exclusively British one. British politicians and military leaders like to imagine that they have a special relationship with the USA and that they possess a unique degree of influence in Washington, while many Americans regard the British simply as one ally among many. On occasion, the two allies have declined to support one another, as the British found to their cost during the Suez crisis of 1956. Much has depended on the personal relationships established between US Presidents and British Prime Ministers. Nevertheless, no alliance is entirely tension-free, and by international standards that between the United Kingdom and the United States is unusually solid.

Further reading
David Reynolds, 'A Special Relationship? America, Britain and the International Order since the Second World War', *International Affairs*, vol. 62, no.1, Winter 1985–86, pp. 1–20

James K. Wither, 'British Bulldog or Bush's Poodle: Anglo-American Relations and the Iraq War', *Parameters*, vol. 33, no. 4, Winter 2003/2004, pp. 67–82

SPIRAL MODEL, see **ARMS RACE**

STRATEGIC ARMS LIMITATION TREATY I (SALT I)

The 'Interim Agreement Between the United States of America and the Union of Soviet Socialist Republics on Certain Measures with Respect to the Limitation of Strategic Offensive Arms', more commonly referred to as the Strategic Arms Limitation Treaty I (SALT I) was signed in Moscow on 26 May 1972, and entered into force on 3 October 1972. It was designed as an interim measure to last for five years while negotiations continued for a more comprehensive agreement limiting the construction and deployment of **nuclear weapons**. The agreement obliged the two parties not to construct additional fixed land-based intercontinental **ballistic missiles** (ICBMs), and not to convert older launchers into more modern launchers capable of carrying heavy ICBMs. A protocol to the agreement restricted the United States to 710 submarine-launched ballistic missiles (SLBMs) and 44 modern ballistic missile submarines, and the Soviets to 950 SLBMs and 62 modern ballistic missile submarines. Additional launchers on submarines above those totals could only be deployed as long as equal numbers of land-based launchers or launchers on older submarines were destroyed. The agreement stated that both parties should not interfere with the other party's 'national technical means of **verification**' (e.g. imagery satellites) to ensure compliance. The greatest weakness of the agreement was its failure to address the then-emerging technology of multiple independently targetable re-entry vehicles (MIRVs), which allow more than one warhead to be placed on a single launcher and directed against different targets. The limits placed by SALT I on launchers did not therefore prevent a subsequent substantial growth in the number of nuclear warheads possessed by both the USA and USSR.

Further reading
Thomas Graham Jr and Damien J. LaVera, *Cornerstones of Security: Arms Control Treaties in the Nuclear Era* (Seattle: University of Washington Press, 2003)

Thomas W. Wolfe, *The SALT Experience* (Cambridge, MA: Ballinger, 1979)

STRATEGIC ARMS LIMITATION TREATY II (SALT II)

The 'Treaty Between the United States of America and the Union of Soviet Socialist Republics on the Limitation of Strategic Offensive Arms', commonly known as the Strategic Arms Limitation Treaty II (SALT II), was signed in Vienna on 18 June 1979. It was the result of the commitment made in **SALT I** to negotiate a comprehensive agreement between the USA and USSR on 'strategic offensive arms' (in other words, **nuclear weapons** and the means of delivering them). Both parties to the treaty undertook to limit the number of their intercontinental **ballistic missiles** (ICBMs), submarine-launched ballistic missiles (SLBMs), heavy bombers, and air-to-surface ballistic missiles (ASBMs) to an aggregrate number not to exceed 2,400, which was to be reduced to 2,250 by 1 January 1981. Unlike SALT I, SALT II addressed the issue of multiple independently-targetable re-entry vehicles (MIRVs). This was done by stipulating that each state was not to test or deploy ICBMs with a greater number of re-entry vehicles than had previously been used in that type of ICBM, and was also not to test or deploy SLBMs with more than fourteen re-entry vehicles, or ASBMs with more than ten re-entry vehicles. Within the maximum aggregate total of 2,400 ballistic missiles and bombers, each state was to be allowed 1,320 MIRVed ballistic missiles and heavy bombers equipped with **cruise missiles** with range of over 600 kilometres. Of these only 1,200 could be MIRVed ballistic missiles. An additional protocol to the treaty prohibited both sides from deploying mobile ICBM launchers and from deploying cruise missiles with a range in excess of 600 kilometres on sea- or land-based launchers. The treaty never came into force. Following the Soviet intervention in Afghanistan in 1979, the US Senate refused to ratify the treaty. Although initially President Carter and later President Reagan stipulated that they would nevertheless abide by it, in May 1986 Reagan, citing Soviet violations of the treaty, announced that this would no longer be the case.

Further reading

Thomas Graham Jr and Damien J. LaVera, *Cornerstones of Security: Arms Control Treaties in the Nuclear Era* (Seattle: University of Washington Press, 2003)

Thomas W. Wolfe, *The SALT Experience* (Cambridge, MA: Ballinger, 1979)

STRATEGIC ARMS REDUCTION TREATY I (START I)

The 'Treaty Between the United States and the Union of Soviet Socialist Republics on the Reduction and Limitation of Strategic Offensive Arms', more commonly referred to as the 'Strategic Arms Reduction Treaty I' (START I) was signed on 31 July 1991 and entered into force on 5 December 1994. Its entry into force was delayed by the break-up of the USSR, which resulted in three new states holding **nuclear weapons** – Ukraine, Belarus and Kazakhstan. A protocol in 1992 converted the treaty from a bilateral one into a five-party multi-lateral one under the terms of which Ukraine, Kazakhstan and Belarus agreed to become non-nuclear weapons states. Russia thereafter assumed control of all the former USSR's nuclear arsenal. START I sought to reduce the number of strategic offensive arms held by the USSR (and later Russia) and the USA. The signatories committed themselves to reducing the quantities of their weapons so that after seven years, the number of delivery systems (intercontinental **ballistic missiles** (ICBMs), submarine-launched ballistic missiles (SLBMs) and heavy bombers) would not exceed 1,600 each, including a maximum of 154 heavy ICBMs. In addition, the parties agreed to limit the number of warheads on these weapons to 6,000, with sub-limits of 4,900 warheads for ballistic missiles, 1,100 warheads for deployed mobile ICBMs, and 1,540 for heavy ICBMs. For the pur-poses of **verification**, each side was obliged to provide the other with all telemetric information broadcast during flight tests. In addition, the treaty provided the signatories with the right to conduct inspec-tions of each other's facilities in order to ensure compliance. Numer-ous such inspections have taken place. The treaty also established a Joint Compliance and Inspection Commission to resolve questions relating to treaty compliance and to agree upon any further measures felt necessary to enhance the effectiveness of the treaty.

Further reading

Thomas Graham Jr and Damien J. LaVera, *Cornerstones of Security: Arms Control Treaties in the Nuclear Era* (Seattle: University of Washington Press, 2003)

US Department of State, *START I Treaty*, http://www.state.gov/www/global/arms/starthtm/start/toc.html

Strategic Arms Reduction Treaty II (START II)

The 'Treaty between the United States of America and the Russian Federation on Further Reduction and Limitation of Strategic Offensive Arms', commonly referred to as the 'Strategic Arms Reduction Treaty II' (START II) was signed on 3 January 1993. Russia withdrew from START II in June 2002 after the United States' withdrawal from the **Anti-Ballistic Missile Treaty** earlier that month. The treaty is, therefore, not in force. START II would have continued the reductions in strategic offensive arms begun by **START I**. The US and Russia were to have reduced the numbers of their weapons so that by 31 December 2004 the numbers of warheads attributed to deployed intercontinental ballistic missiles (ICBMs), deployed submarine-launched ballistic missiles (SLBMs), and deployed heavy bombers did not exceed 3,500. Within this limit, the treaty laid out a sublimit of 1,750 for warheads attributed to deployed SLBMs. All heavy ICBMs and ICBMs with multiple warheads were to be eliminated.

Further reading

Thomas Graham Jr and Damien J. LaVera, *Cornerstones of Security: Arms Control Treaties in the Nuclear Era* (Seattle: University of Washington Press, 2003)

US Department of State, *START II Treaty*, http://www.state.gov/www/global/arms/starthtm/start2/st2intal.html

STRATEGIC CULTURE

Strategic culture refers to the pre-conditioned preferences and habitual practices of members of a given community when determining **national security strategy**. People in different countries and different institutions will tend to approach **security** issues in different ways. Academic studies of strategic culture disagree as to exactly how to define it and as to which factors are the most significant, but among the most often cited are history and tradition, geographical position, the broader national culture in which decision-makers are located, and the institutional structure in which they work. These factors will predispose strategists towards certain kinds of solutions to problems, which in this way constitute their strategic culture.

Strategic culture works at various levels. One can speak of national strategic culture and also of sub-national strategic cultures, such as those of different branches of the armed forces. Thus, it has been claimed that American strategists display a preference for the 'strategy of annihilation', tending towards the maximum use of force in solving military problems, whereas British strategists tend towards a softer approach. This reflects both historical experience (notably the greater British experience of 'small wars') and varying capabilities (the alleged American preference for maximum force being possibly a product of their greater ability to use it).

At a lower level, one can observe differences in strategic preferences between different institutions: the navies of different countries may in some instances share more similar strategic cultures with each other than they do with the armies and air forces of their own countries. Strategic culture is never homogenous or entirely deterministic: one's presence within a given community does not guarantee one's adoption of its strategic culture, nor is that culture the sole determinant of strategic decisions. It reflects tendencies and preferences rather than rigid absolutes. Furthermore, strategic culture changes over time. British strategic culture today is not identical to British strategic culture a hundred years ago. Some commentators argue that the malleable and indeterminate nature of strategic culture limits its use as an analytical tool. Others argue that strategic culture can persist over considerable lengths of time, and that without reference to it, it is sometimes difficult to understand why strategists make the decisions that they do.

Further reading

Colin S. Gray, 'Strategic Culture as Context: the First Generation of Theory Strikes Back', *Review of International Studies*, vol. 25, no. 1, January 1999, pp. 49–69

Alastair Iain Johnston, 'Strategic Culture Revisited: Reply to Colin Gray', *Review of International Studies*, vol. 25, no. 3, July 1999, pp. 519–523

STRATEGIC OFFENSIVE REDUCTIONS TREATY (SORT)

The 'Treaty between the United States of America and the Russian Federation on Strategic Offensive Reductions', more commonly referred to as the 'Strategic Offensive Reductions Treaty' (SORT) or the 'Moscow Treaty', was signed on 24 May 2002 and entered into force on 1 June 2003. It is to stay in force until December 2012, at which point the two parties may extend it or supersede it with another treaty. Compared with previous treaties on strategic offensive arms,

SORT is remarkable for its extreme brevity (under 500 words). It obliges the signatories to reduce their nuclear warheads so that by 31 December 2012 the aggregate number of such warheads does not exceed 2,200 for each party. The fact that the treaty, unlike **START I** and **START II**, makes no reference to delivery systems, such as **ballistic missiles**, means that it is possible for the parties to remove the nuclear warheads from their launchers and refit the launchers with conventional warheads. This provision allows for the possibility of nuclear warheads being refitted at a later date should the need arise, and so makes SORT a somewhat weaker treaty than START I and START II. The treaty contains no **verification** provisions, but does state that START I, and thus implicitly its verification measures, remain in force.

Further reading
Thomas Graham Jr and Damien J. LaVera, *Cornerstones of Security: Arms Control Treaties in the Nuclear Era* (Seattle: University of Washington Press, 2003)
The White House, *Text of Strategic Offensive Reductions Treaty*, http://www.whitehouse.gov/news/releases/2002/05/20020524–3.html

STRATEGY
Strategy is the art of applying means to the achieving of ends. As such, almost any human endeavour involves strategy of some kind. In the field of **security** studies, the term is generally applied more narrowly to the application of military power to achieve political goals. It is distinct from tactics, which are the manner of use of armed forces in battle. This distinction was noted by Carl von Clausewitz, who wrote that 'tactics teaches the use of armed forces in the engagement; strategy, the use of engagements for the object of war'. Military theorists also speak of the 'operational level of **war**', which lies between tactics and strategy. At a higher level still, 'grand strategy' refers to the application of all the resources of **national power**, economic and diplomatic as well as military, in pursuit of **national interests** in both **peace** and war.

Strategists' choices are shaped not only by the facts at their disposal, but also by **strategic culture**, in other words the pre-conditioned preferences and habitual practices of members of a given community. Followers of Clausewitz concentrate on destroying the enemy's armed forces in battle. Others, such as the ancient Chinese strategist Sun Tzu and the twentieth-century British writer Basil Liddell Hart, prefer an 'indirect approach', endeavouring to force the enemy to submit with the minimum of fighting. While there are some general principles of strategy whose application tends to produce positive results, such as surprise and concentration of force, strategy is an art and not a science. There are no rigid rules which determine success or failure. Strategy requires the strategist to link policy and military action during conditions of great uncertainty. It is subject to the workings of the 'fog of war' and 'friction'. These terms, introduced by Clausewitz, refer respectively to the lack of information which exists about the true situation during war and to the myriad of obstacles which tend to disrupt even the best laid plans, such as human weaknesses, equipment failure, and bad weather. As Clausewitz wrote, 'everything in war is very simple, but the simplest thing is very difficult'.

Further reading
Carl von Clausewitz, *On War*, edited and translated by Michael Howard and Peter Paret (Princeton: Princeton University Press, 1976)
Colin S. Gray, *Modern Strategy* (Oxford: Oxford University Press, 1999)
Edward N. Luttwak, *Strategy: the Logic of War and Peace*, revised and enlarged edition (Cambridge, MA: Belknap, 2001)
Peter Paret (ed.), *Makers of Modern Strategy: from Machiavelli to the Nuclear Age* (Oxford: Clarendon Press, 1986)

SUDANESE PEOPLE'S LIBERATION ARMY (SPLA)
Based in southern Sudan, the Sudanese People's Liberation Army (SPLA) was created in 1983 with the aim of overthrowing the Islamic government in Khartoum and establishing a secular state. This aim has now changed to that of achieving independence for the south, which is ethnically and religiously distinct from the north. Both the United States of America and Uganda have provided military and political aid to the SPLA to help it achieve this goal. In an effort to attract further international support, the SPLA has recently been trying to reinvent itself as a democratically oriented organization, and in 2005 it signed a peace agreement with the government of Sudan, under which the southern half of the country has acquired autonomous status within the country and will be permitted to hold a referendum on independence after six years. It is expected that this will result in the creation of an independent southern Sudan at that point.

Further reading
Sharon E. Hutchinson, 'A Curse from God? Religious and Political Dimensions of the Post-1991 Rise of Ethnic Violence in South Sudan', *The Journal of Modern African Studies*, vol. 39, no. 2, June 2001, pp. 307–331
Claire Metelits, 'Reformed Rebels? Democratization, Global Norms, and the Sudanese People's Liberation Army', *Africa Today*, vol. 51, no. 1, Fall 2004, pp. 64–82

SUICIDE TERRORISM

Suicide terrorism is a form of **terrorism** in which the terrorist deliberately kills himself or herself in the process of carrying out his or her attack. This is normally done by detonating explosives attached to his or her body or by detonating explosives in the vehicle in which he or she is travelling. Other methods may also be used, such as the crashing of airplanes into buildings, as witnessed in America on 11 September 2001. Suicide terrorism tends to be much more deadly than other forms of terrorist activity, in part because the willingness of the terrorist to self-destruct makes it far easier for him or her to bypass **security** systems, which are normally designed with the assumption that a potential attacker will wish to escape alive.

Suicide terrorism first came to international prominence in the early 1980s as a result of **Hizballah's** terrorist campaign in Lebanon. It then spread to Sri Lanka, where numerous suicide operations have been carried out by members of the **Liberation Tigers of Tamil Eelam (LTTE)**, and to Israel and Palestine, where the tactic has been used by groups such as **Hamas** and the **Al Aqsa Martyrs Brigade**. Since 2003, the incidence of suicide terrorism has increased dramatically, with a vast increase in the practice by insurgents in Afghanistan and Iraq. The increasing use of suicide terrorism reflects a perception among terrorist groups that the tactic is effective, and also an understanding that it represents the best method of causing harm to Western military forces who are far better armed and protected than the insurgents, and who cannot be easily hurt by other means.

Experts disagree as to why people agree to become suicide terrorists. Some argue that the key factor is religious or ideological fanaticism, especially a belief that heaven awaits the martyr. However, many suicide terrorists have been associated with secular organizations such as the LTTE. Similarly, arguments that suicide terrorists are motivated by poverty, revenge, psychological disorders, or social and sexual inadequacy, have been contradicted by evidence suggesting that they are for the most part reasonably well-educated, highly socially integrated, and apparently thoroughly normal individuals. Some commentators thus argue that the prime motivation is a misplaced sense of altruism, and a belief by the terrorists that in killing themselves they can further a just cause. Author Robert Pape in particular argues that suicide terrorism is a rational response to foreign occupation rather than a consequence of religious fanaticism. Other writers dispute his conclusions, and the issue remains unresolved.

Further reading
Mia Bloom, *Dying to Kill: the Allure of Suicide Terror* (New York: Columbia University Press, 2005)
Farhad Khosrokhavar, *Suicide Bombers: Allah's New Martyrs* (London: Pluto, 2005)
Robert A. Pape, *Dying to Win: the Strategic Logic of Suicide Terrorism* (New York: Random House, 2005)
Ami Pedahzur, *Suicide Terrorism* (Cambridge: Polity, 2005)

SWARMING
Swarming is the method by which networks of small dispersed groups coalesce for short periods of time to maximize their strength for a specific purpose. As such it is a tactic closely associated with **netwar**. In a military context, the term refers to **tactics** in which small military units coordinate their activities so as to strike a target simultaneously from all directions. The units assemble steathily and rapidly, conduct their attack, and then disperse once again. Swarming tactics have been used for centuries, but are nowadays facilitated by modern communications systems. While they can be used in conventional **war**, they are more often associated with **guerrilla warfare** and **insurgency**.

Swarming may also be used by political groups. Anti-globalization protesters, for instance, have been highly successful swarmers. Multiple independent groups, often across many countries, communicate via the internet and coordinate their activities, agreeing to converge on a single point at a single time for a mass demonstration. Even if those in authority become aware of the plan and wish to disrupt the demonstration it is exceedingly difficult to do so, as there is no central command and there are too many groups converging from too many different locations. The problems associated with disrupting swarming make it a highly effective tactic.

Further reading
John Arquilla and David Ronfeldt, *Swarming and the Future of Conflict* (Santa Monica: RAND, 2000)
Sean J.A. Edwards, *Swarming on the Battlefield: Past, Present and Future* (Santa Monica: RAND, 2000)

TACTICS, see STRATEGY

TALIBAN

Taliban is the name of an extremist Islamic movement which ruled most of Afghanistan from 1996 to 2001. The name 'talib' (plural 'taliban') means 'student', and its use to describe this particular movement derives from the fact that the majority of the original Taliban who created it were students in Afghan Islamic schools (*madrassas*) in Pakistan. The Taliban came into being in 1994 as a response to the increasing lawlessness of Afghanistan, which had fallen into the hands of corrupt warlords after the collapse of the previous Soviet-backed government in 1992. Led by Mullah Mohammed Omar, the Taliban rapidly seized control first of Kandahar province in southern Afghanistan, and within several months, of about half of the country. In September 1996 they captured the capital, Kabul. Thereafter, most of Afghanistan, excepting the north-eastern sector, which was occupied by a rival force known as the Northern Alliance, was under Taliban control.

The Taliban consists almost entirely of ethnic Pashtuns, who constitute around 40% of the Afghan population. Pashtuns from Kandahar province have always dominated the governing council of the Taliban, known as the Supreme Shura. The movement's rapid rise to power can be explained by a number of factors. First, it was able to exploit popular discontent with the corruption of the warlords. Second, it built on Pashtun resentment of the fact that the government in Kabul was dominated by Tajiks. Third, it received substantial financial and military aid from the Pakistani **intelligence** service, the Inter-services Intelligence (ISI), and from Saudi Arabia. Fourth, wherever it gained control, it restored order and brought **peace** and basic **security**. However, the Taliban also enforced an extremely radical version of Islamic law, which banned most forms of entertainment, including television, music, and kite-flying, and segregated women from men, prohibiting women from working or from going to school. The repressive nature of Taliban rule, plus its almost exclusively Pashtun composition, prevented it from acquiring deep support across the country, and may have contributed to its rapid collapse in 2001.

From 1996, the Taliban provided refuge to Osama bin Laden and his **Al Qaeda** organization. After the United States bombed Al Qaeda training camps in Afghanistan in 1998, relations between bin Laden and the Taliban became even closer. When the US government demanded that the Taliban hand over bin Laden after the terrorist attacks on America on 11 September 2001, Mullah Omar refused. In consequence, the United States attacked, and fighters of the Northern Alliance drove the Taliban from Kabul and most of the rest of Afghanistan in a lightning offensive in late 2001. Since then, the Taliban has regrouped, and in 2006 began once again to pose a serious **threat** to the Afghan government in Kabul, as well as to military forces of the **North Atlantic Treaty Organization** in Afghanistan. Its support, however, remains restricted to Pashtun areas of southern Afghanistan. It is alleged that the Taliban continues to receive aid from the ISI and to find safe havens in Pakistan, and as long as this remains the case, eliminating it is likely to be extremely difficult.

Further reading
Michael Griffin, *Reaping the Whirlwind: Afghanistan, Al Qa'ida and the Holy War*, revised edition (London: Pluto, 2003)
Ahmed Rashid, *Taliban: Militant Islam, Oil and Fundamentalism in Central Asia* (New Haven: Yale University Press, 2000)

TERRORISM
Terrorism has existed for centuries, but has acquired special prominence since the attacks on America on 11 September 2001 and the launch of the **Global War on Terrorism**. The exact definition of terrorism is highly disputed, but in general terms it consists of the use of illegal violence by non-state actors in order to cause terror among civilian populations and thus pressure governments to make political concessions. The use of illegal violence is what distinguishes terrorism from normal political activity, legal/judicial violence, and conventional warfare. Some commentators include attacks on **security** personnel by non-state actors within the definition of terrorism. For instance, attacks by members of the **Irish Republican Army** on British

security forces have often been classified as acts of terrorism, but many analysts prefer to refer to actions of that sort as **guerrilla warfare** or **insurgency**, and to define terrorism more narrowly as political violence specifically aimed at defenceless parties. Terrorism, as such, is unambiguously seen as wrong by all cultures and countries. Consequently, 'terrorism' is a politically charged term. Those conducting the violence normally wish to be known as 'guerrillas', 'freedom fighters', or 'soldiers', while those resisting it denounce them as 'terrorists'.

The actual term 'terrorism' was originally coined during the period of the French **revolution** to describe the use of terror by the French revolutionary government to eliminate opponents and intimidate opposition. This sort of activity is nowadays referred to as 'state terrorism'. By the middle of the nineteenth century, the word 'terrorism' had changed its meaning, and had become associated with the use of violence against governments by revolutionary movements. This is the manner in which it is now most commonly used.

The political aims pursued by terrorists vary considerably. In the twentieth century, terrorist groups fell into two main categories – ethno-nationalist groups, such as the Irish Republican Army and the **Palestine Liberation Organization**; and ideological-revolutionary groups, such as the Red Brigade and Baader-Meinhof gang. Many combined elements of both. The collapse of the Soviet Union caused socialist-inspired terrorism to decline. So-called religious terrorists, including groups such as **Al Qaeda**, rose in significance at the turn of the twentieth and twenty-first centuries. Some single-issue organizations, such as the Animal Liberation Front, also continue to operate.

Despite fears that terrorist groups may acquire **weapons of mass destruction**, the preferred weapon in the great majority of their attacks is conventional explosives. A tactic which has acquired increasing popularity since it was pioneered in the 1980s by **Hizballah** in Lebanon and the **Liberation Tigers of Tamil Eelam** in Sri Lanka is the use of **suicide terrorism**. The most famous example of suicide terrorism to date is the attacks on the U.S. World Trade Center and Pentagon on 11 September 2001. The number of terrorist incidents worldwide has fallen since a peak in the mid-1980s, but the number of suicide terrorist attacks has increased substantially. Another change in recent years is that terrorist attacks have on average become more deadly. The world is therefore experiencing fewer acts of terrorism than in the past, but very possibly more deaths resulting from them. This reflects the fact that modern terrorist groups such as Al Qaeda appear to be less discriminate in their targeting than those during the **Cold War**, and also more interested in causing maximum harm.

Terrorism poses particular problems for liberal democracies. The existence of a free press ensures that terrorists can easily obtain publicity for their actions and views. The relative lack of restrictions on the movement of people, goods, and money in modern societies makes it comparatively easy for terrorists to hide from the gaze of the security forces.

In the late twentieth century, terrorism became increasingly internationalized and cross-bred with **organized crime** rings. Whereas once terrorists operated solely or primarily within one country, many groups now have cells and funding bases spreading across numerous countries, and can launch attacks anywhere in the world. This makes it very difficult for individual countries to fight terrorism. A successful **counter-terrorism** strategy requires an international response.

Further reading
Bruce Hoffman, *Inside Terrorism* (London: Victor Gollancz, 1999)
Jonathan R. White, *Terrorism: An Introduction*, 3rd edn (Belmont: Wadsworth, 2002)
Paul Wilkinson, *Terrorism and the Liberal State* (Basingstoke: Macmillan, 1986)

THREAT

From the perspective of **national security**, a threat is someone or something with the potential to harm **national interests**. Theoretically, national security policy should be derived from an analysis of threats, leading to a series of suitable responses to reduce the amount of harm the threats cause or to prevent them from causing harm at all. Threats can be contingent or non-contingent. Contingent threats are in part dependent on one's response to them; they may cause a large amount of harm, only limited harm, or no harm at all, according to what one does. The threat of military attack by a hostile power is an example. Non-contingent threats will cause harm regardless of what one does. Natural disasters, such as earthquakes, are examples of these (although some analysts deny that natural disasters can properly be considered 'threats' because they lack intentionality – see below). Threats may also be divided into objective and subjective categories: the former represents the danger which really exists; the latter represents the perception of it. Three factors determine the extent of the real or perceived threat: capability, intention, and control. To constitute a threat, an actor must have both the capability of causing harm and the intention of doing so. In addition, much depends on the degree of control the threatened person believes that he or she has over the danger.

As with **risk**, the perception of threat is often faulty. This explains why many in the Western world now feel more insecure than during the **Cold War**. For many years the threat to national security was clear and was defined largely in conventional military terms as the danger of attack by the Soviet Union and the Warsaw Pact. Now, the situation is more uncertain, and threat analyses have changed, to focus more on **terrorism**, **rogue states**, and the **proliferation** of **weapons of mass destruction**. Some commentators also argue that the main threats to **security** now come from other new directions, such as **pandemics**, global warming, and mass **migration**.

Further reading
D. A. Baldwin, 'Thinking about Threats', *Journal of Conflict Resolution*, vol. 15, no. 1, March 1971, pp. 70–78
Raymond Cohen, *Threat Perception in International Crisis* (Madison: University of Wisconsin Press, 1979)
Thomas W. Milburn and Kenneth H. Watman, *On the Nature of Threat: a Social Psychological Analysis* (New York: Praeger, 1981)

THREE BLOCK WAR
'Three Block War' is a phrase created by US Marine Corps general Charles Krulak to describe the sort of urban conflict situation in which he believes Western armed forces are likely to be increasingly involved in the twenty-first century. Future **war**, according to Krulak's model, will be overwhelmingly urban. Within the space of three contiguous city blocks, armed forces may find themselves having to carry out three different types of military operations: conventional combat against **insurgency** in one block; **peacekeeping** operations to separate warring factions in the next; and humanitarian assistance in the third. Operations of this sort will blur the distinctions between war fighting and **peace operations**, and will require soldiers to display exceptional flexibility. While the Three Block War model closely fits

the experiences of the US armed forces and its allies in parts of Iraq and Afghanistan in the early twenty-first century, it remains to be determined how typical this will be in the future.

Further reading

General Charles C. Krulak, 'The Strategic Corporal: Leadership in the Three Block War', *Marines Magazine*, vol. 28, January 1999

Lieutenant Simon Cocksedge, 'The Three Block War and Future Conflict: Some Implications for the Rifle Platoon', *Australian Army Journal*, vol. 3, no. 1, Summer 2005–06, pp. 267–272

TOTAL WAR

Total war refers to a **war** in which a state has mobilized all available human and economic resources for its war effort. The *levée en masse* (mass conscription) introduced by the French Republic in the revolutionary wars of the late eighteenth century is often cited as beginning an 'era of total war' which culminated in the Second World War of 1939–1945. Throughout this period, states' ability to mobilize their societies increased dramatically, allowing them to pull more and more of the population, including women, into the armed forces and the war economy, thus permitting war to further approach 'totality'.

Total war takes place when states demand the complete, unconditional surrender of their opponents. The absolute stakes force belligerents to exert proportionally absolute efforts to achieve victory. Wars fought for more limited aims will produce more limited exertions. Total war may thus be defined not only by the totality of war mobilization but also by the totality of the war aims. In addition, because defeat means total defeat, there is less incentive to abide by moral and legal restraints on the use of force. Total war is therefore accompanied by a process of **escalation**, in which the list of legitimate targets expands until it encompasses the entire enemy population. This process reached its logical culmination with the dropping of two atomic bombs on Japanese cities in August 1945. At this point, total war became synonymous with what Carl von Clausewitz termed **absolute war**, that is to say a war in which all moral and political restraints have been abandoned.

Total war can be contrasted with **limited war**, which is war fought for goals which fall short of the complete destruction of the enemy, and fought without using all the resources available to the state. Since the end of the Second World War, fear of the consequences of escalation into nuclear war has warded off total war, at least as far as Western states are concerned. For them, limited war has once again become the norm.

Further reading
Jeremy Black, *The Age of Total War, 1860–1945* (Westport: Praeger, 2006)
Hans Morgenthau, 'Total War', in Hans Morgenthau, *Politics among Nations: The Struggle for Power and Peace*, 7th edition (Guildford, CT: McGraw-Hill, 2005)

TRANSFORMATION

Transformation refers to current policies designed to restructure the armed forces of the United States and other **North Atlantic Treaty Organization (NATO)** members in accordance with the dictates of the **Revolution in Military Affairs (RMA)**. Transformation aims to make armed forces smaller, but more powerful and more easily deployable. The large, heavily armed formations which characterized Western armed forces during the **Cold War** are seen as obsolete, as well as hard to deploy rapidly overseas. Transformation will reduce numbers of personnel and heavy equipment, but aims to compensate with the use of precision weapons and **network-centric warfare**, meaning that although military forces will be smaller they will in theory be more capable. The ease with which Anglo-American forces destroyed the Iraqi army in 2003 may be seen as a vindication of the transformation approach. However, the subsequent difficulties confronted by the British and Americans fighting the Iraqi **insurgency** have been construed as suggesting that small, high-technology armed forces may not be well placed to cope with **asymmetric warfare**.

Further reading
Stephen J. Cimbala, 'Transformation in Concept and Policy', *Joint Force Quarterly*, no. 38, Summer 2005 pp. 28–33
Office of Force Transformation homepage: http://www.oft.osd.mil/

TRANSNATIONAL CRIMINAL ORGANIZATIONS, see ORGANIZED CRIME

TREATY FOR THE PROHIBITION OF NUCLEAR WEAPONS IN LATIN AMERICA AND THE CARIBBEAN

Sometimes referred to as the Treaty of Tlatelolco or as the Latin American Nuclear-Free Zone Treaty, the Treaty for the Prohibition of Nuclear Weapons in Latin America was signed on 14 February 1967 and entered into force on 25 April 1968. The contracting parties, which now include thirty-three states in Latin America and the Caribbean, undertake to use exclusively for peaceful purposes all nuclear material and facilities under their jurisdiction, and not to test, use, manufacture or otherwise acquire **nuclear weapons**, nor to permit the storage or deployment of nuclear weapons on their territories. Originally confined to Latin American states, in 1990 the treaty was extended to cover the Caribbean and the words 'and the Caribbean' were added to the title. Two additional protocols have been signed. According to Protocol I, signed in 1977, those outside powers with territories in the region – the UK, Netherlands, France, and United States – undertook to apply the provisions of the treaty to their territories. France, despite signing Protocol I, has not ratified it. In Protocol II, the then nuclear weapons states – France, Peoples' Republic of China, UK, USA, and USSR – agreed to respect the denuclearization provisions of the treaty and not to use or threaten to use nuclear weapons against the contracting parties of the treaty.

Further reading

Thomas Graham Jr and Damien J. LaVera, *Cornerstones of Security: Arms Control Treaties in the Nuclear Era* (Seattle: University of Washington Press, 2003)

US Department of State, *Treaty for the Prohibition of Nuclear Weapons in Latin America and the Caribbean*, http://www.state.gov/t/ac/trt/4796.htm

TREATY ON OPEN SKIES

Originally negotiated by the then members of the **North Atlantic Treaty Organization (NATO)** and the Warsaw Pact, the Treaty on Open Skies was signed on 24 March 1992 and entered into force on 1 January 2002. Over 30 states have now signed the treaty, which finally brought into being a concept first proposed by the US government under President Eisenhower in 1955 as a **confidence and security building measure.** The treaty allows signatories to conduct, and obliges them to accept on 72 hours notice, overhead flights by unarmed observation aircraft, which may be equipped with optical, infra-red, and radar imaging cameras. Each state is assigned a quota for the number of overflights it may carry out and an identical number which it must receive. States are obliged to hand over all information gathered during an overflight to the country over whose territory they flew.

Further reading
Federation of American Scientists, *Open Skies Treaty*, http://www.fas.org/nuke/control/os/index.html

Thomas Graham Jr and Damien J. LaVera, *Cornerstones of Security: Arms Control Treaties in the Nuclear Era* (Seattle: University of Washington Press, 2003)

ULSTER DEFENCE ASSOCIATION (UDA)

The Ulster Defence Association (UDA) is the largest of the loyalist paramilitary groups operating in Northern Ireland. Until it was banned in 1991, the UDA was a legal organization. To maintain the pretence that it was not involved in terrorist activities, these were conducted under the alternative title of the Ulster Freedom Fighters (UFF). In practice, the distinction between the UDA and UFF, in so far as it ever had any meaning, no longer exists. Founded in 1971, the UDA developed out of various vigilante organizations which had sprung up to protect Protestant communities from attacks by the **Irish Republican Army (IRA).** Very rapidly, the UDA moved beyond this protective mission and began carrying out aggressive acts of sectarian **terrorism** against Catholics in Northern Ireland, killing over 100 people between 1971 and 1999. Often the targets were chosen purely for the fact that they were Catholic rather than because of any connection with the IRA. The UDA has refused to disarm in response to the **peace** process in Northern Ireland, and is reported to be active in **organized crime**, including drug trafficking and extortion. At its peak the UDA had some 40,000 members, but it has declined significantly in recent years, and has also been much weakened by internal feuding and power struggles with other loyalist paramilitary organizations, such as the Ulster Volunteer Force (UVF).

Further reading
Steve Bruce, *The Red Hand: Protestant Paramilitaries in Northern Ireland* (Oxford: Oxford University Press, 1992)
Ian Wood, *Crimes of Loyalty: A History of the UDA* (Edinburgh: Edinburgh University Press, 2006)

UNILATERALISM, see MULTILATERALISM

UNIPOLARITY

Unipolarity describes an international order in which there is only one dominant power. It is thus often associated with **hegemony**, although theoretically it is possible to have a situation in which a single state possesses sufficient power for the system to be unipolar, but lacks the resources to be considered truly a hegemon. Unipolarity can be contrasted with bipolarity, in which there are two major powers, and multipolarity, in which there are three or more. The **Cold War** was an example of a bipolar international system, with two great powers – the United States and the Soviet Union. The early twenty-first-century world is often described as unipolar due to alleged US economic and military hegemony. Some analysts disagree with this description. They argue either that we currently live in an era of multipolarity, with several centres of world power, including the United States, the European Union and China, or that such an order will soon emerge.

There is further disagreement as to whether unipolarity, bipolarity, or multipolarity provides the greatest international stability. Hegemonic stability theory suggests that hegemony allows the dominant state in a unipolar order to create and enforce rules for a stable international system. There is, however, no guarantee that others will accept this, and they may form new alliances and blocs to re-establish a **balance of power** or to create a new system based on **multilateralism**. Unipolarity may thus prove to be short-lived.

Further reading
Ethan B. Kapstein, 'Does Unipolarity Have a Future?', in Ethan B. Kapstein and Michael Mastanduno (eds), *Unipolar Politics: Realism and State Strategies after the Cold War* (New York: Columbia University Press, 1999), pp. 464–490

Krauthammer, Charles, 'The Unipolar Moment', *Foreign Affairs*, vol. 70, no. 1, 1991, pp. 23–33
David Wilkinson, 'Unipolarity without Hegemony', *International Studies Review*, vol. 1, no. 2, Summer 1999, pp. 141–172

UNITED NATIONS (UN)

The United Nations (UN) came into being on 24 October 1945. With over 190 members, it is the largest of all international organizations. The UN Charter, signed in June 1945, lays out the aims of the organization, as follows: to maintain **peace** and **security**; to develop friendly relations among nations; to achieve international cooperation in solving international economic, social, cultural and humanitarian problems and in promoting respect for human rights and fundamental freedoms; and to be a centre for harmonizing the actions of nations in the attainment of these common aims.

The UN has six principal organs: the Security Council, the General Assembly, the Economic and Social Council, the Trusteeship Council, the **International Court of Justice**, and the Secretariat. Subordinate to these are a plethora of other bodies, such as the **International Atomic Energy Authority**. Drawing on the failure of the League of Nations in the inter-war period, the founders of the UN decided to strengthen the new organization by granting powerful executive authority to the Security Council, which under the UN Charter has the primary responsibility for matters of peace and security. The Security Council consists of fifteen members, five of whom (China, France, Russia, the United Kingdom, and the United States of America) are permanent members with veto powers. The remaining ten members are elected by the General Assembly for two-year periods and lack veto powers.

The Charter of the UN is an important element of **international law**. Among its most important provisions is Article 2, which obliges members to refrain from the **threat** or the use of force against other states. Article 51 maintains states' right to self-defence if attacked, but other articles make it clear that it is the responsibility of the Security Council to identify aggressors and also to identify threats to and breaches of international peace and security, as well as to decide what enforcement measures should be taken. This means that under the terms of the Charter it is illegal for states to take military action against others in circumstances other than self-defence without the approval of the Security Council. In the event that the Security Council determines the existence of a threat to international peace and security, it may pass a resolution stipulating what action should be taken. This may involve the dispatch of a **peacekeeping** mission, or may involve coercive measures such as **economic sanctions** or military force. In this respect, the UN Security Council in theory acts as the mechanism for the enforcement of global **collective security**.

In practice, for much of its history the UN found it difficult to take effective action to fulfil its collective security function. This was largely a product of **Cold War** antagonisms, which meant that either the Soviet Union or the United States was likely to veto any proposals for collective security action requested by the other. The UN-led operation to reverse North Korean aggression against South Korea from 1950–1953 was a unique exception with no parallel until the UN endorsed the use of force to expel Iraq from Kuwait in 1990/91. The UN focused instead on peacekeeping missions, of which 14 were sanctioned by the Security Council prior to the end of the 1980s. Since then, the end of the Cold War has made it possible for the UN to take a much more activist approach, and in the past fifteen years the number of UN **peace operations** has increased substantially. In addition, the UN has expanded the scope of its peace operations to move beyond pure peacekeeping to incorporate **peacemaking** and **peacebuilding** efforts. Nevertheless, many critics believe that the UN is still failing to achieve all that it could. In particular, they note the UN's failure to take effective action to bring the **wars** in the Former Yugoslavia to an end in the 1990s and its inability to prevent the **genocide** in Rwanda in 1994. How to reform the UN to make it more effective is a matter of continuing debate.

Further reading
Newton R. Bowles, *The Diplomacy of Hope: the United Nations since the Cold War* (London: I. B. Tauris, 2004)
Karen A. Mingst and Margaret P. Karns, *The United Nations in the Post-Cold War Era* (Boulder: Westview, 1995)
United Nations website: http://www.un.org

UNITED NATIONS CONVENTION ON THE LAW OF THE SEA (UNCLOS)

The United Convention on the Law of the Sea (UNCLOS) was signed in 1982, and came into force in 1994. It was the final product of three

United Nations Conferences on the Law of the Sea. UNCLOS I, held between 1956 and 1958, produced four conventions on territorial seas and contiguous zones, high seas, continental shelves, and fishing and conservation of living resources on the high seas. UNCLOS II, held in 1960, ended in failure. UNCLOS III, which terminated in 1982, then finalized agreement on a number of outstanding issues.

UNCLOS divides the world's seas into various types: internal waters, territorial seas, contiguous zones, high seas, international straits, and exclusive economic zones. Waters enclosed within straight lines connecting the outermost points of land of a nation's territory (known as 'baselines') are considered internal waters, over which states exercise exclusive **sovereignty**. In the case of archipelagos, states have sovereignty over waters enclosed by straight baselines drawn between the outermost points of the outermost islands of the archipelago, potentially enclosing very large areas. Beyond this, waters up to 12 nautical miles from the baseline are 'territorial seas'. States exercise sovereignty over territorial seas, but, unlike in internal waters, the ships of other states are allowed to traverse territorial waters provided that their actions are not prejudicial to the **security** of the coastal state, a right known as the right of 'innocent passage'. Extending beyond territorial seas, in a zone up to 24 nautical miles contiguous to territorial waters (known as a 'contiguous zone'), states may exercise such control as is necessary to prevent infringements of their customs, immigration or sanitary laws. Outside the territorial seas and contiguous zones are the 'high seas'. All states are guaranteed lawful uses of them. International straits consist of seas linking together two areas of high sea. Surface, underwater and air passage through, under and over the seas is guaranteed in international straits, even if the straits are enclosed by the 12 nautical mile limit on territorial waters. Finally, states may establish an 'exclusive economic zone' (EEZ) up to 200 nautical miles from their coast, in which they may claim exclusive rights of economic exploitation, such as fishing. Similarly, coastal states have exclusive sovereign rights for exploiting resources of their continental shelf, to the outer edge of the shelf, up to 200 nautical miles from the shore.

To date, about 150 states have ratified UNCLOS III. The most significant state not to do so is the United States of America, although the USA does accept many of the convention's provisions as part of customary **international law**. American refusal to ratify UNCLOS III reflects a long-standing division in the law of the sea between the concepts of *mare liberum* (open sea) and *mare clausum* (closed sea).

Traditionally, great naval powers and those with important maritime trading interests, such as the USA, have promoted the former and sought to restrict the rights of states to deny them access to sea areas. By contrast, weaker states have often sought to expand their territorial rights and to limit the rights of others in the waters off their coasts. UNCLOS III represents a compromise between the competing visions of *mare liberum* and *mare clausum*, but American rejection of it reflects a strong belief in the United States that it has veered too strongly towards the latter. American ratification of UNCLOS III is unlikely in the near future.

Further reading
'Convention on the Law of the Sea: History and Major Provision', *International Debates*, vol. 3, no. 4, April 2005, pp. 100–104 and 128
David M. Keithly, 'The Law of the Sea Revisited', *Low Intensity Conflict and Law Enforcement*, vol. 7, no. 3, Winter 1998, pp. 121–134
The Law of the Sea: Obligations of State Parties under the United Nations Convention on the Law of the Sea and Complementary Instruments (New York: United Nations, 2004)

VERIFICATION

Verification is the process by which people judge whether others are complying with an agreement. This is done in a number of ways. States may verify the compliance of others by means of remote monitoring via their own **intelligence** assets, such as satellites, aircraft, and signals intelligence collection systems, known collectively as 'national technical means' (NTM). Alternatively, the terms of some treaties allow more intrusive methods of verification, permitting states to make on-site inspections of other states' facilities or even to carry out continuous on-site monitoring. **Arms control** treaties may place responsibility for verification on the parties to the treaty themselves or on an international organization. Examples of international verification organizations include the **International Atomic Energy Authority** and the Organization for the Prohibition of Chemical Weapons. Some non-governmental organizations also monitor state compliance with international treaties, an example being the group Landmine Monitor, which monitors compliance with the **Ottawa Convention**.

Verification serves several purposes. In the first place, knowledge that a treaty contains solid verification procedures may encourage states to sign the treaty, as they can have some confidence that other parties will comply with the terms (although if the procedures are too intrusive, they may discourage some potential signers). Second, it detects non-compliance. Third, it deters non-compliance, as states will be aware that this may be detected. And fourth, it demonstrates compliance and thus builds trust between parties. Verification thus acts as a **confidence and security building measure**.

The development of efficient NTM to verify compliance played a vital role in making arms control possible during the **Cold War**. Verification processes in the late Cold War became gradually more intrusive, as seen in the examples of the **Conventional Forces in Europe Treaty** and the **Intermediate-Range Nuclear Forces (INF) Treaty**. No verification system is foolproof, and verification is not synonymous with enforcement. Nevertheless, efficient verification of agreements makes a significant contribution to the maintenance of international **security**.

Further reading

Steve Tulliu and Thomas Schmalberger, *Coming to Terms with Security: A Lexicon for Arms Control, Disarmament and Confidence-Building*, UNIDIR/2003/22 (Geneva: UNIDIR, 2003), Chapter 10 'Verification and Compliance', pp. 185–226

United Nations Institute for Disarmament Research, *Coming to Terms with Security: A Handbook of Verification and Compliance*, UNIDIR/2003/10 (Geneva: UNIDIR, 2003)

United Nations Institute for Disarmament Research, *Verification of Disarmament or Limitation of Armaments: Instruments, Negotiations, Proposals*, UNIDIR/92/28 (New York: UNIDIR, 1992)

WAR

Despite its prevalence, war defies easy definition. Stripped down to its essentials, it may be seen as a prolonged state of violent conflict between two or more organized groups, although even most of these features can be contested for one reason or another. A single act of violence does not suffice to make a war, but the degree to which the conflict must be prolonged is debatable. Violence is normally deemed fundamental to any definition of war, but the word is also used to describe conflicts which involve no physical violence, such as economic war and **cyberwarfare**. Organization of some sort is also essential to war – combat between individuals is not war. However, there is no agreement as to the scale of organization required to make a conflict a war. Traditionally, the term has been primarily used to describe conflicts between states, but it is also now used to describe struggles between states and non-state actors, such as **guerrilla warfare**, as well as struggles between much smaller groups, such as gang wars, and to describe campaigns such as the 'wars' on drugs and **terrorism**.

According to the great Prussian military theorist Carl von Clausewitz, 'war is an act of force to compel our enemy to do our will'. War, said Clausewitz, was an 'act of policy', a 'continuation of policy by other means'. This definition classifies war as a rational act. It would be absurd, Clausewitz noted, for a state to wage a war without considering its purpose and how it planned to achieve this. However, history suggests that this absurdity is often the reality. For, as the Prussian himself recognized, war in practice is highly affected by emotions. States and other organizations may wage war as much to satisfy the emotions of their leaders or their public, or to save face or to avoid looking weak, as for any material goal, and they rarely make accurate assessments of the likely costs and benefits of their actions. Furthermore, once war begins, **strategy** often gives way to mere tactics, as those fighting focus purely on military victory and lose sight of the original political purpose of their efforts. Consequently, the description of war as a rational activity is questionable.

There are numerous explanations of the causes of war. Some focus on human nature, which is seen by many observers as inherently violent. This view would suggest that conflict among humans is inevitable. Others, by contrast, argue that war is a cultural rather than a natural phenomenon, which suggests that it could in due course be eliminated from human society. A third set of explanations concentrates on the material benefits which humans seek to gain from war, such as territory or booty, and suggests that wars take place because they are considered profitable by those who wage them. Meanwhile, yet another explanation sees the causes at least of inter-state war as lying in the structure of the international system, in particular the existence of **anarchy**. No single one of these explanations is sufficient, and they are not for the most part mutually incompatible. The causes of war are extremely complex, and consequently there is no easy method of eradicating it.

Many commentators argue that the nature of war is currently undergoing a fundamental change. Wars between states are becoming less common, and **asymmetric warfare** is becoming the norm. Concepts such as **netwar, fourth generation war**, and **cyberwarfare** are allegedly altering the way in which wars are fought. This analysis is not accepted by all. In fact, since the end of the Second World War the great majority of wars throughout the world have been fought within rather than between states, so this phenomenon is nothing new. What is new is that since the end of the **Cold War** the incidence of both inter-state wars and internal wars, such as **civil war** and **insurgency**, has declined substantially, as has the damage done by those wars. The reason for this precipitous decline in war is not clear. Explanations include the end of Cold War rivalries, US **hegemony**, the spread of democracy, and the increasing willingness of international organizations to engage in crisis prevention and **conflict resolution**. Whether the decline will continue remains to be seen.

Further reading
Carl von Clausewitz, *On War*, edited and translated by Michael Howard and
    Peter Paret (Princeton: Princeton University Press, 1976)
John Keegan, *A History of Warfare* (London: Hutchinson, 1993)
Quincy Wright, *A Study of War*, 2nd edition (Chicago: University of Chicago
    Press, 1965)

WAR ON TERROR, see GLOBAL WAR ON TERRORISM (GWOT)

WAR TERMINATION
War termination refers to the process by which wars come to an end. Despite the importance of the subject, far less attention has been given to war termination than to studying the causes and conduct of **war**. Once war has begun, those waging it tend to focus their attention on defeating the enemy in battle, and to assume that once military 'victory' is achieved war termination will take care of itself. As a result, very little attention is given to thinking about how to translate victory on the battlefield into **peace**.

War termination can take a number of forms, such as ceasefire, surrender, formal peace treaty, withdrawal, or extermination. These can come about in one of three ways. First, one side can be completely destroyed. Second, one side can realize that its struggle has become pointless and lose the will to resist. At this point it surrenders, either unconditionally or after a period of negotiation, or alternatively, if it is able, simply withdraws from the combat. Third, both sides can reach a point of exhaustion and negotiate a settlement, either by themselves or with the help of a third-party mediator. The first scenario is relatively rare. Even in cases such as the end of the Second World War, where one side surrendered unconditionally, the defeated party still had some capacity to resist at the moment of surrender. The second and third scenarios are more common. Research into the ending of wars over the past 200 years suggests that some 68 per cent of inter-state wars, and 48 per cent of all wars, involve negotiations between the belligerent parties. War termination is sometimes, therefore, described as a process of bargaining.

In most cases the negotiations will begin because the weaker side realizes that it is losing and wishes to find some way of cutting its losses. As a general rule, wars tend to last beyond the point when this realization should logically occur. Psychological pressures, such as fear of defeat and a desire to avoid looking weak, tend to encourage leaders to overestimate the possible benefits of continued resistance and to underestimate the probable costs. Often they will choose the path of **escalation** rather than admit defeat. Successful war termination depends on finding ways of correcting such misperceptions about the costs and benefits of further fighting through a combination of coercion and negotiation. The weaker party should be made aware of the inevitability of its defeat while also being offered some positive incentives for ceasing combat. In this regard, face-saving formulae are often decisive. If a method can be found by which the weaker party concedes to most of the demands of the stronger party, but in such a way as to maintain honour, war termination will be easier to achieve.

Further reading
Fred Charles Iklé, *Every War Must End*, revised edition (New York: Columbia University Press, 1991)
Paul R. Pillar, *Negotiating Peace: War Termination as a Bargaining Process* (Princeton: Princeton University Press, 1983)
Major Chione Robinson, 'A Theory of War Termination for Peacekeepers', *Canadian Forces Journal*, 2000, pp. 81–94

WEAPONIZATION OF SPACE, see MILITARIZATION AND WEAPONIZATION OF SPACE

WEAPONS OF MASS DESTRUCTION (WMD)

The phrase 'weapons of mass destruction' (WMD) refers to **nuclear weapons, biological weapons**, and **chemical weapons**. These are believed to be qualitatively different to other weapons due to their destructive potential and indiscriminate nature. The conflation of nuclear weapons with the other two is somewhat misleading as biological weapons and chemical weapons lack the destructive power of nuclear weapons. Furthermore, so-called conventional weapons, such as bullets and high explosives, have in the past killed, at present do kill, and in the future will probably continue to kill, far more people than WMD. It is debatable whether the categorization of WMD is a meaningful one, and whether it is wise to focus so much on WMD at the cost of paying less attention to other weapons which in reality do much more harm. For this reason some analysts prefer alternative terminology such as Chemical, Biological, Radiological, and Nuclear Weapons (CBRN), and Nuclear, Biological and Chemical Weapons (NBC), although these suffer from a similar weakness in suggesting some parallel between the three.

Preventing the **proliferation** of WMD is one of the highest priorities of the **national security** policies of many countries in the post-**Cold War** era. There are particular fears that a **rogue state** might donate WMD to a terrorist organization in order to allow it to carry out a particularly destructive act of **terrorism**. Despite the prevalence of this fear, it is not entirely obvious why a rogue state would wish to act in this way, since it would invite its own destruction in retaliation. Nevertheless, anxiety about such a scenario was fundamental in persuading the United States and the United Kingdom to adopt the doctrine of **preventive war** after the terrorist attacks of 11 September 2001.

A wide variety of **arms control** agreements restrict the production, stockpiling, deployment, and use of WMD. Most notable in this context are the **Non-Proliferation Treaty**, the **Biological Weapons and Toxins Convention**, and the **Chemical Weapons Convention**. A number of formal and informal international groups, such as the **Australia Group**, also exist to restrict the export of WMD and materials required for their production.

Further reading

Joseph Cirincione, with Jon B. Wolfensthal and Miriam Rajkumar, *Deadly Arsenals: Tracking Weapons of Mass Destruction* (Washington, DC: Carnegie Endowment for International Peace, 2002)

Malcolm R. Davis and Colin S. Gray, 'Weapons of Mass Destruction', in John Baylis, James Wirtz, Eliot Cohen, and Colin S. Gray (eds), *Strategy in the Contemporary World: an Introduction to Strategic Studies* (Oxford: Oxford University Press, 2002), pp. 254–285

Steve Tulliu and Thomas Schmalberger, *Coming to Terms with Security: A Lexicon for Arms Control, Disarmament and Confidence-Building*, UNIDIR/2003/22 (Geneva: UNIDIR, 2003)